More When I Know You Better

ISBN: 978-962-937-636-9

Published by
    City University of Hong Kong Press
    Tat Chee Avenue
    Kowloon, Hong Kong
    Website: www.cityu.edu.hk/upress
    E-mail: upress@cityu.edu.hk

Printed in Hong Kong

More When I Know You Better

THE LIFE OF ALBERT SANGUINETTI
1923–2009

By Stuart Wolfendale

香港城市大學出版社
City University of Hong Kong Press

Contents

Preface

U nlike most people, Albert Sanguinetti stipulated that after his death, his ashes should be scattered and that no tablet or memorial should be erected in his name. Not even a small head stone in an obscure churchyard or a name to squint at in a hundred on the wall of a columbarium. Baulking though at thorough obliteration from the human record, he set out in his will provisions for "a writer be selected … to write and edit a book … relating events and my activities", and most people do not do that either. He made this provision because, he said, many friends and acquaintances had persistently asked him to do so during his life and that he particularly owed it to Gibraltar and Hong Kong to record historical events in which he had been involved.

It came to pass that Sanguinetti's nephew and trustee, James Gordon, who lives in Gibraltar, approached me to put this biography together. I had been introduced to Sanguinetti in late 2008 to discuss writing his life story from his own account, supported by documents. Writing a history from this base is not as easy as it might sound, requiring energy and persistence from both parties. Sadly, these were fading in Sanguinetti and when he went into hospital, the project was dropped. Ten years later, I have had the chance to carry it through for him.

I am grateful for the earlier research done by Brian McElney and for his anecdotes on his long friendship with Sanguinetti, and for a further version of his early years provided by Virginia Blackburn. Much information and support was given to me from Gibraltar by James Gordon and here in Hong Kong by his friend and trustee, Gladys Li. Sanguinetti would have been 99 years old this year, had he lived, so there is almost no one left from his earlier life to recall him. Of his later years, I learned much from his loyal friends Peter and Audrey Ho and from the companion of his last decade who generously and poignantly brought back his memories for me.

The archive I have worked from consists of boxes of Sanguinetti's files containing correspondence, press cuttings, magazine articles, memoranda, transcripts of statements, interviews, invitations, meeting minutes, and various court judgements that he kept because they had involved him, related to him, or simply interested him. This includes notes he made on these documents. While some of the information in the text is not associated with a particular citation or official case number, the majority of the quoted and referenced material can be found in these files. Where these documents have been in Hong Kong and to hand, I have included citations referring to the archive by the number of the box that the document has been kept in. Some information, including that transmitted in emails, is kept in Gibraltar.

Thirteen years on from his death, the world Sanguinetti lived and worked in has been significantly altered. Hong Kong is 25 years on from colonial rule and much more integrated with the motherland. While he had been an ardent supporter of the Common Law, he was also a friend to the China of his day and had backed the negotiations for the Joint Declaration in the 1980s. It is impossible to guess what his opinions of today's world would have been, and this book makes no attempt to do so, focusing instead on the man himself and the life he lived.

I refer to him as Sanguinetti throughout the text which is the usual practice in a biography and because I did not want to imply, by use of his first name, any long friendship. I met him only occasionally, over a matter of weeks, but that was a privilege and a delight, and I only wish there had been time to hear more of this story from his own lips.

Stuart Wolfendale
Hong Kong, August 2022

Abbreviations

AACR	Association for the Advancement of Civil Rights
BBC	British Broadcasting Company
CA	Criminal Appeal
HK	Hong Kong
HM	Her Majesty's
HRH	His Royal Highness
ICAC	Independent Commission Against Corruption
ICJ	International Commission of Jurists
IRD	Inland Revenue Department
KLFA	Kenya Land and Freedom Army
QC	Queen's Counsel
SC	Senior Counsel
UCL	University College London
UK	United Kingdom
US	United States

Family Tree

(showing five generations of direct descendants)

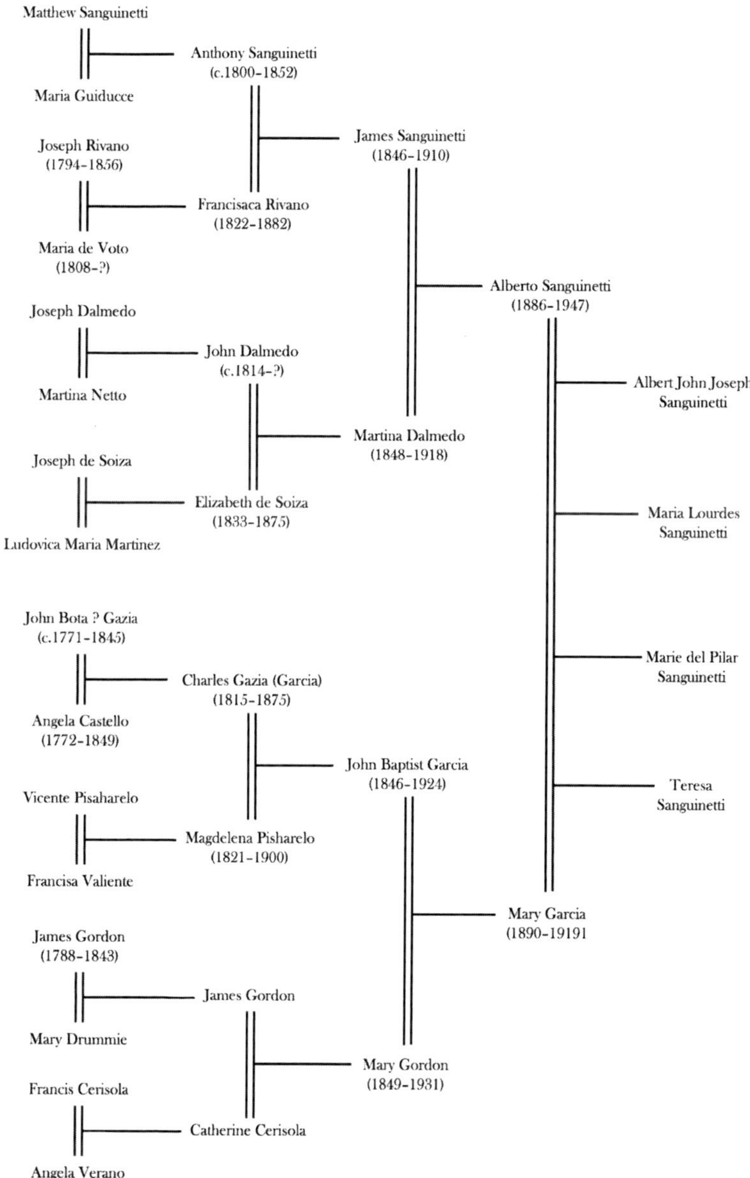

Childhood on the Rock

Albert Joseph Angel Sanguinetti was born in Gibraltar on 3 October 1923. Flamboyant yet fastidious, social and bookish, canny but generous, careful of detail though careless of convention, he was a fascinating compound of that tiny colony of huge repute. Taken from Spain by the British under the Treaty of Utrecht in 1713, this curiously small community, clutching a monolithic promontory of up-ended Jurassic limestone, is famous for its role as garrison, naval base, and sturdy outpost, locking up the entrance to the Mediterranean in the interest of British naval control. Those are its starchier, gunboat features. Its real flavour is an accumulated population of Spaniards, Italians, Portuguese, Maltese, Moors, Jews, and indeed the British. It was from this compact cosmos of peoples that shot Albert Sanguinetti's star. He dropped the name "Angel" on his confirmation—a name he may have taken some ribbing for as he grew up—and replaced it with John. Childhood pictures suggest a profile more cherubic than angelic. It was not a characteristic that even his warmest friends would say he developed in later life.

Sanguinetti came from an Italian line. His father, Alberto, was born in 1886 and was the great-grandson of Mateo Sanguinetti, later called Matthew, a ship's captain from Genoa who settled in Gibraltar with his wife and son around 1812. The Gibraltar Census Return of 1834 shows Matthew Sanguinetti, a 62 year old in shipping, living with his two sons at 13 Road to the Lines. This was very close to the Moorish Castle on the western side of the Rock of Gibraltar (the famous 426-metre-high monolithic limestone promontory, from which the territory gained its moniker "the Rock"), overlooking the town of Gibraltar and the bay, and the Spanish town of Algeciras. Being in shipping, it might have been expected of him to live in Catalan Bay, which is on the eastern side of the Rock and where many of his fellow Genoese had developed a distinct fishing community, but he chose to live on the opposite side, closer to the army and naval bases as well as the developing business centre. This may have been a reflection of his aspirations and would have been more advantageous to his sons' occupations in leather and carpentry.

It would have been a very serious decision for Matthew to uproot his family from the long traditions of Genoa and move to a new community. However, Gibraltar was very familiar to Genoese traders. Ships from Genoa were often there to register under the British flag. The British had made a series of agreements with Ottoman satraps along the North African coast, and the flag granted the Genovese protection against Barbary pirates. So, the captains came and went and sometimes settled. The great wealth and power of Genoa in the Middle Ages had rested in its trading ships and fighting fleet so these ship captains had become "captains of the people" and a form of inherited nobility.

It was this *ancien regime* which the French occupation under Napoleon was abolishing in Genoa. By 1805, France had annexed it to its own Empire. Men were being forced to enlist in the French Army, so many families left to avoid this. Gibraltar was seen as a refuge and a place of opportunity. British command of the Mediterranean was ensured by the victory at Trafalgar in 1805, and the years following were a booming period as the inhabitants found ways around the blockades set up by both Napoleon and the British. The dockyard was also fully stretched with repairing damaged ships, and a new Naval Victualling Yard developed at Rosia Bay. Matthew moved to Gibraltar at the same time as Sanguinetti's maternal family, the Garzias, who also uprooted and began a new life there. Giovanni Baptista Garzia from Finale, on the Gulf of Genoa, arrived in Gibraltar about two years earlier than Matthew, in around 1810.

Matthew's son Anthony married twice. His second wife was Francisca Rivano. The Rivanos, also Genoese, afford the earliest traceable ancestor of Albert Sanguinetti. In the archive of St Mary the Crowned Cathedral in Gibraltar, the first local birth for the Rivano family is recorded for 1700. Several generations later, Francisca's second child was James, Sanguinetti's grandfather, born in 1846. He was only six years old when his father Matthew died. At 22 years old, he married Martina Damedo in St Mary the Crowned, and they had eleven children. James became a successful carpenter and cabinet maker. His business grew, and he moved closer to the main trading area of the town. He died at the age of 63 in 1910. A carpentry business located on Main Street is still operating under his name and those of his sons.

Alberto, Sanguinetti's father and eighth of the eleven children, was born in 1886 and married Mary Garcia (the spelling had altered) in 1922, which united these two prominent families in the Gibraltar community. Alberto developed his own trade, dealing in leather, but went on to build up a portfolio of house and business ownership. His brother Avelino also had a shop in the centre of the town on Main Street called "The Green Room", established in 1870, selling goods including leather, bicycles, motorbikes, pianos, and gramophone records.

Charles Garcia, Sanguinetti's maternal great-grandfather, developed a tobacco business called "Carlos Garcia, Enijo Gibraltar". Advertisements for it can be traced in old trade directories, and tobacco wrappings from the period carry the trademark of "Carlos Garcia". Tobacco was a very prosperous trade in Gibraltar, even when the other aspects of its economy had difficulties. Prosperity lay in the Spanish trade which was developed to include cigars. In 1814, "only about thirty-one people were employed in rolling tobacco leaf".[1] By 1850, about 2,000 people were employed, including whole families, in crowded tobacco factories. Conditions were unhealthy, the wages were very low and the few families who organised the trade "were disproportionately rich".[2]

In 1841, Charles married Magdelena Pisharello, aged 20. She gave him eight children, the third of which, John Baptist (their first son and Sanguinetti's grandfather), was born in 1846. He continued his father's trade in tobacco, deliberately starting at the bottom as a tobacco chopper and working his way up. By 1891, his business was so prosperous that he needed to expand his workforce. While he had still been chopping tobacco, he married Mary Gordon and had 11 children. Mary Gordon brought into the Sanguinetti family a connection of which Sanguinetti was always proud. She was a descendant of William Gordon (1854–1922) who had been the US Consul in Medellin and a representative of British companies in Colombia. From him, Sanguinetti inherited a gold Mayan cross. In fact, the Gordons had arrived in Jerez, Spain, around 1750, Scottish Jacobins escaping the Hanoverian succession in Britain. They became prosperously involved in the sherry trade. Lord Byron records a happy meeting with a Mr Gordon who showed him around his vaults in 1807, and by 1809, they were partners in Sandeman & Co. There are now two marquises and a count in Spain with "Gordon" names.

Mary Garcia, Sanguinetti's mother, born in 1890, was the youngest of Mary Gordon's children. Mary married Alberto on 12 December 1922 in the Gibraltar Registry Office. One of her brothers, John, and one of her sisters, Enriqueta, were witnesses. They would remain close to her and her family throughout her life. John ("Uncle John"), along with their sister Victoria ("Aunty Vicky"), was to play a pivotal role in Sanguinetti's upbringing and in the financial support for the family. The name of "Uncle John" was widely used of John Garcia by family members regardless of whether he was a true uncle or not, a tradition that was to be followed by Sanguinetti himself, as he too became known as "Uncle Albert" by children of his close friends and associates.

Unfortunately, things had gone terribly wrong in business for John Baptist, leaving Mary, John, and their nine other siblings destitute. John took over what was left. Having sampled poverty, he was more determined than most to succeed. By making astute use of the many contacts he had established throughout the years, his business flourished. He purchased prime loose tobacco from North America and Cuba and produced a favoured blend of cigarettes in Gibraltar that was exported throughout Spain and North Africa.

He managed to establish a good customer base and sold cigarettes to well-established traders. His major client was Spanish entrepreneur Juan March Ordinas with whom he had a very close connection. Indeed, there is clear evidence of a long-standing friendship between the two found in their correspondence dating from 1915,[3] and an invaluable outcome of this was that the family would become March's agents in tobacco. Such was the degree of connection between Juan March and John Garcia that some of March's vessels were registered in Gibraltar in the name of John Garcia, to benefit from being flagged as British and coming under the protection of the Royal Navy.

Juan March began life as a tobacco smuggler. He was an unusually perceptive and swift businessman and interloper who often ran his affairs in the margins of the law. He prospered under the Spanish monarchy, was imprisoned by the Republic, and fled to Gibraltar. He generously financed Spanish leader Francisco Franco and the Falangists, and arranged troop airlifts during the Civil War. He acted as a go-between for the British and Franco to keep Spain out of the war, and declassified documents from the United Kingdom show that he funnelled US$10 million from the British to Madrid for that purpose. Even before the war, March was writing to Garcia that "honourable English merchants came to see me in my house in Palma on behalf of the English government seeking my moral assistance in certain matters which were of interest to the English government".[4] With the Nationalist victory in 1936, March regained his influence through the favour of

Franco, and in 1944, he became a supporter of Don Juan de Borbon. He owned newspapers and funded political parties, and his business empire became huge. He was believed to be the seventh richest man in the world after the Second World War. It is telling that the title of Pere Ferrer Guasp's book on him published in 2004 is *Joan March, la cara oculta del poder* (*Juan March: The Hidden Face of Power*).[5] Over his life, March also put together a very large and valuable art collection.

Some of the funds which were to accrue to Sanguinetti later in life had their origins in the tumult of modern Spanish history, though his uncle made his money in other ways too. When John Garcia returned from Madeira after the Second World War, he had retired from the tobacco business and dedicated his time to managing his properties and providing mortgages to commercial entities in Gibraltar. He already owned a residential building at Engineer Lane, and little by little, he purchased numerous buildings at Cooperage Lane, located between the entrance to the Main Street and Irish Town in Gibraltar, where most of the tobacco activity was located. He ended up owning all of the buildings on the south side of Cooperage Lane and its corner building at the entrance to Main Street. He developed these buildings into offices and housing in 1952. It was quite an ambitious project in those days and it proved successful. John Garcia became quite a wealthy man. The Sanguinetti families came to represent a considerable collection of properties in Gibraltar and these holdings helped give Sanguinetti standing in a closed fortress city where status was incredibly important. This is memorialised in the prominent and distinguished family tomb in North Front Cemetery, dating from 1870, which Sanguinetti himself regularly visited and showed to any visitors whenever he was in Gibraltar, out of an abundance of pride in his family.

Albert Sanguinetti's later life as a lawyer was largely dedicated to the common man, but from childhood, he was fascinated by aristocracy and princely style. Even if it was only to chuckle over, it pleased him that he might have had distinguished origins. As well as in Genoa, the name of

Sanguinetti has been one to conjure with in Bologna, where the most recent owners of the sixteenth century Palazzo Aldi Sanguinetti are a family of note. Sanguinetti declared himself to be a cousin of Doria Sanguinetti, whom he called upon in the Palazzo on sea voyages home later in life.

His most striking claim to grand connection on his father's side was being a descendant of a pope. The pope in question, Leo VI, was not one of the most distinguished, or even discernible, successors of St Peter. In his *The Popes: A History*,[6] John Julius Norwich does not even waste ink on Leo by naming him. His reign lasted for about eight months between 928 and 929 AD and he was murdered by Marozia Theophract, who had the louche distinction of being mistress, mother, and grandmother of popes. She virtually controlled the papacy for about a decade, and Leo was enthroned as a fill-in stooge until her appalling son, not then even ordained, became of age to occupy St Peter's throne.

Little is known of Leo except that his family name was Sanguine. They were of good Roman stock and his father was a notary apostolic to the Vatican. The family owned a residence in Rome called the Tower of Sanguine, and Sanguinetti spoke of a ruin in the city that bore his coat of arms. In his brief reign, Leo VI managed to make a call to arms to defend Rome against Arab raiders and, though it is surprising there would be any call for it, forbade castrati to marry. In fact, much later, during his time in Hong Kong, Sanguinetti told Oswald Cheung, QC, that he was descended from a pope. Cheung shot back: "Well, now we know why you are such a bastard."[7] Unusually, there is no record of the customary, sharp Sanguinetti riposte.

Further, if a papal connection was not enough, Matthew Sanguinetti's wife, Maria Guiducce, was said to have been descended from Cardinal Guiducce, Archbishop of Toledo and Primate of Spain. This claim seems to have been clinched for Sanguinetti by the Cardinal's epitaph in Toledo which bears the words "Natural de Gibraltar".

Sanguinetti did not grow up in a family as numerous as his father's and grandfather's. He was the oldest of four, the only son and brother to his sisters—Maria Lourdes, born in 1925, Marie del Pilar, who came along two years after that, and finally, in 1933, when Sanguinetti was nine, Teresa. The family home was on Engineer's Lane, just off Main Street and close to the centre of the town. It was owned by John Garcia who lived across the road at Gavino's Passage with his unmarried sister Vicky. Sanguinetti and his siblings were close to their uncle and auntie, and they were forever going in and out of the Garcia household.

James Gordon, Sanguinetti's nephew, recalls that Uncle John was a distinguished-looking man, tall and slim, very well dressed and, in later years, with a shock of white hair. He did not marry and have children so he became close to his nephew. Sanguinetti was very comfortable spending time in Gavino's Passage where he was very clearly cared for. Eventually, he ended up living there, although he maintained the usual relations with his immediate family across the street. He really liked what the Garcia household had. John Garcia was able to afford a high standard of comfort, including a large house with many quality pieces of art, domestic helpers to take care of Sanguinetti, and even a chauffeur at the boy's disposal. There is no doubt this way of living influenced his personal style, and from an early age, he had a great interest in everything historical. He had a love for antiques and works of art, and devoured books, particularly on history.

Even in his original home at Engineer's Lane, Sanguinetti never knew want. The family employed a nanny, a maid, and a washer woman, and his sisters had their own dressmaker. In their earliest years, they also had a private tutor. His father, on the other hand, was of the "pennies maketh pounds" persuasion and put great store in the value of small money. His sister Maria Lourdes recalled that while their mother was generous to the women who came to the house to sell flowers and vegetables and to the water carriers, these people would time their visits for when Alberto was not at home. To his nephew, James, Sanguinetti described his father as strict. The relationship does not seem to have been close.

The Sanguinettis and the Garcias clearly lived more comfortably than many Gibraltarians, who, on the whole, put up with cramped flats, built around a communal courtyard with water delivered by carriers in barrels. Streets in the city centre were narrow, and there were markets everywhere. The Spanish crossed the border for the day each morning to run fruit and vegetable stalls. Some of those who crossed the border chose to stay.

Similarly, there were many Jews who had crossed the seas to the Rock for good. One of the lesser-known lights in the Gibraltar cosmos are the Sephardic Jews from Morocco. When Spain periodically refused to supply food to Gibraltar, it turned to Morocco.[8] The Sephardic Jews there, expelled from Spain in 1497, happily supplied provisions but some wanted to settle in Gibraltar. One of the Treaties of Utrecht, which ended the War of the Spanish Succession in 1713 and ceded Gibraltar to Britain, said that Jews and Moors could not reside in Gibraltar, and the British authorities tried to enforce this. However, the Moroccan ruler, in turn, threatened to stop the food supply so this provision of the treaty was abrogated. There is now an influential Jewish community in Gibraltar, and one of the greatest Gibraltarians, Sir Joshua Hassan, the first Chief Minister and father of self-government, is a member of it.[9] It was John Garcia, perceptive and beneficent, who lent Hassan the required funds to set up his chambers, which are now the largest in Gibraltar.

Given the variety of peoples who had by this time congregated in Gibraltar, the town was a cacophony of languages and dialects. In the Sanguinetti household, Spanish was the predominant language, but Albert was taught English at school. This was another mark of exception, for only the best private schools used English. Most of the population spoke Spanish with varying grasps on English, and the older generation had hardly any at all. It was not until after the war, when the authorities realised the importance of a collective identity, and the loyalty that came from it, that English was taught more thoroughly to the entire population.

To say that Sanguinetti grew up bilingual is an understatement of his prodigious ability to master new tongues. He even began learning Latin from an early age by the grace of a detailed fascination with the Catholic Church.

Gibraltarian cuisine was as varied as its tongues, having Spanish, Italian, British, and North African influences, and the family would themselves make frequent visits across the border to Spain in their Uncle John's car, stocking up on provisions. Uncle John was one of the first people on Gibraltar to purchase a car, but he never learned to drive and used a Spanish chauffeur, Antonio, to take him around the Rock to visit family and to travel into Spain.

When the children outgrew their private tutor, the girls went to a private school, and Sanguinetti attended Christian Brothers Preparatory Private School at Line Wall Lane, in the centre of the town, at a location that is now a bank. The fees were paid by his Uncle John. He was a day boy.[10] First established in 1835, it was the school of choice for better off families but also had a reputation for strictness and the use of the strap. One British lawyer who spent some of his childhood on the Rock recalls in his blog: "The Christian Brothers ran the school with a rod of iron or more accurately, with straps of leather, which they applied generously to over exuberant boys."[11] In later years, Sanguinetti would chafe against excessive authority, a rebellious streak that might have had its beginnings here. However, the Christian Brothers provided him with a classical education, which also expanded on his Church Latin.

Sanguinetti's fascination with the church is not altogether surprising. The family was devoutly Catholic and went to Mass every Sunday at the Cathedral of St Mary the Crowned as well as on prominent holy days in the Church calendar. Sanguinetti was baptised and took his first holy communion there. When he lived with his Uncle John, priests regularly called at their house, and Garcia frequently purchased indulgences and offered masses for the repose of the souls of his deceased relatives. Sanguinetti later grew to have a rather unsettled relationship with the Catholic religion, but at that point and with no choice in the matter, he was a regular attendee.

He became an altar boy, which extended his involvement with the liturgical life of the Cathedral. Depending on his seniority, an altar boy would support the bishop and clergy in a variety of ways, such as preparing the communion table, arranging the sacred vessels, holding the holy book for the priest to read from, assisting with the incense, and ringing the hand bell during the consecration. Altar boys would lay out vestments for the clergy, process with them, and hold the hems of their garments off the floor when they genuflected. There was altogether much fetching and carrying as the mass progressed and, in doing this in the days before the liturgical changes of Vatican II, Sanguinetti would have had to understand Latin to keep pace with his duties.

This was put to good use, and Sanguinetti was made a senior altar boy. There exists a picture of six of them in profile with heads turned to the camera.[12] Sanguinetti is at the head of the line, and, though not a tall man, he was the tallest and the stockiest, suggesting he was one of the oldest. In the image, he has around his shoulders a white pleated scarf known as a "vimp" which a trusted altar boy would have been invested with so that he could handle the bishop's crozier and mitre during a ceremony without them coming into contact with his uncovered, unordained hands. Fourth along the line behind him is the smallest boy, Alfred Vasquez. He is not wearing a vimp, but this apparently did not slow him in his later career as a QC, knight, and Speaker of the Gibraltar Parliament for 22 years.[13]

This detailed involvement in unworldly grandeur in the service of august and robed adults took a hold on the imagination of a boy so admiring of style and aesthetic. A lifelong fascination with the history and liturgy of the Roman Catholic Church was dug in deep here. In the beginning, there was a childish enthusiasm which involved dressing up and playing at being adults. Sanguinetti led his friends in these ecclesiastical re-enactments, and he even had a ready supply of missionary work. His school friend Raphael Massias, from a mercantile Jewish family, for instance, would visit him in the hopes of obtaining a ham sandwich, something that was obviously forbidden in his own home. Sanguinetti would promise him this tempting non-kosher treat, but before asking the maid to make the sandwich, he would have to baptise Raphael. The two would repair to a bathroom where Sanguinetti, with great gravity, in careful accordance with the sacramental rite and in the name of the Trinity, would baptise Raphael, conveniently as Raphael since it was also a Christian name, over the bathroom sink. Once received into the faith, Raphael could sinlessly have his ham sandwich.

Sanguinetti may have been liturgically fluent, but in boyhood, he had a mild speech problem. At school, his nickname was "Buto", in place of "bruto", or brute. He could not pronounce his "r"'s, hence the diminution, and although it was not a nickname he was fond of, it was to last throughout his life. When he returned to Gibraltar in later years, he remained "Buto" to his associates, "Albert" or "Alberto" to everyone else.

John Garcia remained close to the rest of his family. Uncle John provided his brother-in-law with the car and driver for family trips across the border to Spain. When they gathered together for celebrations such as Christmas, the car would again be on loan to deliver presents of chocolates to family and friends. The family would all come together to celebrate the festival and piled in their contributions—Aunty Vicky would buy the turkey and Alberto would supply a ham, while Aunty Enriqueta and her husband William Canto would contribute Spanish tea cakes. It was in many ways a charmed existence. There were also friends who would reappear throughout Sanguinetti's life. Among them, Lydia Armstrong, a few years younger, remembered him as "a popular boy with a fantastic memory, so good it would make other boys jealous". Even then it seems that he stood out from the crowd. Another friend was Willie Piccone,[14] also younger, who described him as "eccentric but good fun". After Sanguinetti's death, Piccone mentioned to another old Sanguinetti friend Anthony Lombard: "I have a thousand anecdotes to tell about him. His friends would understand them, knowing Albert."[15]

CHAPTER TWO

Scattered by War

It was a mellow, sunny life for a child but one which was overshadowed by the approach of war. Two major conflicts were to have an impact on the Sanguinettis and the first of these was the Spanish Civil War, which broke out on 17 July 1936. It lasted for three years and saw a Nationalist alliance of Falangists, monarchists, and conservatives under General Francisco Franco overthrow the leftist republican government. Fighting began in southern Spain, uncomfortably close to the Rock. Spanish troops from the Spanish protectorate in northern Morocco landed at Algeciras, just across the bay, while there was conflict very near the Gibraltar border. Hostilities raged at La Linea and San Roque, which the Sanguinettis had visited many times. Gibraltarians who had been caught out by the speed at which the war broke out and who were in Spain had to flee back, while Spaniards, escaping the tumult, also crossed the border into Gibraltar, straining resources and creating a refugee crisis. By January 1937, the Nationalists had gained control of Andalusia and the flood of refugees abated. Sanguinetti, now 12 years old, had been given a taste of conflict and the upheaval it brought.

Sanguinetti's life was formed and spent in the British Empire. It benefitted him, addled him, and often aggravated him. Gibraltar was one of Britain's rare European possessions, but Sanguinetti was of a stock—Latin and Catholic—which the standard Briton looked on with mistrust and unease.

Gibraltarians were not treated by the British with the same brusqueness and condescension as the Africans of Kenya or the Chinese in Hong Kong, but the imbalance in the relationship was similar, and Sanguinetti was not to escape it personally until he went to those two places where the natives posed real or imagined threats to the British far greater than anything Sanguinetti's Genoese roots had to offer.

There was a dulling inevitability to colonial arrangements, even in a small and loyal possession such as Gibraltar. The expatriate British civil administrators and military personnel and their families, exerted a political and, gallingly, social superiority over the locally born population. In Gibraltar, the imposition was not cruel or insufferable but still deeply unsatisfactory, particularly to the local business and professional families like the Sanguinettis, who saw themselves as at least the equals of the British around them. If anyone looked down on him because his surname was not English, they were in for an eruption. His superior knowledge of genealogy, carried on a powerful wave of contempt, made whoever belittled him quickly regret it.

An anecdote is attached to Sanguinetti which has it that he was introduced to Queen Elizabeth and, in explaining his name to her, he said: "Ma'am, my ancestors were rulers in Bologna when those of others were mere shepherds in the fields!" This exchange is as unprovable as it is unlikely, but it does suggest the resentment felt against assumptions of superiority amongst expatriate British residents in Gibraltar. There was only the slightest of representation for locals on the City Council, and the civil service was closed to them. The British also expected to be served first in shops.

A long-standing example of the local-expat divide was the Garrison Library, founded by officers of the garrison in 1792. This was exclusively used by the expatriate military and government officials. Gibraltar residents, however respectable or well educated they might be, however unlikely they were to deface the books or decamp with them, were not allowed to use the Library. This caused enormous resentment, and the resident Gibraltarians set up the Exchange and Commercial Library in 1803 for their own use. A memorial plaque shows the names of founders including Sanguinetti's great-great-grandfather James Gordon and his brother John. Inexorably, this alternative became a rival. Since there was no other forum, the Exchange and Commercial Library and its committee soon developed as a seedbed for local politicians and as a pressure group for reform.

Gibraltar was ruled in the conventional colonial fashion with a Governor through the Letters Patent from the Crown, assisted by an Executive Council. There was a significant nudge towards self-government in 1921 with the establishment of a City Council, most of whose members were appointed. In 1934, there was a call for a majority to be elected members, but this was rejected. Significantly, the call was repeated by the Exchange and Commercial Library in 1937.

When the Second World War broke out, there were fears that Spain would side with Germany and capture Gibraltar. Its strategic importance for the British was clear, so Britain invested heavily in aid for Spain to prolong its neutrality and began to fortify the Rock. This meant improving its naval facilities and building an airfield over what had been its racecourse. Then, with the situation in France deteriorating, the decision was taken to evacuate Gibraltar of all but its most essential residents to make way for an expanded garrison. The evacuation policy and dispersal of the population to Britain, Jamaica, Morocco, and Madeira was, paradoxically, to do more to forge a sense of Gibraltarian nationality than anything that had gone before.

Approximately 70 percent of Gibraltar's population was evacuated in a matter of weeks to accommodate the military personnel required to safeguard the Rock. The kingdom of Morocco was a French protectorate and the closest place for Gibraltarian families to take refuge. Alberto, who stayed behind in Gibraltar, booked first-class tickets for two cabins on the SS *Mohamed-Ali-Kebir*, and the family embarked on 12 June 1940 for Tangiers. In all, 13,500 evacuees crossed the Strait between 22 May and 24 June 1940 and were spread out across nine towns in French Morocco. The Sanguinettis booked into a bearable hotel, and their intention was to stay there until called back to Gibraltar, a plan totally tipped over when the French surrendered to the Germans. On 3 July, in the port city of Mers-el-Kebir in northwest Algeria, the British sank the French fleet to prevent it from being taken over by the Germans. What fragile hospitality existed in now Vichy Morocco was shattered. The Gibraltarians were thrown out. Sanguinetti and the family were herded at gunpoint by French colonial troops onto the Tangiers docks. Empty British freighters which, ironically, had just disembarked French troops evacuated from Dunkirk, were forced to take on this new set of evacuees and ship them back to Gibraltar.

The Morocco evacuees triggered a crisis when the freighters docked. The Gibraltar government refused them entry for fear that, once off the ships, they would be difficult to send away again. Crowds gathered in John Mackintosh Square in the centre of Gibraltar as the news broke. Barrister Joshua Hassan, assistant librarian of the Exchange and Commercial Library, took leadership of a new powerful pressure group, the Association for the Advancement of Civil Rights (AARC), which challenged the Governor's legal right to deport native Gibraltarians. Two city councillors, accompanied by the acting president of the Exchange and Commercial Library, went to see Governor Sir Clive Liddell to ask that the evacuees be allowed to land.[1] After receiving instructions from London, Liddell allowed the landing as long as the evacuees went out again when other ships arrived to take them away from the Rock.

Hassan's insistence on "civil rights" in the title of the new movement was an astute move signalling that its intended scope of political involvement was a wide one. The next Governor, Sir Frank Mason-Macfarlane, was positively encouraging of the AACR as a legitimate grievance group and gave them opportunities for organisation which prompted them to become the dominant political party in Gibraltar for 30 years.[2]

This short time back on the Rock was not an easy interlude for the Sanguinetti family. They could not return to their home on Engineer's Lane and instead took up residence at Gavino's Passage. On 10 August, the Sanguinettis, this time including Alberto, Uncle John, and Aunty Vicky, embarked on the *Neuralia* for Portuguese Madeira, while Aunty Enriqueta and her daughter, Lourdes, and son, Pepe, made their way to London. The England-bound ships were not escorted and so they had to sail well out into the Atlantic to avoid German U-boats.

In Madeira, the family stayed in the New English Hotel in Funchal before renting a home in Estrada Monumental. Madeira was a charming and welcoming destination, with considerably more space for the family to live in than they had found in cramped Gibraltar and, sustained by income from John Garcia's rental properties, they were able to live quite well. The properties were looked after by a cousin who stayed behind with the military and were easily let because of the influx of military personnel.

Most evacuees who went to Madeira adapted well. There was plenty of good food of a sort they were used to and the setting was more Latin than the other destinations they might have gone to. The Gibraltarians got together frequently at social and, in particular, religious events. The primary drawback was that relatives in Gibraltar could not visit as such traffic could compromise Portugal's neutral status in the war.

During this time, young Sanguinetti read anything he could get his hands on, which was mostly history books. People found it interesting to get together with him because his skill as a raconteur meant that he could entertain them with tales constructed around what he had read. Many of his friends said that he had a talent for this.

He also continued his schooling and completed secondary school while abroad. He quickly picked up Portuguese. Lydia Armstrong, who was to remain a friend and would re-enter Sanguinetti's life again in coming years, recalled that they would test his photographic memory by showing him a page in a book and taking it away. He would always be able to repeat it word for word, a facility that would serve him well in his later days in law school and as a barrister.[3]

By this time, Sanguinetti was in his third year in Madeira, and though the peace and the charms of Funchal would please him well enough when he was travelling in later years, he was now finding it rather dull. After the first batch of returnees from England arrived in Gibraltar in April 1944, departures from England were halted because of D-Day. To offset this disappointment, returnees were allowed from Madeira and the first batch left in May 1944.[4] The 19-year-old Sanguinetti had gone before them, returning in January 1943 via Lisbon, where he practiced his Portuguese. A postcard from there, sent back to the family in Madeira, attests to excitement and a sense of release.

> Dear Auntie, Daddy, Uncle John, & Mummy
>
> At last you find me here in Lisbon after a rather bad journey but nevertheless now I am in the best of spirits and enjoying myself very much. There are rumours that we are sailing tomorrow on board a Belgian ship, which I fear are definitely [*sic*]. Here we are staying in a 2nd class hotel, where there are lots of seamen, of all nationalities. I shall be writing to you from Gib. very soon. All my comrades are very good to me. Lisbon is marvellous. Tons of kisses.
>
> Albert

He was quickly drafted into the Gibraltar Regiment after his return. For a man who was to spend his life questioning authority and disputing the application of rules, this proved an uncomfortable turn of events. Sanguinetti hated it. He was repelled by guns and shunned violence. He repeatedly fainted on parade either from genuine distress or by faking it, thereby causing chaos. The unhappy episode was brought to a close by finding him employment as a clerk in the cashier department in Her Majesty's Dockyard. There is a suggestion, which could only have originated with Sanguinetti, that he acted as a king's messenger during this time. These diplomatic bag carriers are today usually retired senior diplomats and military men. Even if requirements were a little looser then, given colonial prejudices, why would a young Gibraltarian clerk, militarily incompetent and given to fainting fits, be sent around a dangerous world carrying intelligence crown jewels? Sanguinetti, remembering running errands round the dockyard with mildly classified bits of paper, probably decided to be satirical about his role.

The rest of the Sanguinettis and Garcias made their way back to Gibraltar before the war ended. However, the years had wrought changes, and the family had not endured the hostilities unscarred—Aunty Enriqueta, in London, had gone through the Blitz, while cousin Pepe Canto, Enriqueta's son, had ended up in Edinburgh, where he became ill and died, marrying his long-time Gibraltarian girlfriend, Bertrind Garcia, on his death bed. Gibraltar itself had also changed and was to do so a great deal more in the coming years.

There was to be a lot more politics, and the environment would become more heated on the road to self-government. After the war, there was an increase in the size of the City Council to six elected members, balanced by six unelected members. All of them, including the Attorney General, would be on a new Advisory Council to the Governor. However, the AACR was now pressing for a fully elected City Council. They took a delegation to London for this purpose, and the pressure was on for a full constituted Legislative Council, along the lines of those in other colonies.[5]

Sanguinetti did not stay on to be part of this. For a young man with flair, a gift with words, a passion for history, and obvious dreams of travel, the war had stunted his growth, and he was dangerously underqualified with a school certificate from Madeira. The businesses which his family had been involved in do not seem to have attracted him. His outspoken concern for the truth and his eccentric approach to money may have made him an unsuitable maneuverer in the byways of commerce. What attracted him to law in the beginning is not clear, but it was a path he was bound to look down at least. Some prominent Gibraltar politicians, like Joshua Hassan, and other people he knew, like the Triay family and John Alcantara, were lawyers. Hassan was a local Jew who had gone to London to read law and come home again in 1939. This may have attracted Sanguinetti's attention. There is also the assertion that most barristers are simply frustrated actors, and Sanguinetti was not one to shy away from a bit of drama. While his early theatrical instincts seemed to have found a boyhood expression in the Church, his attitude to Rome lurched, and there was most certainly no priestly vocation. However, affection for the rituals of the liturgy seemed to have persisted, so perhaps the barrister stood in for the celebrant.

Whatever it was that inspired him to pursue law, it was now obvious to the rest of the family, especially Uncle John, that they had a young man of unusual ability on their hands. Sanguinetti, upon whom dealing in leather or tobacco or even property would not have sat well, had decided on a living that no family member had previously been involved in.

As a lawyer, he does not seem to have been an exact fit to start with, and, like many who study law, he had to find his own approach. Sanguinetti had a recall of detail, but he rejoiced in the tradition and the flow of precedent. He was at his core a romantic. A sign of an apprentice love of colour over process comes in a talk given many years later to young lawyers by one of his closest friends and protégés, Hong Kong barrister Gladys Li, SC.[6] She brought to light the unflattering result of an early tutorial for Sanguinetti at University College, London (UCL). She found a double-sided sheet of paper in his handwriting inside a book he had given her.[7] He had been set a question on a quotation from Montesquieu which was not actually written out but which was probably followed by the customary imperative to "Discuss". At the top of Sanguinetti's response to this prompt, the tutor had written in red ink: "This introduction to your answer is too long, full of historical detail.

What the examiner wants mostly is a consideration of the doctrine as it exists today." At the end, he wrote:

> You would have done better to consider the modern position under three distinct headings: 1. Legislative and executive functions. 2. Legislative and judicial functions. 3. Executive and judicial functions. Only by so doing will you make sure of covering all relevant points, many of which you have consequently omitted in your answer.

Sanguinetti seems to have taken the criticism to heart, and he developed down his legal career an acute sensitivity to the distinction between executive and judicial actions. This is also highlighted in his later roles as Assistant Attorney General in Gibraltar and a Crown counsel in Hong Kong.

To begin on this path, the first thing for him to do was to go to London to study law at UCL. Uncle John supported him in the endeavour. Thus, in June 1945, Sanguinetti made for the hub of the waning Empire, and his adult life was underway.

CHAPTER THREE

London Calling

I n June 1945, Sanguinetti arrived in London with the hope of reading law at UCL. Getting to London from Gibraltar in the first place would have been a test in itself. There was no question of travelling by air. The objective was to get overland to Calais or Boulogne and then to the Channel ferry. Some of the journey was by train and some by car. In Spain and France, the roads were in an atrocious state after a decade of war. This was a trip that Sanguinetti made at least three times, including in 1947 when he had to go back to the Rock after the death of his father. In fact, Willie Piccone, a friend from Gibraltar whose family owned the premier Bristol Hotel there and who was in London to do a degree in engineering, remembers driving with Sanguinetti back to Gibraltar in an old Ford Prefect with the engine overheating, punctures and other problems, and having to use petrol coupons to buy fuel.[1]

Petrol, food, and clothes rationing was fairly universal in immediate post-war Europe. In Britain, it was not lifted entirely until 1954, and there were also foreign currency exchange controls which severely limited the amount of money that could be carried out of the country. Sanguinetti's passport[2] shows an application for £17 in July 1947 for his journey back to Gibraltar.

There is a tendency to describe London after the war as drab and damaged. The country was broke, there had been a falling off of maintenance in the housing stock and streets during the conflict, and there were bomb sites which would take years to completely re-develop. There were some devastating winters, particularly in 1947, and the air was so much dirtier than today. Sanguinetti would have experienced the Great Smog of 1952 which lay over the city like a suffocating blanket for five days in December 1952 and blinded it.[3] There were economic austerity measures which affected the middle class. Among the working class and in their neighbourhoods, poverty was no greater than before the war, though political consciousness was. Yet for a young man whose only urban experience outside Gibraltar had been Lisbon, London would have felt like a vigorous cosmopolitan power house, still the mountain top of government and imperial power.

Before he could be accepted by UCL he had to sit a matriculation examination, one which is taken at the end of secondary school education. The examination he took at his school in Madeira was not recognised as adequate to exempt him from the English qualification. In England, at that time, the examination was called School Certificate, and to achieve an exemption from it, he would have to gain a Credit in five subjects under it, four of which were English, maths, science, and a language. He consulted a palmist on whether he would pass. This could have been out of mischievousness, curiosity, nervousness, or all three. Sanguinetti was capable of any of them. He came out of the reading full of good cheer.[4] She said he would pass — and he did. This he must have achieved within a year, as he began studying in the UCL Faculty of Law in the winter term of 1946.

No matter how far London and the law were to bring Sanguinetti out of his chrysalis, he never left behind his Gibraltar friends during his time there, or ever after. If he could at times be a social climber, he was always a loyal and unforgetting one. His early accommodation was shared lodgings at 8 Bedford Place with other Gibraltar chums including Raphael Massias. On Sundays, still a practicing Catholic, Sanguinetti would join his fellow Gibraltarians, including Willie Piccone, at mass at Westminster Cathedral, then a group would meet for lunch at Lyons Corner House at the Strand and Trafalgar Square.[5] The three London Corner Houses, along with two Maison Lyons, were as packed with London life as they were with chocolates, fruit, wines, cheeses, flowers, hams, cakes, and pastries. They were huge establishments with a food hall on the ground floor and three or four floors of restaurants above. They employed up to 400 staff, including the famed "Miss Nippy" waitresses, and would have been a social thrill for the Gibraltar gang.

All of this changed though when Sanguinetti was introduced to a restaurant called Madame Porte's, located behind Foyle's bookshop on Charing Cross Road. This restaurant sold horse steaks, which were not subject to rationing. From then on, Madame Porte's became the group's regular weekend haunt.

Sanguinetti was capable of reaching back into his Gibraltar past as far as the ecclesiastical play acting. He would meet up with Raphael and his brother Mesod in Mesod's rooms to chat over the day's events. There was no risk of Raphael being converted this time. They converted the room instead into a mock law court. Raphael took the part of the judge, Mesod would be the victim or the accused, and Sanguinetti would take on the role of the practicing barrister, alternating between defence or prosecution, and in both roles, substituting a white towel for the barrister's wig. Sanguinetti's deep voice would resonate throughout the house to such an extent that he attracted an audience. He would open the door to find the two landladies eavesdropping outside. "It's part of my training", he would say to them, "for my professional career".[6]

Sometimes on Saturdays, time was spent with a girlfriend called Audrey. She is one of the few women of whom it is said Sanguinetti had a romantic attachment.[7] He kept her away from the rest of the crowd, who thought he was jealous that one of them might try to steal her away. He could have been shy to show himself with a girl and how far or not the affair had progressed. Little is known about Audrey, although Willie Piccone recalled that she was employed as a secretary. To ensure that Sanguinetti's lady friend was not imaginary, one member of the gang followed Sanguinetti one weekend and was able to report back that, yes, Audrey did in fact exist. The relationship seems to have continued for a couple of years and then references to her cease.

Sanguinetti was now 23 years old, on his own, comfortable with the financial support of John Garcia, socially extroverted, and apparently quite confident in his own abilities. He began to develop his own brand of adulthood. To him, there was no reason why his lodging, a rented room in a terrace in Bloomsbury, should not display the same comforts as his family homes in Gibraltar. He filled it with furniture and paintings from antique shops and auction houses, which in those days would have been within the pocket of a well-financed student. It was a standard he would maintain throughout his life wherever he lived.

The settings and society of London brought out in him a taste for sartorial display which would also stay with him wherever he went. Sometimes, his clothes fitted the circumstances to perfection, sometimes they elevated them, sometimes they contradicted them as though he was saying that there were other places he would rather be—indeed, places that were *better* to be. In London, Sanguinetti's standard day dress would be a dark pinstripe suit, usually with a waistcoat, stiff white shirt with detachable collar, rolled up black umbrella with a knobbly cane handle, and, until about the mid-1950s, a bowler hat. On other occasions, there would be striking silk waistcoats, silk ties and handkerchiefs flopping out of pockets, and top hats. It was around this time that he began to smoke a pipe, which was then a more popular symbol of maturity than it might be today.

He was handsome, with a full head of black hair, and the overall effect stood him out from the crowd to the point where people did not realise he was a student. In fact, there was the occasion of a UCL reception, which was attended by the then Provost, David Pye, and Roy Marshall from Barbados who was then doing a doctorate and teaching at UCL and later became vice-chancellor of Hull University. Marshall's wife pointed to

Sanguinetti and asked Pye if he would introduce her to the new member of staff. "He's not a member of staff", said a bemused Pye. "He's a student."[8]

It was not just at UCL where Sanguinetti was prominent. An important discovery for him was the openness of political debate in Britain and the excitement of the parliamentary arena, which he seemed to take to with all the seriousness of a young convert. Raphael Massias recalls[9] that on Fridays Sanguinetti would often go to the public gallery of the House of Commons during Private Members Bills, which shows considerable fascination with the House, even at its quietest. Compared to the business dress of the later 1940s, Sanguinetti's outfits must have been verging on the Edwardian. Strikingly turned out as always, he caught the attention of Sir Stafford Cripps, then Chancellor of the Exchequer, who was known for his ascetic look. We do not know if he saw Sanguinetti as he glanced upwards from the floor of the House or when he was crossing the Central Lobby, but he asked to meet this dapper young man.

Stafford Cripps, though associated with austerity measures, was the real architect of the economic improvement that followed his retirement and death in 1952. The public respected him for "his integrity, competence, and Christian principles".[10] Although Sanguinetti may have dressed like a courtier, his views were more egalitarian. This brief friendship with Stafford Cripps was pure chance but an important one. England was changing, but the post-war years were still an attempt by the ruling class to continue the 1930s by other means. Having been disturbed by the social stratification of Gibraltar, Sanguinetti was critical of this. Cripps, who was taxing the wealthy, increasing social spending, and nationalising industries, would have found him interesting. As a senior cabinet minister, he introduced Sanguinetti to others of rank in England with whom he could hold his own. These included the Conservative, Lord Mancroft (who held various offices under Winston Churchill), Anthony Eden (former Foreign Secretary and later Prime Minister), and Jeremy

Thorpe (later the leader of the Liberal Party who, despite being tried on charges of conspiracy and incitement to murder which ended his career, remained a lifelong friend).

One of his housemates recalls that, on most Saturdays, Sanguinetti took tea with the former Secretary of State for the Colonies, Oliver Stanley, second son of Tory grandee the Earl of Derby, still a Member of Parliament, and also a member of Gray's Inn. Stanley was one of the best minds in the Conservative Party of the time but was also a sick man and died in 1950. Sanguinetti regularly attended political meetings of all stripes in London and continued to make contact with useful figures across the political spectrum. Apart from commoner politicians, he went on, over the years, to associate with members of the royal families of Belgium, Greece, Iran, France, and even Albania.

Gibraltarian lawyer J.E. Triay[11] observed that "Albert's personality gained him access to wherever he thought he ought to be".[12] Triay, who was of considerable support to Sanguinetti at a moment of crisis and change when he quit the Crown service in Hong Kong for private practice, was also in London now, with a loose group of rising young Gibraltarians of Sanguinetti's generation.

There is a photograph of these young men, strolling in a line along one of London's broader avenues, probably by one of the royal parks. Sanguinetti is at the centre and leading by half a step. Even allowing for the black and white of the photograph, his dress seems unremarkable that day: a tweed sports jacket, trousers that could do with a pressing, and a pullover on top of a fairly ordinary shirt and tie. He wears a curious trilby hat with a crown that is too large for its brim and makes him look, as the English of the day would have said, "continental". To his immediate left is John Alcantara in a very formal brass buttoned blazer with a pocket badge the size of a flag and sharply creased trousers. Back in Gibraltar, Alcantara became a lawyer and member of the Commonwealth Party, founded in 1956, which for a short time posed a challenge to the dominant AACR. He left the Legislative Council to become Registrar of the Supreme Court after civil service posts had been opened up to native Gibraltarians. To the far left of Sanguinetti is Louis Triay in a double-breasted suit looking down thoughtfully. He too became a Commonwealth Party member with his older brother J.J., who led it. Both left after disagreements with the Party, which later collapsed. To Sanguinetti's right is the taller Willie Piccone, who became a hotelier, wearing a raincoat, perhaps feeling a chill. To the far right is a shorter, stocky young man who has a necktie finishing half way down his chest and no interest in dress. He was marked as "Imoss", probably short for Imossi, likely making him a grandson of James Lucas Imossi, the founder of Gibraltar's largest shipping logistics and car importing firm.

This line of young men with close links back home and sticking together in discovery of their guardian's capital were the young hope for Gibraltar's future. They all went back to the Rock for good, except, ultimately, Sanguinetti. At this time, he was making the first of many connections which, in the end, would draw him away.

Studying law at UCL at the same time was Simon F.S. Li,[13] whose extended family had been bankers and businessmen in Hong Kong for generations. They were a central family in what historians have described as the "Chinese gentry" of the British colony. Li was the first in his family to become a lawyer and the first ethnic Chinese to be appointed a High Court and then Court of Appeal judge in Hong Kong. He was later involved in approving the terms of the Joint Declaration leading to the return of Hong Kong to Chinese sovereignty in 1997.[14]

Li was Sanguinetti's first impression of Hong Kong. He shared accommodation with him and others on Gower Street, where he had moved, around the corner from Bedford Place and within walking distance of UCL. Sharing lodgings with like minds is one of the treasures of undergraduate life which can never be replicated afterwards. Great fun was had there, entertaining friends in which Sanguinetti took such delight, and the group titled themselves "the Godless people of Gower Street". It was Li's elder brother, Li Fook Shu, who was studying to be an accountant who introduced the Gibraltarian's to Madam Porte's restaurant.

A bond was forged with the Li family which would help carry Sanguinetti forward. It was encouragement and a recommendation from Li at one of Sanguinetti's turning points in 1958 which brought about his move to Hong Kong.

At UCL, Li was already married to Marie Veronica Lillian Yang who was pregnant with their first child. It was to Li's children that Sanguinetti would become more than anyone's "Uncle Albert". He once saw Lillian Li attempting to cross a very busy road, pushing her child in a pram. Here, we have the first of several instances in his life in which he did battle with the traffic Goliath in defence of pedestrian friends. He walked into the road and brought the traffic to a stop using a combination of toreador tactics with his umbrella, a fearless standing of his ground, and a personal charm which needed to be considerable to penetrate a windscreen. With a characteristic half-bow, he gestured to Li to make her way across.[15]

In 1947, he enrolled as a member of the Honourable Society of Gray's Inn, one of the four Inns of Court to one of which a person must belong to be called to the Bar and practise as a barrister in England and Wales. It was also the year his father died. Sanguinetti went back to Gibraltar for the funeral and helped settle his father's affairs. Alberto had made a contribution to Sanguinetti's expenses in London, and this was always supplemented by John Garcia, to take him beyond the bare bones of student living. Garcia now formally undertook to support his nephew throughout the rest of his university career and his pupillage at the Bar, which was unpaid. He arranged for a handsome allowance, which allowed Sanguinetti to live in a fashion that suited him and, above all, without worry. Those who have no prospect of a private income are often disapproving, but though it may not amount to great wealth, it has the marked advantage of granting both security and independence. Sanguinetti not only felt most comfortable with this, he also put those advantages to creative use beyond himself later in his career.

In 1950, Sanguinetti graduated with an upper second-class honours degree in Laws, the same year that Simon Li also completed his studies. He came top of the year in Roman law, an achievement so impressive that Professor Herbert Jolowicz, one of his lecturers and Britain's foremost scholar of Roman law, urged him to pursue a career in academia, and one can imagine him developing into a suitably brilliant and eccentric Oxbridge don, but Sanguinetti was set on being a barrister. He passed his Bar exams, coming eighth in order of merit in the Bar finals, and was called to the Bar in 1951.

Sanguinetti moved into London House on Guildford Street, Bloomsbury, an institution now known as Goodenough College. It had been established in 1930 as a postgraduate residence for "able young men, coming from the Dominions and Colonies", who were being educated as future leaders in the far flung corners of the Empire. In other words, it was a truly international community assembled from all over the world. It included the Canadian Ronald Macdonald, later a professor at Toronto University and a judge on the International Court of Human Rights, and the Australian John McCrossan, later the Chief Justice of Queensland, both of whom became lifelong friends. Sanguinetti had fond memories of London House and eventually became a life member. Decades later, his great-nephew James Anthony Gordon lived there during his own studies.

There was also a sprinkling of residents from the United Kingdom at London House and these included Leolin Price, who became a distinguished QC. He would speak of Sanguinetti's larger-than-life presence, effortlessly captivating over the dinner table, expansively riding hobby horses such as individual liberty and British constitutional freedoms, both of which he maintained were in danger of being eroded by the government of the day. Despite dressing like a High Tory of old, it was quite clear that Sanguinetti did not ally himself with the establishment. Price wrote a card at Christmas 1955 to him in Gibraltar, lamenting that an invitation to visit him there had never reached him: "I expect you are a Very Important Person in Gibraltar, a social lion and eccentrically yourself."[16] There are those who might have thought this observation a touch sardonic, a poke at egotism, but Price did not mean it that way. It was a recalling of the Sanguinetti they had all enjoyed and expected, and it was an assessment that Sanguinetti would hold of himself, be bolstered to read, but be self-effacing if spoken about. He was acutely self-aware. J.E. Triay, speaking of his development in London said: "He deliberately created his public image in a manner which accentuated his eccentricities." Lourdes Galliano, a friend from childhood said that even the youthful Sanguinetti was full of self-mockery over them.[17] Concluding his postcard, Price wrote: "Whenever I meet anyone from London House, he is avid for news of you." It was the ultimate critique on his impact.

He served his pupillage, the final practical stage of his barrister training in three sets of chambers, all distinguished. The first was at 5 King's Bench Walk, which was where Lady Thatcher served her own pupillage (a point Sanguinetti was keen on) as well as the television personality Sir Robin Day. Now known as Red Lion Chambers, it was established by Fred Lawton in the 1940s and was to be home to Michael Havers, later the Law Officer and Lord Chancellor, as well as the renowned judge Sir Harold Cassel. The second was with I.H. Jacob (more commonly known as Sir Jack Jacob)[18] at 2 Hare Court, where Sanguinetti established relationships that were to be crucial to him in his later career. He was to spend most of his pupillage there.

Jacob himself served as a visiting professor at UCL and became a master of the Queen's Bench in 1957, rising to senior master and Queen's remembrancer. He was also editor of the White Book on the Code of Civil Procedure for over 25 years. This was essentially the bible of rules and was regarded as the outstanding British exponent of civil court procedure in the twentieth century. He ended up as the director of the Institute of Advanced Legal Studies and, like Sanguinetti, his early years were in far-off places. He was born in Shanghai to a family that had previously been based in Iraq. They moved to the United Kingdom when he was 18 years old. His abiding influence on Sanguinetti was to install in him a reverence for the rule of law. He further impressed upon him the importance of knowing not only the law and the facts of the case, but also understanding the courts and the tribunals in which he would appear.

According to one of Sanguinetti's fellow pupils Stella Gergel, Jacob would have his pupils prepare a statement of a case, look at it, and then throw it into the bin, his point being that cases were the pathological side of life and that the real world was not reflected in them. Fellow lawyers believe this had a strong bearing on Sanguinetti's later campaigns to improve the administration of the law in Hong Kong. He remained in touch with Jacob for the rest of his life, as well as with Jacob's son Robin, who became an English High Court judge.[19]

Stella Gergel, who became chairman of the Industrial Tribunal in 1977 under her first married name of Hydleman, and later married Daniel Hollis, QC, was the only woman in the chambers. She recalled the rush in which chamber's members met at the ABC Café in the Strand. Jacob would gulp down a cup of disgusting coffee and depart with another pupil who was to become one of the country's most distinguished lawyers, the future Sir Louis Blom-Cooper, QC, who in later years would stay over with Sanguinetti in Hong Kong on trips to Australia. Stella and Sanguinetti would be left together. The tradition was that the last out would pay but Sanguinetti's chivalric code would allow for no such thing; he became actively upset if it fell to Stella. She remembered how, by then, he was living in the "unlovely" Vincent House student residence in Clerkenwell. "He was the kindest of those around; relaxed, probably because he was not going to stay on in the UK." The two became friends outside chambers, and Stella invited him to dinner at her house when her mother and grandmother were visiting from Australia. Sanguinetti showed up in a blaze of couture wearing a satin black and white striped waistcoat and high collar, carrying an ebony lacquered cane with an extravagant gold knob. Stella's family had never encountered anything like it. As ladies often did, they immediately surrendered to the loquacious Sanguinetti charm.

He also had a brief spell at the Chancery chambers of Michael O'Connell Stranders at 5 New Square, Lincoln's Inn, later to merge with two other sets of chambers, 1 Raymond Buildings and 19 Old Buildings, and emerge as Hogarth Chambers. In 1969, Stranders was in public view as counsel appearing for the London School of Economics for High Court orders against disruptive students who had caused the School to close down. Sanguinetti's expectations of pupil masters were as high as theirs were of him, and Stranders was a man he respected over the short time he was with him.

The most colourful and imperial of events of Sanguinetti's eight years in London was at the end of his time: the June 1953 coronation of Queen Elizabeth II. By his account, he was an usher at the ceremony. Gentlemen ushers who escorted dignitaries to their seats were usually retired senior officers of the armed forces, an identity Sanguinetti was the least likely to fit. However, as a young Commonwealth student, he was probably recruited to some useful function on the periphery of the event. It was this which was supposed to have led up to the conversation with the Queen on sheep herding.

Sanguinetti was a guest at the Coronation Reception to Overseas Visitors held by the Mayor and Mayoress of the City of Westminster at the Dorchester Hotel on 16 June 1953. It was a very large guest list, beginning with sultans from the Gulf and the Malay states and coming towards its end with deserving souls from around the Empire who found themselves in London, including young people like Sanguinetti. He was also invited to a similar reception by the Mayor of Kensington, and by the Archbishop of Canterbury to a tea party at Lambeth Palace. One invitation which would not have been expected by a young Commonwealth law graduate was from the Duke of Norfolk and the Countess of Bessborough to a gathering at Petworth House in Sussex being held by the "County Committee".[20] Lady Bessborough's husband had been Governor General of Canada. Norfolk was Earl Marshal of England and organiser of the Coronation, and it may just be conceivable that Bernard Marmaduke Fitzalan-Howard, sixteenth Duke of Norfolk, a man very conscious of his status in the world and everybody else's, met Sanguinetti and was at least bemused if not impressed. There is no record of anyone else introducing him to the world of the County Committee, who were aristocrats of the deepest dye and scions of the establishment and the rural nobility. Yet, let us not forget J.E. Triay's observation about Sanguinetti gaining access to wherever he thought he ought to be. If he made the trip to Petworth, it may have appealed to his fascination with heredity and rank as well as his sense of history. It might have brushed up against his aversion to class distinction and condescension which he found the most difficult part of the British.

Upon reaching the end of his pupillage, he had to find employment as a lawyer. For this he would ultimately not remain in the British homeland. Stella Gergel's observation that he was relaxed because he was not staying in England indicated an intention easily and already arrived at by this stage. It seems strange to achieve London and then want to leave it. He liked the British best when they were at home and he loved their law, yet he had decided to go back to the colonies even though everything he had seen of colonialism in Gibraltar he had disliked.

There is every likelihood that, though Uncle John had supported him through his studies, the strong work ethic of the Garcia and Sanguinetti families would be expecting him to be earning his own living from now on. However, barristers are the ultimate freelancers of the legal world, and earnings at the beginning of a career can be very slim. Sanguinetti was bright and keen, but he had perhaps seen that, at the English Bar in those days at least, to get on you had to be English and middle class with good school connections. If he eyed a life in London in poverty with disdain, life as an overlooked junior in chambers was certainly not the way to go.

For a colonial boy called to the Bar, the Colonial Legal Service had a certain promise of travel and excitement, and it did proffer a way for Sanguinetti to use his professional skills in aid of peoples who lived in the same or even worse circumstances of social and political disadvantage as he had. Thus, in 1951, he accepted a grant from the Colonial Service, with the condition that, on qualification, he would serve for three years. In November 1953, in this capacity, he embarked for Kenya.

CHAPTER FOUR

A Different Kind of Colony

Sanguinetti was offered a probationary appointment as a Crown counsel by the Colonial Legal Service in Kenya on a salary of £865 a year, plus first-class passages, on 31 July 1953.

He joined the Service on the advice of the Right Honourable Sir Sidney Solomon "Solly" Abrahams,[1] an emeritus advisor to the Colonial Legal Service and one of the collections of distinguished figures Sanguinetti managed to meet in London. Solomon was Chief Justice of Uganda, Tanganyika, and, from 1936 to 1939, Ceylon. He became a member of the Judicial Committee of the Privy Council in 1941. Educated at Emmanuel College, Cambridge, "Solly", like other members of his family, was an accomplished athlete, which he is remembered for as much as, if not more than, his legal career. His younger brother Harold competed in the Olympics, an episode featured in the film *Chariots of Fire*.[2] Sir Sidney was an enormously popular father-figure to members of the Service. Sanguinetti spoke of the kindness and guidance he gave to legal officers. He wrote of him following his death in 1957:

> The name of Solly was a byword amongst legal officers in the Service and no matter what one's troubles were one could always look with confidence to Sir Sidney for wise and kind advice. On numerous occasions I have come across officers of the new

generation who, like myself, were fortified by Sir Sidney's counsel before being posted abroad for the first time.[3]

Still, Kenya was a curious choice for Sanguinetti. The posting was not an unqualified success. In what were to be the last 20 years of the Empire, Kenya was developing into a brutal and unconscionable example of it, and he did not enjoy the setting.

It was a fertile land for the most part, and because of that, it was a colony in the truest sense of the word. White people came to settle in it and farm. A small high-profile group of upper-class English people had briefly given the "White Highlands" a notoriety for self-indulgence, but the white population there was a mixed bunch, many from southern Africa, who were keen to profit from its agriculture, enjoy its excellent climate, and live in an aristocratic idyll supported by a supply of cheap black labour. The colonisers were actually few — 23,300 whites lived in Kenya compared with the African population of 5.2 million.[4] To award themselves paradise, this group had dispossessed indigenous blacks of their land and reduced them to landless labourers and squatters. In many areas, Africans were confined in reservations. The "White Highlands" policy restricted the ownership of the best farming land to Europeans.

The Young Kikuyu Association was established to assert African rights and recover appropriated Kikuyu land. Jomo Kenyatta became general secretary and editor of the organisation's newspaper, *Muigwithania* (The Unifier). In the 1930s, he campaigned on a range of policies. His methods were peaceful, but he warned that lack of progress would result in "a dangerous explosion — the one thing all sane men wish to avoid".

In 1944, the Legislative Council in Nairobi included one African member — a lonely representative of the ethnic majority. By 1951, there were eight, but the steps towards reform were slow and half-hearted and were overtaken by an alarming challenge to British colonial rule. In 1952, a militant independence revolt erupted. It was instigated by the Kenya Land and Freedom Army (KLFA) composed mostly of the Kikuyu people, Meru people, and Embu people and dubbed "Mau Mau" by the British.[5] In October that year, the British declared a State of Emergency. Jomo Kenyatta, charged with planning the Mau Mau uprising, was arrested, tried, and sentenced in March 1953 to seven years' imprisonment.

The Mau Mau rebellion, which lasted for around four years, was not immediately successful. The loss of European life was alarming for the British but slight. The Mau Mau killed mostly fellow Kikuyu who refused to support it. Many more Africans, Mau Mau or not, were to die in encounters with British forces or in British prison camps.

By the time Sanguinetti arrived in 1953, Kikuyu tribal lands were being cordoned off by spiked trenches up to eight feet high and patrolled by locally enlisted black troops to prevent the circulation of activists. In the month he had been offered the posting, 100 Kikuyu were killed by British troops patrolling tribal lands. Mau Mau suspects were confined in detention camps on the thinnest of suspicions. There were interrogations in which it has now been accepted that the British used torture. In March and early April 1954, captured Mau Mau leaders were persuaded by the British to convince others to lay down their arms. This failed. In late April, over 40,000 Kikuyu tribesmen were arrested by British forces, which included 5,000 imperial troops and 1,000 policemen. Almost as a response, in the following month, the Treetops Hotel, where Princess Elizabeth and her husband had been staying when they heard of King George VI's death in 1952,[6] was burnt down by Mau Mau activists.

By the end of it all, it was estimated that the British had killed about 20,000 Mau Mau militants, of which 1,090 were executed. The worst of the violence was over by 1956, though the State of Emergency was not lifted until 1960.[7]

This then was the situation the fastidious, clubbable, and socially conscious Sanguinetti stepped into. He was a Crown counsel in the Attorney General's Chambers in Nairobi and travelled on circuit to cities like Nyeri, the administrative capital of the Central Highlands. He often commented on how the courtrooms were unpleasant places, badly ventilated and very hot. The atmosphere could be further thickened by tension amongst the African defendants confined in an alien colonial legal building, angered and frightened that they were being denied justice. There were frequent, emotional, sometimes violent eruptions.

From his files, we know Sanguinetti provided legal opinions to African District Councils, largely elected local bodies, on matters to do with licences, merchants, deportation issues, and building applications. He dealt with issues on the hide and skin trade, forest development, and the agriculture trade. He provided coroner's reports on the deaths of military personnel and legal opinions to the Commissioner of Local Government and to the Accountant General and Director of the Establishment.

Between October 1953 and June 1954, Sanguinetti prosecuted 14 cases under the Emergency Regulations of 1952—six were for murder, one for manslaughter, four for the possession of firearms, two for the possession of ammunition, and one for possessing 19 sticks of gelignite. He also prosecuted one rape case. The basic details of these are as follows, all listed in the *Kenya Gazette*.[8]

06 October 1953	Murder trial, Joshua Thetu Ndirango Kinothe
08 October 1953	Murder trial, Muturi s/o Munyuru
14 October 1953	Murder trial, Sabre s/o Marwa
19 October 1953	Manslaughter trial, Joseph Chereti s/o Namasaka
10 November 1953	Murder trial, Ouko s/o Odonco
29 November 1953	Police beating trial, Mbogwa s/o Gathua
12 February 1954	Murder trial, Sindugu Ole Negarne
06 March 1954	Unlawful possession of 19 sticks of gelignite trial, Thika M. Arui s/o Kithiaru

16 March 1954	Possession of firearms trial, Machakos Mwendwa s/o Muli
29 April 1954	Possession of firearms trial, Njaku s/o Kimani and Njenga s/o Kungu
27 May 1954	Possession of firearms trial, Wawkru s/o Kimani and Karanja s/o Mungai
27 May 1954	Possession of firearms trial, Muthahi Githaiga
27 May 1954	Possession of ammunition trial, Shege s/o Gathogo
29 June 1954	Rape trial, Abeli Ngaria s/o Kisarta
29 June 1954	Possession of ammunition trial, Mwangi s/o Muhia/1954; Murder trial of Maree s/o Mukwe

It is interesting to wonder at the fate of these men from so long ago and how a young prosecutor with such a strong sense of native fairness and who had so recently revelled in the political liberty of London looked upon them sensing, as he must have, that what he had to hand for their prosecution was unfair, in some cases plain untrue or provoked by deep illiberality. In the two years leading up to November 1954, "756 Africans were hanged, more than 500 of them for crimes other than murder and 290 for 'unlawful possession of weapons'".[9] Of these figures, Sanguinetti will have been acutely aware.

There was a life of cool verandahs, cooler drinks, pressed whites, evening dress, sequins, and silks and the eternity of partying and sport which was drawn as a screen across the unpleasantness. The only black face to be seen as a reminder of the outside and troubled environment would be out of the top of a servant's tunic. Sanguinetti seems to have done predictably well in this atmosphere.

He kept a black and white photograph dated March 1954. What it says on the back could be "Sunday" or it could be "Lindy"—possibly referring to either the young society woman in a white evening jacket and black dress or the older grande dame in a leopard skin coat featured in the photo. Between them is Sanguinetti, in black tie, hand held waist high, two fingers poised with a cigarette and the other two pinning a programme, looking keen and assured with his company. They are in Nairobi's swanky Trianon Club. There is a pillar, double white doors, and the hint of a cherub in the corner. Counsel is clearly not concerned with native affairs tonight. He wrote "Self, 31" in a corner of the image.

In his collection of photographs of cocktail parties, there are more taken in those 14 months in Nairobi than in any other location. Perhaps there was little else to do. Sanguinetti enjoyed society, and there was no one who could not only work a room but hold it too quite like him.

Fellow Gibraltarian Lydia Armstrong had kept a coincidental track with him and was already in Kenya with her husband, who was working with Cable & Wireless, outside Nairobi. "I would invite him over for kidneys cooked in sherry, one of his favourite dishes", she recalls.

> I tried to match-make for Albert when he was out there but he wasn't having any of it. But he would come and entertain everyone in the house. He would tell farfetched stories tongue in cheek and people would never be sure whether or not they were true. Once, when an epidemic of foot and mouth broke out, Albert told us in all seriousness that when people travelled, they examined your feet and mouth to see if you were suffering from it. People would listen to him in awe.[10]

Impeccable though he always was in black tie with double-breasted waistcoat, his daytime clothes did not match the usual local style in Kenya. He dressed exactly as he had done in London, in pinstriped suit with rolled umbrella and bowler hat. Given the unwanted warmth and odd looks he would have had to bear, this could have been a statement beyond mere eccentricity—"There are better places than this to be."

Armstrong tells of the limits which the political situation imposed on movement and peace of mind. For instance, it was unwise to walk out too far on one's own, and everyone had to learn to handle a revolver. This Sanguinetti certainly did not do. When Armstrong gave birth, there was a policeman in the delivery room, because one of the Mau Mau oaths was to eat part of a human being, the favourite of which was the placenta. Some fears may have been paranoia but others were not. Armstrong once recommended a houseboy to her sister, only later was it discovered that he had taken a Mau Mau oath to kill white people.

All this bore down on Sanguinetti, who was appalled at the way the British treated the Africans and uncomfortable and restless in the climate of feeling around him. In one instance, he went to a local village to view a crime scene. The atmosphere turned sour. We might imagine that he was in this rough and earthy rural spot dressed in a pinstripe and bowler because, once again, the Sanguinetti umbrella was deployed. He unfurled it to keep the villagers at bay and beat a hasty retreat. Even when the surroundings were less hostile, he was uncomfortable in them, even though he brought good sense and kindness to bear. He could never love Kenya.

Kenya's colonial standards, especially in the law, puzzled him. On one occasion, he prosecuted a man who was convicted and sentenced to death. Sanguinetti returned the next day and found him sitting outside the courtroom. "What are you doing here?" he asked. "No one's come to take me away", replied the man. "I don't know what to do."

One recipient of this anecdote suggested that Sanguinetti likely told him to buzz off while he had the chance. This would chime in with the mischievous Sanguinetti wanting to give the underdog his chance, but it would go impassibly against the grain of Sanguinetti the lawyer, who held to obedience of the law and its courts as well as the rightness of maintaining their final judgements, no matter how much he may privately doubt their wisdom. There came a point through, in Kenya in 1954, when his doubts broke into voice.

Gerald Nazareth, born in Kenya and later to become a High Court judge in Hong Kong, was working with

Sanguinetti as a prosecutor in the Kenyan service. If there was suspicion that the colonial embrace might have quietened Sanguinetti, Nazareth's view of him dispels it. Before his death in 2018, Nazareth recalls of him at that time: "Albert was there, just as he was in Hong Kong: an excellent lawyer; a very powerful advocate; a thoroughly good man; a fiercely independent one; and a character in his unique way." [11]

It was this goodness and independence which drove Sanguinetti to contradict the accepted wisdom on the conviction of Jomo Kenyatta. The colonial government felt that the uprising would die down if Kenyatta was tried and imprisoned. They had nothing to charge him with, but, after scratching around in his personal papers, he was put on trial with five others for organising the Mau Mau. Historians John Lonsdale and Adrian Assensoh assert that he was made a scapegoat and that the authorities knew very well that Kenyatta was not behind it. [12] His trial looked like a set-up. The main prosecution witness perjured himself, and the judge, brought out of retirement and paid a hefty £20,000, was alleged to have had a back door to the Governor throughout. [13] In the very small legal world of Nairobi, on the inside of the Crown's chambers, Sanguinetti will have known much of this.

The Supreme Court overturned the inevitable conviction, on a technicality. The government took the case to the East African Court of Appeal, which reversed the Supreme Court's decision. The defence ultimately applied for the case to be heard by the Privy Council in London, but it refused his petition to appeal without providing an explanation. This disturbed Sanguinetti. He kept in his files a letter dated 20 October 1953 [14] from counsel in London to the Attorney General's Chambers in Nairobi describing the proceedings and how the Court, including the Chief Justice and four others, began by being very much in favour of granting a hearing and were somehow turned by the arguments of the Attorney General of Kenya, John Wyatt. "I don't think I have ever seen a case turned about more completely", wrote the counsel A.G. Somerhough. He went on in a huff of satisfaction:

> I may add that Mr Wyatt not only had to cope with a Court which was hostile from the outset but also the gloomiest prognostications from his advisers here. I am glad to say modestly, that I was the sole exception.

British barrister and Member of Parliament Denis Pritt, for the defence, said this sudden refusal from the Court came despite the fact that his case was one of the strongest he had ever presented during his career.[15]

It has been alleged that this turnabout by the Privy Council may have been political rather than legal, something which was almost but not quite unthinkable. Not unthinkable to historian Jeremy Murray-Brown who alleges it[16] and maybe not to Sanguinetti, who regarded the result with the deepest of suspicion. The young man whom Nazareth describes would have been shocked that the law in the colonies could be so manipulated. The man who Nazareth knew then and who others came to know afterwards was incapable of staying silent. In Nairobi, he voiced his concern that from a court in a Kenyan provincial town up to the apex court of the Empire, Jomo Kenyatta had not met with justice.

Inevitably, this placed him at odds with the Kenyan Legal Service. He had laid the groundwork for his own departure. It was something he was to do repeatedly in the first ten years of his career. Whenever he was in employment, there arose a matter of principle which he found unshakeable but would shake him out of office. After the third such occasion, in Hong Kong, he found that the key to satisfaction was not to be in office at all.

At this point though, he needed another job, and he was guided to one back home in Gibraltar by J.E. Triay, who was now in practice there. This left the tricky business of extricating himself from Kenya. He resorted to "Solly" to explain his position, which would ease him out of Kenya. Sanguinetti wrote to him on 19 August 1954:

> Dear Sir Sidney,
>
> The kind help and valuable advice you gave me when I saw you last year before coming out to Kenya encourages me to write to you on a personal matter.
>
> The matter that I should like to bring to your attention is that two days ago I learnt from the Gibraltar papers that the appointment of Assistant Attorney-General, Gibraltar, will fall vacant this year, and I feel that due to my connections with Gibraltar, both linguistically and otherwise, I would be more suitable there than here in Kenya.
>
> I can assure you that I do not intend for a moment to embarrass anyone in the least in connection with a possible transfer to Gibraltar, bearing in mind that I undertook when granted a legal probationership in 1952 to serve for three years in any part of the Colonial Empire, and also being fully aware moreover that the exigencies of the Service must come first. Mr Attorney here has however assured me that although he would be sorry to lose my services, nevertheless, so far as he is concerned, he would certainly not stand in my way if I were to apply for the appointment.
>
> Accordingly today I cabled the Colonial Secretary, Gibraltar, applying for the appointment, and a letter will follow in due course giving particulars and stating that my application is subject to the approval of the Secretary of State and the Government of Kenya.
>
> Needless to say that if I am transferred to Gibraltar and by doing so expenses would have to be incurred in one way or another, by either the Secretary of State or the Government of Kenya, I am prepared to repay such expenses, including, if necessary, the legal probationership fees to the Imperial Government.
>
> Please excuse this somewhat hasty and informal approach, but it is necessitated by the fact that applications for the appointment must be in the hands of the Colonial Secretary, Gibraltar, by the 20th instant.

The statements that "I would be more suitable there than here in Kenya" and "Mr Attorney would certainly not stand in my way if I were to apply for the appointment" were flashing beacons for Sir Sidney that Kenya was as happy to see him go as he was to leave. His keenness to be done with the posting is shown in his unprompted offer to refund his probationary grant. The move was approved of, and the application to the Attorney General's Department in Gibraltar was accepted.

Poor in spirit though Kenya had been for him, there had been some fine parties, and, as he did everywhere, in every aspect of his life, Sanguinetti increased his circle. His time there enriched him in friends who were to reappear later in his life and mean a great deal to him. One of these was Hugh Mills-Owen who, like Gerald Nazareth, was working as a legal draftsman in Kenya. He was later called to the Bar and went on to practise in Hong Kong where he and Sanguinetti became good friends. Mills-Owen went on to become a High Court judge in Hong Kong and later Chief Justice of Fiji. One of Hugh's sons Richard became a QC in Hong Kong and kept up the family connection with Sanguinetti. Another lifelong friend from Kenya was Dermot Renn Davies, who became his pupil and later the Chief Justice of Gibraltar.

Sanguinetti left Nairobi for Gibraltar in December 1954, with a short break in Rome along the way. It would be understandable to think that Sanguinetti's aversion to the distinctions and discriminations overlaid by colonial rule grew in his upbringing and certainly the roots of his dislike would have been laid there. However, the scale and immediacy of strong arm imperial rule under emergency laws, which he worked with in Kenya, unveiled to him a colonialism operating with greater deviousness, military intensity, and intolerance of dissent than usual to maintain its authority. Kenya taught him to recognise new dangers in the colonies in which he went on to serve.

CHAPTER FIVE

Home to Higher Office

The Gibraltar government position had been advertised on 10 August 1954. By the end of the year, Sanguinetti was back home in the substantive post of Assistant Attorney General, acting up as Attorney General.

He lived in an official residence, a house on the higher reaches of Engineer Road on the upper Rock, called Tewalfan. Today it is called Humphrey's Bungalows. The view across the Straits is bliss. A four-bedroom house up at this location now commands a very high price. For Sanguinetti, this was a satisfyingly correct place for him to be at last and a most appropriate gathering spot for his thriving social circle which took life the moment his feet touched the Rock.

Dr Cecil Isola, a Gibraltarian he had originally met in London as a student, recalled many evenings when he and his wife, Mary, dined with Sanguinetti and how tastefully the house was decorated, with art and antiques that Sanguinetti was accumulating as he moved through the world. Larger soirees were held in the evenings that became known for their hilarity and good nature.[1] Sanguinetti's now established disinclination to extravagance and his preference for spending peanuts on food led him to serve, literally, peanuts at these affairs. Ever aware of the effect he was having, Sanguinetti took pride in this and how a party could go on with a bang just on peanuts. His guests enjoyed the paradox of peanuts and the effervescence of Sanguinetti, in the setting of a decorated garden, with marble busts lining the path. The evenings became so well known throughout the Rock that friends who had been accidentally left off the invitation list would feel no embarrassment at all about demanding to be put back on again.

Tewalfan was also the scene of more profound gatherings. Sanguinetti's passion for history and antique items led him to become a leading member of the Gibraltar Archeological Society. In that capacity, he entertained the distinguished archaeologist Gordon Childe when he lectured to the society in Gibraltar. Childe stood out in his field for being the first to apply what has been described as Marxist interpretations to archeology.[2] Although he was not pro-Soviet, he was highly critical of capitalism and Western government, saying it was "full of fascist hyenas". It was typical of Sanguinetti to have brought such a controversial figure under his roof, and it was an evening of proud and treasured memory. He entertained other visitors of note there and in the town by virtue of his office and his ex-officio membership, as acting Attorney General, of the Governor's Executive Council. Membership of "Exco", towards the end of Sanguinetti's tenure, consisted of the Governor, the Deputy Garrison Commander, the Colonial Secretary, and the Attorney General as well as four members nominated by the elected members of the Legislative Council.

The political and constitutional situation which Sanguinetti returned to in 1954, though still unsettled, was improving for local Gibraltarians. There was, however, resentment over the treatment of the wartime refugees and the length of time it had taken to return them to Gibraltar. The last group, from a camp in Northern Ireland, was not repatriated until 1951. The experience had forged a new identity as Gibraltarians. The fear that the gains made during the inter-war years were slipping away or, at best, stagnating created a new wave of political activism after 1945. The struggle led to the establishment of the Legislative Council in 1950. From this vital point, political development would become a process of evolution.[3] Sanguinetti was part of this, albeit through an interesting route—namely, a formative constitutional crisis that blew open in October 1955. It began when the government attempted to rush through a Revenue Bill that would have increased import taxes on certain items. There was expected to be a tied vote between elected and appointed members but an appointed member, Peter Russo, suddenly voted against the Bill, defeating it six to four. The Governor, General Sir Harold Redman, did as all cornered soldiers are want to do and made an immediate counterattack by using his reserve powers to override the vote. All five elected members of the Legislative Council—Joshua Hassan, A.R. Isola, Albert Russo, A.W. Serafty, and J.E. Alcantara—resigned in protest over what they saw as an abuse of power. All these men were of the same Gibraltar stock as Sanguinetti, colleagues and some fellow members of the small Bar Association who knew him well, yet his files carry a memo to the Governor advising him that his action in using the reserve power against them was lawful.[4] As a law officer, he was in the middle of a tug of war between the local establishment, his world, and the colonial government, his adopted loyalty. His advice as acting Attorney General was factual, in accordance with the law, but not what everyone wanted to hear. At this stage in his life, he had developed strength and adamancy in defending a position, and this led to conflict with some in his circle.

It would be misleading to describe Sanguinetti's relationships with his friends on the Rock as a stream of balmy get-togethers, punctuated by hilarious parties. There were postures and emphatics in Sanguinetti which seem to have provoked irritation and the occasional poking from his more conventional friends. Some of them, including Louis Andlaw, as officers in the Gibraltar Regiment, had been on an exercise on the Rock and they staged a pretend attack on Sanguinetti's house late at night "as a prank".[5] These men must have known about his brief and unhappy membership of the regiment and his open contempt for soldiering. This prank, bordering on bullying, could have been an unarticulated disapproval of his attitude. They must have hoped he would laugh along with them, but he did not. The sense of affront to his dignity led to a high temper, and he called the police. He lectured them on soldiers being officers and gentlemen. He demanded a written apology from all of them, an unusual requirement from friends, followed by a threat that he would press for their arrest if he did not get one. This bruise to Sanguinetti's self-esteem lasted beyond the night. Andlaw reports that he gave the required apology because he was to be married two weeks later and feared his wedding would be marred by the affair.

All came to be forgiven on both sides, of course. Friends of years' standing learn to close one eye, and all Sanguinetti's Gibraltar brethren accepted his peculiarities, not only because he too acknowledged them in amusing flourishes of self-denigration but because, from other quarters of his soul, came such an outweighing wealth of friendship, knowledge, kindness, and fun. One who knew him well in Gibraltar and speaks of him with great praise put it in a private memo: "Many of his friends in Gibraltar readily excused Albert his failings and idiosyncrasies. His warmth and his friendship were in no way diminished, notwithstanding his foibles."[6]

His post and his ex-officio membership of the Executive and Legislative Councils kept him in the hothouse of political reform through the 1950s. Immediately after the embarrassment of the reserve powers fiasco, the Colonial Office and Redman were so keen to patch up relations that when the AACR, on a London visit, gave the Colonial Secretary their manifesto for further reform, it was largely accepted. The reforms of 1956 gave the Legislative Council a majority of elected seats and an independent speaker as chair. This was a watershed in modern Gibraltar history. It was only a matter of six more years before departmental government was taken over by local ministers and Gibraltar was effectively self-governing.

Sanguinetti sat at the centre of political development yet his work in the courts in such a small place as Gibraltar was more prosaic. The cases he prosecuted were such misdemeanours as breaches of a probation order, larceny, and common assault. In the Supreme Court, he handled a lottery fraud allegation. Out of the usual run of things, he prosecuted a murder on a cargo ship called the *Geddington Court* and a libel case against the *Gibraltar Post* newspaper,[7] which was defended by Joshua Hassan, Executive Councillor and Mayor of Gibraltar, to demonstrate what a small world it was that he worked in. In *Pizarello v Attorney General*,[8] a case which set an interesting if probably rarely needed precedent for his own profession, Sanguinetti established that a barrister's chambers were not an educational institution for the purposes of allowable deductions of tax.

He gave opinions on behalf of the Crown on residency permits, trade disputes, agreements on social insurances for Spanish workers, stevedoring, transport and dock labour, town planning, law drafting, and amendments to existing and coming legislation. Yet, it was his legal vision, framed in history and delivered with eloquence which left its mark on Gibraltar more than the bread and butter of his job.

At the ceremony for the opening of the legal year in October 1955, Sanguinetti, acting as Attorney General, gave the reply to the speech by the retiring Chief Justice Sir Roger Bacon, who was giving way to incoming Chief Justice, Sir Hugh Flaxman. The rolling inclusion of principle with history and a dash of humour was archetypal Sanguinetti. It was clearly not the sort of oration they heard every day in Gibraltar, and it left an impression that was to last for years in the tight circle of law and government. To leave us in no doubt of that, Anthony J.P. Lombard, a former Mayor of Gibraltar, said in his very full four page obituary of Sanguinetti in the *Gibraltar Chronicle*[9] that the speech was remembered to that day. It was probably the most significant speech outside a courtroom that he ever made. The most remembered part is a treatise on Sanguinetti's vision of his profession and the flavour of the passion in which he held it.

> Your lordship has given us sufficient food for thought. The duties and responsibilities of membership of the profession at any time and in any society are many. Amongst the most important duties which a lawyer has, is to see that which is right and fair is done

irrespective of personal considerations. "Fear" it is said "is not a good companion", and no one better than a lawyer knows how true this saying is. Throughout history it can be seen that lawyers have not considered any price too high to pay before sacrificing those sacred principles of Righteousness and Justice which are the true heritage of the profession. In spite of these historical facts there have been great, clever, and at the same time good men who in one way or another have not been charitably inclined towards the profession. It was only recently that I was going through the lives of these celebrities and was interested to see what they had to say about law and lawyers. Shakespeare said, "The first thing we'll do is to kill all the lawyers." "I never spoke evil of any man behind his back", declared Dr. Johnstone, "but I think that man is an attorney". However, notwithstanding such views, no one can gainsay that lawyers as a whole don't stand for what is fair, just and right. A lawyer's sense of duty is his life's compass and its magnetic pole, Justice.

It was that sense of duty to his client and to the society in which he lived, which prompted Cicero to defy the military dictatorship of Sulla, when he undertook to defend Rufus. And when James I was trying to introduce the vague and ill-defined principle of Roman jurisprudence "that which the Prince desires is law", into English law, that great lawyer Sir Edward Coke, declared before that prince the famous words of Bracton, "that the King is under God and the Law". Unselfish devotion to duty was the main factor that induced Malherbes to defend his sovereign Louis XVI before the revolutionary Tribunal of Paris and to follow him soon afterwards to the guillotine.

No wonder then that 20 centuries ago it was said, "We are the slaves of the law that we may be free." Cicero and the 12 tablets of Rome concluded by stating that "the safety of the people lies in its supreme laws".

To these supreme laws the profession in England has contributed in no small measure and will continue to do so when necessary, especially when the liberties of people are at stake. Respect due the law by governor as well as by governed seemed as it was and is, the only sure shield for reasonable freedom and the maintenance of the integrity of all members of the body politic.

Unfortunately, the respect due to the law from governors was not always forthcoming. As acting Attorney General, Sanguinetti advised the Governor as to the legality or otherwise of his actions, as he had in the case of the reserve powers in 1955. He had delivered encouraging news on that occasion, but the duty can cut both ways. He had always been on good, even social terms with Governor Redman and recalled outings with his family into Spain. In May 1958, Redman was replaced by General Sir Charles Frederic Keightley, who had led the inglorious though militarily successful attack on the Suez Canal in 1956.[10] We are left with a recollection from Sanguinetti that, at some point, he advised the Governor that what he contemplated doing was illegal. When the Governor told him that he would nevertheless press ahead, Sanguinetti apparently told the Governor that, in that case, he would prosecute him. What triggered this confrontation we do not know but what followed suggests that Sanguinetti's days suddenly became numbered. The outspoken Attorney, speaking out on principle, and quite a bit further by threatening action against Her Majesty's representative, had shaken things up and himself out of a job. A way to terminate his services was soon devised.

The post of Registrar of the Court was advertised with a salary scale that went from less than what Sanguinetti was earning to beyond that. He assumed the new Registrar would start at a lower figure than he was getting so he did not apply. John Alcantara was the only applicant and he got the job — as he would have done anyway. As a member of the Legislative Council from which he had resigned with the collapse of the Commonwealth Party, he had been marked by the administration as developing worryingly anti-English tendencies. He had been particularly embittered by being, as a locally born Gibraltarian, refused entry into the civil service. Now that this barrier had been swept away, he was offered the establishment embrace of the Registrar's post and, to ensure the warmth of it was fully felt, at the top of the pay scale.

Sanguinetti rose to the bait. He pointed out in righteous indignation that the Assistant Attorney General ranked equivalently to the Registrar and the Stipendiary Magistrate and that he had seniority over Alcantara. The government refused to see that equivalency. What was more, they informed Sanguinetti that the post of Assistant Attorney General was to be abolished and that at the end of his contract, they would have nothing more to offer him.

It was fortunate that the turnover in the Colonial Legal Service was sufficiently vigorous for posts to fall vacant with regularity. This time, the opening was offered by Hong Kong. Sanguinetti knew people there who had been with him in Kenya and, above all, Simon Li and his family from his days at UCL. It is claimed that the Lis put in a good word, and it would not be surprising if that had been well heard. In late July 1958, a "savingram", which was a Mad Hatter concoction of a telegram sent by mail, informed him that he was offered a post in the Hong Kong Attorney General's Chambers on a salary of HK$1,650 per month which would increase to HK$1,729 after 31 December, on expatriate terms of pension, quarters, and passage.

On 1 September 1958, Sanguinetti wrote as far up the system as he could go, to Sir Kenneth Roberts Wray, Legal Adviser to the Colonial Office, in a tone both puzzled and with a sense of hurt, explaining that he was only going because he was being shoved. Wray wrote back on 7 October,[11] consolingly, that nobody had reason to think that he was anxious to leave Gibraltar. In Sanguinetti's words: "It was Hobson's choice. Had to accept it."

He was given a send-off by the legal profession with a party at the Mediterranean Rowing Club on 29 August 1958. On behalf of the government legal service, the acting Colonial Secretary presented him with a silver salver. A silver cigarette box was also presented to him by W.M. Isola[12] as senior member of the Bar in appreciation of his work for the profession while in Gibraltar. Isola voiced the feeling of his brother barristers when he stressed the cooperative spirit in which Sanguinetti had performed the duties of his office. "He had found himself in embarrassing situations which he had met with a thorough determination to act justly and independently."[13] On what those situations were, Isola did not elaborate. Presumably the cause of his leaving was among them, but the remark suggests that the politics of the post, tugging him between government and community, must have been its most trying part.

More informally and raucously, 45 of his friends, all male, grouped together to give him a hearty send-off, across the border in Spain, at the restaurant Miraflores. The evening was marked with roaring laughter and impromptu speeches. His friend Dr Cecil Isola, summed up its success: "Albert was a very good person, who was hugely popular, with many friends, because his fellow human beings enjoyed his company and sought him out."[14] Though the numbers dwindled as the years went by, these friends turned out every time he made his way home for a summer visit. Word would spread that Sanguinetti was back on the Rock. "Within 24 hours, everyone knew", says Isola. He compared it to how the word went around like wildfire in the 1930s when a consignment of Cork butter arrived.

The *Vox* newspaper did not celebrate Sanguinetti's going. It berated the government instead. In September 1959, they had no Chief Justice, as yet no Registrar and no Stipendiary Magistrate. Now there was no Assistant Attorney General. This extraordinary famine of attorneys in Gibraltar did not end until 1960 when Denys Roberts was appointed full Attorney General. He only lasted two years before he shouted to the officer in charge of the Queen's Birthday Parade that he had messed it up. Roberts was also moved on to Hong Kong where others and Sanguinetti were gathering.

CHAPTER SIX

Hong Kong: On the Bench

When he left Gibraltar, Sanguinetti took a diversion to Europe and went to the 1958 World EXPO in Brussels before travelling on to Hong Kong. Almost as soon as he arrived in November, he was taken out to his first Hong Kong Chinese meal by Simon Li. It was at the Capital Winter Garden Restaurant, existing now in a shrinking number of memories, and the menu included braised sharks fin, Peking duck, and apple toffee. Sanguinetti came to love Chinese food, telling an interviewer from *Vox* newspaper on one of his trips back to Gibraltar that it was "excellent, surpasses even French".[1]

His first government quarters were in Tower Court near the Lee Gardens Hotel in Causeway Bay (a popular shopping and residential district along the eastern coastline of Hong Kong Island), one of the sweeteners of colonial preference. Expatriate government staff enjoyed heavily subsidised official quarters, higher salaries, pensions based on them, long holidays with pay, and subsidised private education for children. Local employees, where they were of equivalent rank, had none of this. Sanguinetti had arrived in Hong Kong at the beginning of a period of expansion and transformation which was accelerating the economy and alterations in the industrial structure beyond the established patterns of racial and social behaviour. The catch-up process was at times painful.

In 1945, the population of Hong Kong had shrunk to about 600,000. By the time Sanguinetti arrived in

November 1958, there were, on average, 25,000 refugees a month entering Hong Kong from Mainland China running ahead and away from Mao's Great Leap Forward, a five-year economic plan, later abandoned in 1961, which caused anywhere between 30 to 55 million deaths from starvation, execution, and forced labor.[2] In some months, the influx to Hong Kong reached as high as 100,000, and the Census of 1961 put the population at 3.1 million.

The refugees flooding in included wealthy industrialists from Shanghai who had shipped down equipment, bought in new, and re-established their large textile factories in the colony. Local entrepreneurs, benefitting from Korean War boycotts and the closing up of the Mainland, started up smaller factories with the barest of facilities and, if they were to be successful, demonstrated remarkable flexibility in reinventing themselves when market demand for products shifted. The immigration surge furnished thousands of peasants and workers who provided the labour pool for these endeavours. An industrial revolution was taking place in Hong Kong.

Although it is tempting now to see colonial governments as villains, the Hong Kong government was playing a sensibly considered part in this industrial explosion. To house the enormous population increase, they took, with some hesitation at first, the daring step of building huge resettlement estates of extremely basic accommodation, followed by whole new towns. They also encouraged the private sector landlords, almost all local Hong Kong Chinese, to re-develop their pre-war properties by erecting high rise buildings. The physical infrastructure of the colony was maintained and expanded to match the changes. The provision of utilities was reliable and predictable. A high level of public order was generally maintained and the rule of law operated. Yet as the work and profits omelette was being whisked together, eggs were being broken.

There was little or no social security system or old age pension in 1958. Inflation was quite high, but the plentiful labour force kept wages low. Working conditions could be atrocious, and hours were long. Trade union activity was almost non-existent. Corruption was endemic in the lower levels of the government and its services. In the police force, it was so thorough as to be a fine art. The great rush of poor newcomers and new money being made gave rich opportunity to organised crime and its particularly insidious Chinese version, the black society or triads. The working population lived with it all. Employment was high, and a living could be earned in relative safety. It was better than what was behind them, and there was at least the prospect of a break out into wealth ahead.

As a judge and a barrister, Sanguinetti's instinct was to look out for the broken eggshells. For example, though the government put measures in place to protect tenants in rented accommodation, as a magistrate, he had before him unscrupulous landlords who wanted to get rid of their tenants to develop their increasingly valuable real estate by declaring that a building was unsafe, having gone to lengths to make it so or by having bribed an inspector. He was good at and brave in confronting this kind of crookedness, but the legal setting in which he worked was not always encouraging.

The number of barristers in private practice when Sanguinetti arrived in Hong Kong was small. There were two QCs—John McNeill and Leo D'Almada—and a dozen other barristers, making up the junior Bar. The number of solicitors in total was under 100. Barristers had to qualify in England and be admitted to one of the Inns of Court and serve pupillage there, as Sanguinetti had done. They served on four-year contracts with six months of paid leave. The Crown Law Office was also small, with the Attorney General, Solicitor General, Law Draftsman, and not more than 12 Crown counsel. Sanguinetti started as a Crown counsel. Simon Li was the only Chinese Crown counsel. Patrick Yu, a legend in his time and author of *Tales from No. 9 Ice House Street*,[3] had been the first Chinese Crown counsel but had left just before Li joined, on a matter of principle—the government refused to pay him the same as the expatriate Crown counsel of equal seniority.[4]

It was difficult for this small band of lawyers to make contact for the good with the broken parts of society. Legal aid as such in Hong Kong in 1958 was virtually non-existent. In criminal cases, free legal representation was given only to the accused standing trial for capital cases in the High Court and, at the judge's discretion, free legal representation was given to appellants and accused persons whose cases were subject to reservation on a point of law. The common man regarded the police with suspicion and carried with him the traditional aversion to contact with the "official bandits" of government. The sort of justice that liberal lawyers like Sanguinetti wanted to bring was a heard of but far-off notion.

His first case was as a Crown counsel and he did not win.[5] He was prosecuting Detective Sergeant Kwan Man-on and Cheung Chan, a former police constable, in a jury trial before Mr Justice Courtney Reece. Patrick Yu was acting in defence. The charges were that Kwan had conspired with Chan to solicit money corruptly from a ballroom manager and that he demanded money with menaces, charges Kwan denied. The three men had met in a Kowloon café, but according to the defendant, the meeting had been coincidental and he only overheard the odd snatch of conversation between Cheung Chan and the other man, Cheung Kwok-hung.

The jury took just two hours to acquit Kwan and this did not bother Sanguinetti. Maybe he did not have the streak it took to be a ruthless prosecutor. His belief was that a prosecutor presents the facts and evidence fairly, and leaves it to the jury to weigh up. It was not the duty of the prosecution to obtain a conviction in every case, and he punctiliously upheld the legal principle that it was wrong for a prosecutor to coach prosecution witnesses because it gave them ideas to embroider the factual evidence.[6]

As he had intended to be, Sanguinetti was appointed as a magistrate soon after he arrived[7] and held office from April 1959 to July 1964.[8] He was appointed for periods as an acting District Court judge on two occasions, starting on 22 May 1960 and 22 March 1963 and lasting for several months. Acting District Court judge was a novel and unsettling position. In the United Kingdom, a judge is appointed for life or the age fixed for retirement. In colonial administrations, the position was quite different. The judiciary was subject to colonial regulations and government orders. The door was open to pressure from the government. The acting judges could feel constrained in expressing views on matters before them. Demotion to the former substantive appointment was always a threat. This happened twice to Sanguinetti. It forged a mission in him thereafter to change the system and eliminate acting appointments.

The circumstances in which he worked on the Bench were a light-year removed from those of the modern judiciary. On 29 January 2005, he took a guided tour of the old Magistracy building in Central which, for a while, was being shown to the public as a place of historical interest.[9] He noted down some recollections of its functioning days, 40 years before. On the top floor was his first clerk, Mr Kishell, who did handstands and fell over when Sanguinetti walked into the room. There was Court No. 2 where he was to make a statement in 1964 which would again shake things up and shake him out. He was reminded of Hin Sing Lo, the solitary Chinese magistrate, who sat for many years there and died at the age of 101. He was much respected and regarded with affection and acted in the traditions of a Chinese mandarin. Lo had actually sat the Chinese imperial civil service examination in Guangdong in his youth. He was very lenient in his sentencing. He would admonish those convicted with "[y]ou have dared to disturb the tranquility and peace of this oasis of Hong Kong" then give them an absolute or conditional discharge. At the morning adjournment, he served tea and biscuits on the Bench itself. Just as Sanguinetti was delighted by Lo, he disliked a magistrate called Van Rees. This man was also an auxiliary policeman. He went out hunting for illegals at night who could well appear before him in the morning. This may have been in the tradition of William Caine, the first Chief Magistrate of Hong Kong (1841–1844), who was also head of the police force he had formed, but, even in 1959, that sort of rough and ready duality had become bizarre. When Sanguinetti appeared before Van Rees as a defence counsel, in a typically theatrical expression of disapproval, he walked out of his court. Van Rees asked to see him in his chambers but, when Sanguinetti arrived, he was told the magistrate was having tea with the diocesan bishop, so he left. "I refused to attend on him in chambers", Sanguinetti wrote. He went on to explain:

> I said he could make an appointment with my clerk to see me in my chambers and I would decide whether to charge a fee. Later he tried to be friendly and use my first name. He was posted to Fiji where they burned down his court.[10]

Sanguinetti was alarmed by the lack of legal aid, the severity of sentencing, and the anachronistic punishments at his disposal as a magistrate. "I was absolutely stunned when I first came here in 1958", he said in an interview with Margaret Chan of *iCubed*, titled "Does Punishment Work", the year before his death.[11] "They were given…the cane, simply for begging. For being destitute—for not having parents to look after you. Can you believe that?"

His views about corporal punishment were solidified when 22-year-old Lee Shu Chung, who had been convicted 30 times already, appeared before him in the South Kowloon Court in 1961 on two charges of larceny from delivery vans on 11 and 18 April.[12] The man's record dated back to 1948 when he was convicted at age nine for begging, and in the following ten years, he had been given 126 strokes of the cane, chiefly for begging, and 12 strokes for being destitute. "Probably this corporal punishment has made you anti-social. It seems you have never been given a chance in life", he told the accused, who readily agreed with him.[13] Lee pleaded guilty, and Sanguinetti decided he should be given a chance and asked for a probation report. He placed the youth on probation for 18 months to live in a Discharged Prisoners Aid Society Hostel, and gave him HK$20 from the poor box. He also sentenced him to one day's prison which meant he was released at the end of the court sitting. He told him: "Now don't be foolish and throw away your chance. Many people want to get into the hostel but could not do so. You are lucky in a way."

Lee did not follow up on his luck. He went on to offend again, and Sanguinetti took it philosophically. He told Chan that Lee had so much ill treatment, it had probably been too late. He campaigned for corporal punishment to be abolished.[14] In 1970, in an appeal against sentence, which included caning, in which he acted for the appellant, the Court set the sentence aside and held that caning was a departure which should only be made in consultation within the judiciary.[15] This was not followed. More than 125 males were caned between 1979 and 1990.[16] It was not abolished until 1991.

From the Bench, Sanguinetti saw the range of unjust practices and petty corruption which blighted the lives of the working class. In the South Kowloon Magistracy, he sat in an evening session in Court No. 1 where hawker cases were heard. It was a hurried and tawdry business. Cases that were only remotely similar, dozens of them, were taken en bloc. All the defendants would raise their hands in a unanimous plea of guilty and the magistrate would fine each hawker the same amount, simultaneously. In some ways, it was a neat response. Hawking was an indispensable service to an immigrant population which had money but not enough to spend in stores or street-front shops. The scope of demand and supply was far beyond the cumbersome hawker licencing system. Hawking was an important way of making a living, an alternative to the factory, and a commercial beginning for the more entrepreneurial, the period version of a start-up. So the hawkers came back again and again to be fined. It was a running cost along with the protection money they might pay to the street-level triads. In one case, Sanguinetti expressed his sympathy for Cheng Kam-yip, indicating that he "realised the difficulty people like yourself have in making a living", but also had a duty to enforce the law.[17]

En bloc guilty pleas may have been pragmatic but they were not just. The casual cynicism of this process was never going to survive Sanguinetti's inevitable disapproval. He insisted on each case being taken on its own with individual pleas, and mitigation and fines levied depending on the circumstances. This approach meant that a great deal more time was spent in dealing with these cases. The Court sat very late, which Sanguinetti was prepared to do in the interests of justice, but the Court staff were not, in the interest of getting dinner. He was particularly unpopular with the shroff clerks who collected the fines and had to stay the latest. There were mutterings of a strike. Sanguinetti was not conciliatory. He upped the game by imposing fines of dollars and cents in odd numbers. Every transaction involved scratching in the bottom of purses and pockets. Long queues formed, the accounting escalated, and the office would run out of change. The staff grudgingly accepted the new regime, and Sanguinetti went back to round figures. How long the proper way of pleading was maintained there immediately afterwards is uncertain because, like the can kicked down the road, troublesome Sanguinetti was soon transferred, but he had made the point, and the malpractice was, before long, stopped entirely.

Care had to be taken in determining where Sanguinetti was to be transferred. T.L. Yang[18] was sitting in the Causeway Bay Magistrates' Court when the principal magistrate, Derek Cons (who might later have become Chief Justice), asked Yang (who became Chief Justice instead) to come over from the Central Magistracy and take over Sanguinetti's court in Causeway Bay. Some sort of swap was involved. It has to be appreciated how prized a spot the Causeway Bay Magistracy was. It was centrally air-conditioned. The magistrates each had their own toilet. The Central Magistracy, in contrast, had window type air-conditioners and toilets were shared. This was a match to Sanguinetti's flammable self-esteem. He thought he was being victimised. He refused to let Yang into his court, physically barring his entrance. Yang was the most pacific of men and a magistrate so fighting back was not a choice. Cons had to go down to Causeway Bay and sort the matter out, which mostly involved assuring Sanguinetti that he was not being victimised. This may have been Yang's first taste of a roused Sanguinetti, but it would not be his last. Yet they were friends for the rest of Sanguinetti's life, two men who were clearly in different realms temperamentally but still came to enjoy an intimacy of mutual confidence.

While Sanguinetti lost his temper with bureaucracy, hierarchy, and what he saw as manifest colonialism, he rarely lost it with the common man or woman. He could lavish on them as much good humour and charm as he would on a countess at a cocktail party. Sitting on the Bench gave him the opportunity to show some grace to ordinary folk, sometimes in small ways but ones that touched hearts. He also defended them with a passion which could go beyond bounds. In his early career as a magistrate, it did just that in the cause of a hawker named Tam Fun who pleaded guilty before him on 23 June 1961 in Causeway Bay.[19] He cautioned and discharged her. However, during the course of the hearing, she had complained that police corporal Shum Hung, the arresting officer, had maliciously damaged her property, used abusive language, and assaulted her. Sanguinetti asked her if she wanted to charge the police corporal. She most certainly did, so he got her to swear a complaint and made it so that he tried it himself. Although corporal Shum Hung denied the allegations,[20] Sanguinetti found him guilty and fined him HK$15 for using abusive language in a public place and ordered HK$1 compensation. On the damage charge he was conditionally discharged and was acquitted of assault.[21]

The police were not happy. The Crown counsel for Shum Hung stated that that Sanguinetti "let his sympathies run away with him" and that "his verdict was quite unreasonable".[22] The case went on appeal before Ivo Rigby, then a senior High Court judge, who later became Chief Justice, too. Sanguinetti had made the point that the policeman was represented by Crown counsel and the woman had no one, therefore he regarded it as his duty to cross-examine the witnesses.

This absence of legal representation was a preoccupation of Sanguinetti's which was with him throughout his career and his contribution to legal aid reform was probably one of the greatest he made. Rigby sympathised with his position. However, in his judgement,[23] he quoted Sanguinetti's own words, which paraphrased a 1945 judgement from the Master of the Rolls that he should "not descend into the arena of dispute and side with one party against the other". "But despite the very words used by the Magistrate", wrote Rigby, "I am satisfied that that is exactly what he did do." The appeal was allowed. Sanguinetti's passion had got the better of him.

To policemen in front of him either as witnesses or defendants, he could be hard and fair. In a statement of findings,[24] he found two policemen guilty of taking an HK$20 bribe and given them 14 months each. On the other hand, in 1960 in the District Court, Sanguinetti let off a police officer for unlawful and malicious wounding, stating: "I do not find… that the offence has been proved beyond reasonable doubt against the defendant… He may have acted unreasonably… that is another matter."[25] Earlier that same year, he had indicted and fined a police constable for giving false testimony[26] and almost a year later, in April 1961, he "criticised the police for depriving a man of his 'personal liberty by unnecessarily detaining him for 11 days'".[27] His criticism of the force did not stop there. In February 1963, Sanguinetti questioned the link between the number of arrests a policeman made and his chances of promotion.[28] However, later, in 1972, he would write an article for the *South China Morning Post* indicating his support for increasing pay and improving conditions of service for the police force to curb crime.[29]

As a principled pain to the procuratorial authority, he was unchanging. The Attorney General even took him to appeal because he had refused his request to give conditional pardons to prosecution witnesses, promises one might presume in some backstairs deal.[30] In his magistrate's findings of the case sent to the higher court, he made a point of law that this was a prerogative not at the magistrate's discretion.[31] An admirer, signing himself "Charles", wrote a note and pinned it to Sanguinetti's copy: "Excellent…you are a past master at drafting such cases stated."

People on the margins easily caught his attention. He listened carefully in July 1960 to the circumstances of a Muslim Indian police constable who wanted to affirm rather than swear on the Koran because he was "unclean" and his knees were uncovered, and he allowed it.[32] Sanguinetti was particularly impressed by the man's supporting story of an Indian sergeant major in the Hong Kong police who, according to an 82-year-old watchman Ali Ditaa, had not been so fastidious and had collapsed and died in the Supreme Court 30 years before for swearing in that condition. A bit of the ceiling fell down too for good measure. Sanguinetti thought it prudent for all concerned to stick with affirmation.[33] The law continued to be colour blind through Sanguinetti's eyes no matter how distasteful the circumstances. In his judgement in November 1959 over an Indian businessman demanding money with menaces,[34] Sanguinetti found that whatever reprehensible means or actions the man took, he may have had a legitimate claim to what he demanded. "Not an easy decision to reach", he wrote.

For the lustful, he had compassion. In the prosecution of a club for illegally allowing visitors to pay to watch pornography, one witness complained bitterly that he had paid his HK$10 but that the police had raided the place before he was able to watch the film, called *The Sexual Life of Robinson Crusoe*, which must have been somebody's film of the book written by Humphrey Richardson.[35] Sanguinetti listened to his misfortune gravely. Since he had to view the film himself to decide whether it was pornographic, he invited the witness into his chambers to watch it with him and the man's misfortune over his HK$10 was reversed.

He always appreciated counsel who came before him who demonstrated ingenuity and contributed to his own stock of anecdotes. There was one which he delighted in and told with glee on occasions both suitable and not. A man was up in front of him for an act of indecency in a public toilet. His defence lawyer, with full control of his facial expressions, explained to Sanguinetti that his client was crossed eyed and so, while standing in the urinal, had touched the penis of the man standing next to him in mistake for his own. If asked what the outcome was, this was one of those occasions when, having dropped a racy teaser into the conversation, he might have said one of his favourite lines: "More when I know you better."

He would also enjoy talking about how he was once the butt of unintended ridicule when before him was a New Territories peasant. In the early 1960s, the "NT" was still remarkably remote. There were only three roads and a single-track railway up there, and the population had not yet been educated by TV courtroom dramas. It was, therefore, not surprising for the peasant—presumably in the Fanling District Court—to ask what the mandarin was doing sat there with cauliflower on his head.[36] There are accounts of this tale being told in more than one corner of the Empire and one might wonder at this peasant's familiarity with a crop not grown in those parts. Still, Sanguinetti dined out on it for years, and he said that the common man's impression of judicial regalia persuaded him that it needed doing away with, something he advocated, though not particularly vigorously.[37] Coming from one who enjoyed getting dressed up, it may have sounded hollow.

Inevitably, Sanguinetti attracted the attention of the Chinese, particularly its press, largely over his handling of hawkers. In February 1964, one press report told the story of how he acquitted hawker Chang Ping-kwai after she was arrested without warning for obstructing the pavement outside Western Market with two boxes of vegetables.[38] Constable number 84 was prosecuted for false testimony against her. He had denied seizing her plastic bag of water but another constable, who must have had a dim view of his colleague, broke the usual "omerta" and said he did. It was not on the evidence list, but the bag was given back to Chang. Sanguinetti is quoted saying that she had been "driven from post to post … prosecution becomes persecution".

Members of the public wrote to him hoping that, in traditional fashion, his magisterial powers might work for them. On 19 October 1963, for instance, Kwong Ngau, a workman in Sai Wan Ho, wrote to him about how a shoe merchant was persecuting him by setting up a love trap and spreading rumours of indecent assault.[39] This merchant's men had caused him to lose jobs and harassed him in his home. Doing what he could, Sanguinetti had scrawled a quick note on the letter: "Referred to police."

Tsang Ying, a police corporal in Tsim Sha Tsui, wrote to ask for help over his delayed promotion. An orphan refugee from the Mainland, he now had four kids. He had lost out in the interviews of 1962 and had not been nominated for those in 1963. "How kind and solicitous you have always been about my welfare", he says, indicating that they had obviously crossed paths before. "Put a word in to AC Sutcliffe, who I believe is a great friend of yours." The calculating Tsang seems to have been worth promoting, even though he must have blotted his notebook along the way, because he was right about Assistant Commissioner Sutcliffe. "Great friend" may have been stretching it, but Sanguinetti liked Sutcliffe because he was an intelligent and honest cop. He wrote to him on his retirement as Commissioner of Police in 1974, and Sutcliffe wrote a warm and appreciative response.[40] On it, Sanguinetti noted: "He is in full agreement on lenient sentencing policy for drug addicts and traffickers…he said he could not say so at the time (Not the first one)."

From one Chen She Tu, Sanguinetti appears to have been able to command discipleship. He wrote to Sanguinetti telling him he was "the only kindness [*sic*] judge in HK".[41] He offered to serve him for the rest of his life. Could he or his wife work "in your family"? "And if you don't want that—could you introduce me into a job at the Hilton and if they don't want me, introduce to another job either mean or noble."

Though these letters highlight his impact on those he helped, in his two periods as a District Court judge, he did not hear cases that proved to be jurisprudentially remarkable. That was not the nature of the job. However, his rulings in some cases did establish interesting precedents for Hong Kong. For example, he held that if you used words admitting to a debt from a dishonoured cheque (which could not normally be pursued because of the statutory lapse of time), then the debt could indeed be pursued.[42] In a complicated Tenancy Tribunal appeal, he held that if a rent collector—someone with the sole job of collecting the rent—knows there is a breach of tenancy and collects the rent nonetheless, it is not a waiver of the breach on behalf of the landlord, but if an estate agent with some general responsibility for the property does so, even though the landlord still does not know, it is a waiver.[43]

He also decided that works done to premises could be so extensive that the building was entirely new and therefore not subject to Part 1 of the Landlord & Tenant Ordinance, applicable to pre-war premises.[44] In another case,[45] he held that when the bailiff is levying distress—confiscating goods—for rent, they are an officer of the court. This contrasted with the position in England where the bailiff is the agent for the landlord. In this case, the rent had been paid just before the action by the bailiff so the confiscation was unlawful but the bailiff was protected.

In the trial of Assistant Revenue Officer Ko Chik-nam, on a charge of dangerous driving, the defendant challenged his statement made to the police because it was taken by a Chinese officer with very bad English but the defendant did not give evidence.[46] Judge Sanguinetti commented on his not giving evidence and maintained that in the circumstances, he had a right to comment even though, ordinarily, a judge would not, lest it cast the defendant in an unfavourable light.

On 22 March 1964, an anonymous resident wrote to Sanguinetti about the proceedings of a coroner's inquest into the death of a five-year-old boy,[47] saying simply: "I really admire you for the splendid way you conducted the enquiry." That he acted as coroner is one of the least remembered of Sanguinetti's functions. In this role, he had both the opportunity and duty to comment critically on public policy and management when they caused death. His remonstrations had an impact in particular on industrial safety and hospitals. The death of a workman killed by a blasting accident, for instance, led to a verdict of accidental death caused by negligence.[48] Sanguinetti pointed out that there was no government department responsible for ensuring that the special conditions covering such work were complied with. Soon afterwards, there was.

In 1960, he began criticising the conditions in the casualty departments of public hospitals. At that time, there were few large-scale general hospitals—none at all in Kowloon—and no hospital authority, just smaller hospitals of mixed origins and capabilities, all under pressure from immigration. That year, a man had been thrown out of a delivery lorry. He developed gangrene in his leg because treatment was withheld in an overwhelmed hospital, and he later died.[49]

In March 1961, the death of a six-day-old baby prompted further comment from Sanguinetti about the terrible conditions in the casualty departments. He questioned a prominent doctor involved, Harry Fang, later Sir Harry Fang, orthopaedician, crusader for rehabilitation of the disabled, and senior unofficial member of the Legislative Council, which caught the public's attention. The case was the lead story in the *Hong Kong Standard* on 19 March 1961, which included Sanguinetti's earlier comments from the lorry case.

> On June 30th last year in a hearing on the death of a lorry attendant, the Coroner, Mr A.J. Sanguinetti made the following remarks "Whilst I am not at all happy or for that matter, not at all satisfied, that the deceased was properly attended to … I can well appreciate the difficulties that the medical and other staff have in the very crowded hospitals in the colony, but I would like to suggest that some system, some means should be worked out by the authorities concerned to safeguard that treatment prescribed to any individual patient should in fact be carried out with certainty."[50]

The following day, the same newspaper ran an editorial further highlighting Sanguinetti's point. Across the top of a copy, James Lee wrote in red ink: "Dear Albert, This is a feather in your cap, Best wishes."[51]

There was a downside to being a coroner, however. You could be called out at all hours to view a body, mainly to decide whether an autopsy was required. Sanguinetti was, not surprisingly, averse to this. Fairly late one evening, he was contacted by the prison authorities at Pik Uk and asked to come out to view the body of a prisoner who had been found dead. Sanguinetti baulked at the trip from Causeway Bay on a ferry across the harbour and then to the far reaches of Clearwater Bay Road. He refused. "Let the mountain come to Mohammed", he said, to confound them. Contrariness can have its comeuppance though, and out there in the far reaches of the Prisons Department, someone had understood the allusion. To his amazement, at around midnight, the doorbell of his government flat at Tower Court rang, and he opened it to two prison officers saluting him and holding between them the body of the deceased prisoner. The anecdote, which Sanguinetti frequently relayed because he enjoyed telling a story against himself, sadly does not go on to tell whether the body was invited in.

As strong as any aversion to viewing corpses in the depths of the night was Sanguinetti's dislike of any arrangements coming from the Chief Justice, Sir Michael Hogan.[52] There is no record of where this dislike came from. Friends of Sanguinetti have described his hostility to some people as feuds or vendettas, but these processes need causes and, at least in Hogan's case, one does not present itself. Hogan had a far from easy career in the Colonial Service and was not one to be looked down on. He served in Aden and then Palestine, both of them turbulent territory. He was Attorney General of the Federated Malaya States and Administrator of the Federation immediately after the High Commissioner, Sir Henry Gurney, was assassinated in 1951 during the Emergency, the communist guerrilla war against colonial rule.[53] Hogan also had in common with Sanguinetti a brilliant memory with a powerful recall of detail. Yet whatever Hogan did, he appears to have offended Sanguinetti's principles of liberty and independence.

As a magistrate, Sanguinetti attended meetings of magistrates chaired by the Chief Justice. The Commissioner of Police and the Attorney General also attended these meetings. Sanguinetti and Arthur Garcia, another magistrate who was later a High Court judge and Hong Kong's first Ombudsman, objected as a matter of principle to having the Commissioner of Police and Attorney General, who were prosecuting authorities, sitting in on these meetings while the legal profession involved with defence was not represented at all. Their objections were overruled by Hogan. Thereafter, Sanguinetti and Garcia adopted a policy of what they called "satyagraha", passive resistance after the fashion of Mahatma Gandhi,[54] and refused to contribute to the proceedings in any way, sitting there passive and mute. This became tiresome, so Sanguinetti often arranged to be absent from Hong Kong on the days fixed for the meetings. Satyagraha could be conducted from Macau.

His antagonism towards judicial arrangements in general and Hogan in particular did not bode well for a future on the Hong Kong Bench, and from September 1963 to July 1964, Sanguinetti flamed out from government service, for the last time. The spark was a characteristic one. Annoyed by the trappings of hierarchy, he regularly parked in the spaces reserved for puisne judges at the Kowloon Magistracy. The flame was then fanned by his reaction to a circular issued by the Chief Justice to magistrates on sentencing for minor traffic offences.

The origin of this circular was a moment out of Gilbert and Sullivan. Hogan had been talking to a visiting French admiral who, *en passant*, said he had been advised that in Hong Kong it was easier to plead guilty to a parking offence, even though you thought yourself innocent. Why a French admiral should have been concerned about parking cars on Hong Kong streets was not clear, but the Chief Justice was affronted by the suggestion from a foreign dignitary that the courts were a push over on traffic. On 15 August 1963, he issued a circular[55] through the Chief Magistrate. While he did not wish to say anything "which would detract…from the power and authority of a magistrate to exercise his own…judgement", he thought it was "incumbent on Magistrates to impose penalties that will act as a deterrent". By the following Sunday, the contents of the memo were the subject of not exactly friendly comment in the "Tiger Talk" column of the *Hong Kong Standard*, with a peculiarly specific reference to motorists who might park in areas reserved for judges. The column was usually written by reforming crusader solicitor Brian Tisdall, and the suspicion that he learned what he had from Sanguinetti was strong.

On 28 September, the Chief Justice asked Sanguinetti to come and see him. The setting of the meeting was unfortunate. Hogan regarded it as an interview rather than a conversation. He asked High Court judge Alastair Blair-Kerr to be present as a witness, which did give force to Sanguinetti's allegation that it was an inquisition. Hogan began by asking him if he parked wrongly at the Kowloon Magistracy. Sanguinetti said he would only answer that to a court hearing or a judicial committee of inquiry. To further question as to whether he knew he was breaking the law and would he stop it, Hogan got the same response. Questioning then shifted. Had he disclosed the circular to the *Hong Kong Standard*? Sanguinetti said he had not but that he "may or may not" have chatted about it to colleagues or "at a dinner party".

This was Hogan's version of events in a note he wrote afterwards.[56] Sanguinetti, in a counter note,[57] remembered it differently. He said he had admitted the parking but would not explain it nor give any assurances lest he abrogate any legal right that might be subsequently established by a judicial committee or a court hearing. On the circular, he would only discuss that before a commission set up under Colonial Regulations. However, because Blair-Kerr had been present, he claimed he had been the subject of accusations of impropriety and dishonesty.

Escalation was rapid. Hogan fired back with questions like "well did you or didn't you?", "who was present at the dinner party?", and "have you chatted like this in the past?" Sanguinetti said he had already answered these questions. Hogan took that as a refusal. Sanguinetti declined to say more to him because he was seeking permission under Colonial Regulations to ask for a Legal Opinion.[58]

The Colonial Secretary replied to that request by asking for the full details of the case. For help with the draft and for advice, Sanguinetti went back to his roots and asked his old friend J.E. Triay in Gibraltar. Triay gave him both, and he was an honest friend who read the land ahead. "If you have ways and means of profitably withdrawing from the service, you may possibly be a happier man for availing yourself of them", he wrote, incisively.[59] As to the future, the Registrar's job in Gibraltar was a "stepping stone", but for that Sanguinetti would have to "be careful not to offend the powers that be, and maintain cordial relations, irrespective...It is not my impression that you would or could do the same." They were taking in a new partner at his own firm, but he was sure Sanguinetti would be too expensive.

On 8 February 1964, Sanguinetti told the Colonial Secretary that he was suing the Chief Justice.[60] Permission was unsurprisingly denied on 27 February. His career on the Bench would now clearly never survive the next contract review, but he must have decided that he could not go in silence. What he saw as the independence of magistrates being reduced for the convenience of departmental policy was a malpractice that needed to be known. On previous occasions, he had upbraided prosecutors and policemen before him for telling him they believed the accused deserved a strong sentence. To Sanguinetti, the circular was a powerful organised move in that direction.

On 9 March, before he began hearing three traffic cases, he made a statement in open court, in Court No. 2 in the Central Magistracy, citing the Chief Justice's circular as a "departmental circular and a direction to magistrates". He said that he would deal with the cases in front of him "'in justice, according to the law', although he ran the risk of disciplinary action".[61] He went on to find all three not guilty and discharged them.

Three days later, in a highly unusual move, the acting Chief Justice, Ivor Rigby, took time out at the beginning of his own day in court to issue a rebuttal to Sanguinetti.[62] The circular was not departmental, he said, and was not from the government to magistrates. It was a regular communication from the Chief Justice, and it was purely guidance and not a directive. In the English press, the *South China Morning Post* took against Sanguinetti, asking "why then all the fuss?",[63] while the *Hong Kong Standard* supported him but mostly over why the circular had been "secret" in the first place.

After his return from leave, the Chief Justice set in motion the machinery to rid himself of this turbulent magistrate. The Colonial Secretary wrote to Sanguinetti on behalf of the Governor on 7 May to inform him that his dismissal was being contemplated on the grounds that:

> On 9th March 1964, whilst holding the office of magistrate, you published a statement from the magistrate's bench which represented, contrary to the facts that you had received, by way of a departmental circular, a directive which conflicted with your judicial and magisterial functions and duties.

He was asked to exculpate himself. Now the campaign was about how he was to go out through the door. Was he to walk or be thrown?

On 12 May, he wrote to the Colonial Secretary, "after much heart searching", to propose that he retire from government service under the usual conditions. On 24 May, with Triay's help, he wrote a ten-page document setting out the grounds on which he exculpated himself.[64] He got a reply to both on 22 June saying he had failed in his exculpation (a word in which the civil service seemed to take a surgical delight) and until he retracted or corrected his statement, he was not going to get retirement. In the meantime, a judicial commission was being appointed to consider the matter on 17 July.

The feisty Sanguinetti, angered by his treatment and indignant over the colonial government's attitude to the judiciary, might have been expected to welcome the arena of a judicial commission trying a judge. In fact, the more compelling interest at this point seemed to be to retire, and walk out the door with a pension and benefits. Perhaps at this stage in his career, he was not the man of independent means he was to become. The benefactions of his Uncle John and the revenue from Gibraltar would not come to him until later. At this point and facing the unnerving risks of a freelance life, the pension may have been a necessity. On 29 June, he wrote to the Colonial Secretary asking "to receive a draft of the form of correction His Excellency has in mind".

His proposal to do a deal was not met magnanimously. It was suggested in a reply on 4 July that he should say he "erred gravely in representing the circular as a directive and … regard the statement as unjustified and withdrawn". Sanguinetti baulked at these words as "harsh and oppressive".[65] This was a difficult point for Sanguinetti. J.E. Triay wrote to him on 9 July telling him frankly to build up no hopes of a fair result from the Commission and that he and his brother J.J. had decided to offer him a place in the firm believing they would "get on with one another without too much friction".[66]

The Hong Kong government may have been less sure of the outcome than Triay was and seems to have feared that if it overplayed its hand, Sanguinetti might just be reinstated. Whatever drove them to it, a compromise was arrived at in which, though he could still consider the circular a directive, Sanguinetti would concede that it was "not requiring magistrates to do something they should not properly do" and "to construct this was not justified by the contents". His Excellency was satisfied. In a letter dated 18 July, it was agreed that all the correspondence between them since that of 12 May should be regarded as compliance with Colonial Regulation 68 and that Sanguinetti's part of it be regarded as a "reply to complaints". Retirement could be proceeded with, "in the public interest", a reason which delighted Sanguinetti for the rest of his life.

This left the judicial commission, which had been prepared under the now set aside Regulation 60, without a purpose. The former Chief Justice of Kenya from 1954 to 1957, Sir Kenneth O'Connor, had been brought into Hong Kong to chair the commission. Following Sanguinetti's departure from Kenya, in 1957, O'Connor had presided over the trial of Dedan Kinmathi (who, like Kenyatta, had played a significant role in the freedom movement) and had sentenced him to death. Considering how small the colonial legal world was, he certainly would have recalled Sanguinetti and perhaps not with favour. O'Connor, now retired, was put up in the Mandarin Hotel for six weeks. He was not allowed to say why he was in Hong Kong but the press speculated that he was there to adjudicate on civil service salaries, which were under review. To O'Connor's surprise and bemusement, several civil service delegations turned up demanding to see him. After he left Hong Kong, having explained limply that he had been there to make business contacts and that plans had not materialised, he described the city as a mad house.

Sanguinetti formally retired in November 1964, after soaking up leave owed to him. Sometime before he left but after the decision was announced, Sanguinetti's favoured and favouring paper, the *Hong Kong Standard* published an article about him by Sally Keswick on 26 July. She was writing about the home of this outspoken and eclectic magistrate to see if it reflected his unusualness. She was not disappointed.

From his arrival in Hong Kong in 1958, Sanguinetti collected antiques, often on expeditions to Hong Kong's famous Cat Street with his friend, solicitor Brian McElney,[67] on a Saturday afternoon, in the hope of picking up the odd bargain. As the years went by, he concentrated on Japanese art. McElney recalled an occasion when they both wanted to buy one group of "inro" (small segmented containers for pills or other items) and "netsuke" (pouches for tobacco paraphernalia or writing equipment). The dealer seems to have not dealt with Japanese art before. He was asking about HK$1,000 for the item, which was a steal. They bought quickly and split the lot down the middle.

In addition to collecting, Sanguinetti had a natural ability for displaying these objects. He would spend hours arranging and re-arranging displays and taking a very long time to place just a few pieces, like an Ikebana master. He read widely on Japanese art in particular and built up a considerable expertise.

Apart from patrolling Cat Street, he kept an eye on the goods for sale at the local auctioneer Lammert Brothers. This long-established firm used to sell the effects of dead expatriate residents of Hong Kong, and there were occasional bargains to be had, especially if you knew your European antiques. On one occasion, a George III silver tea caddy with its original silver key was for sale described as "an oval tin box". Sanguinetti could not attend the auction, but he left a bid with the auctioneer for HK$70. McElney warned Sanguinetti that if his bid was exceeded, he would jump in and buy it at up to a much higher price. Amazingly, this gem went unnoticed and was knocked down to Sanguinetti. However, it turned out that Sanguinetti had been somehow undercharged, and McElney had to settle that difference. As a consolation, he promised to leave McElney the tea caddy in his will—a promise he kept.

The results of his collecting, up to that point at least, were now laid open to an amazed Sally Keswick. There were about 3,000 items in his government quarters at Mount Nicholson. In the living room alone there were 15 Chinese lacquer tables from the eighteenth and nineteenth centuries, a gold thread silk carpet from Beijing, rugs from Bokhara, Teheran, Shiraz, and Mongolia, and some Cambodian decorations. Over the mantelpiece was a family treasure, a pre-Renaissance Florentine painting. Around the hallway and other rooms were Siamese Buddhas, Tibetan tankas, a Faberge piece, a fifth-century BC Ionian miniature, an eighteenth-century Chinese marble screen, and a Chinese emperor's Chippendale replica table, one of a sequence made for his concubines. Representing Japan were a seventeenth-century samurai's armour, Noh and Kamakurah masks, and Tokugawa art pieces. Over various surfaces was a treasury of stones—agates, jades, jaspers, turquoises, topazes, carnelians, and corals—and pieces in ivory, gold, and silver, as well as a quite distinct and vivid collection of 150 antique fans.

Keswick said it was not an easy home to describe: one living room, one dining room, two bedrooms, and 3,000 antiques. It fitted a description of one envious aesthete she quoted: "What you missed of the good things in Cat Street is at Sanguinetti's."

All of this now needed securing and storing—he was vacating his Mount Nicholson quarters and the colony. Taking stock, Sanguinetti had his newly acquired Hong Kong pension, another from his Gibraltar service, and a tiny amount for his time in Kenya. At 41, he was three times retired with no job, no accommodation, and a large reputation. To contemplate this picture, he went back to Gibraltar.

CHAPTER SEVEN

To the Bar

Sanguinetti used his outstanding civil service leave to depart from Hong Kong in September and sail home via Singapore and Suez. Back in Gibraltar, it is not clear at what point he made the decision to go back to Hong Kong. He declined the offer of a place by the Triay brothers, but he presumably listened to a lot of advice from his friends and John Garcia. Friends back in Hong Kong had been encouraging him to return and go into private practice, which they were convinced he would make a success of. Brian McElney had offered him temporary accommodation in his own flat in "Rockymount" at 39 Conduit Road, and that was one solicitor who would certainly send him briefs.

He was sufficiently a personality on the Rock to be interviewed in the *Vox* on 20 November 1964 by Nancy Vaughn, and he gave her the impression that he was still very much in business in Hong Kong. He told her his flat there had three bedrooms, two baths, and a sitting room with two terraces and that he was looked after by a cook, a *valet de chambre*, and a cleaning woman. In present day terms, Sanguinetti was building his brand in Gibraltar. At that point, he did not have a flat at all in Hong Kong. He was probably describing his last civil service unit, and McElney's would have been similar in size, though whether he was going to lay on a *valet de chambre* was unlikely.

Vaughn was trying to present her readers with the real Albert Sanguinetti, and she was not getting very far.

> I wasn't able to storm that little ivory castle in which the real Albert hides himself. There was no hesitation in utterances but clever evasion, a change of subject, a sidetracking, or a blunt. No not that, no, no names, don't mention that.

To a question about how in demand he was as an eligible bachelor, he sidetracked to Persia, which he had visited in late 1962 as part of a vacation that had also included Lebanon. The girls there were "coquettes", he said. There was a female friend called Lilly, who had been divorced three times and wore Dior and Schiaparelli. He volunteered a photograph which Vaughn admired. Had he popped the question to Lilly about becoming number four? He had "probably done that ten times already".

"Lilly" seems to have been a rather modest description of Princess Pari Arfa of Iran, a descendant of a family of senior officials of the previous Qajar dynasty, including a distinguished diplomat and poet, and possibly the daughter of General Hassan Afra who was a powerful figure in the early years of Shah Mohammed Pahlavi's reign.[1] Sanguinetti probably visited Princess Pari Arfa again on his way back to Hong Kong the following February. She adored him and came to meet him in Hong Kong several times over the years though feelings eventually became one-sided on her part, notwithstanding his earlier claims of unanswered proposals. A letter dated 29 November 1970, which remains in the possession of the Gordon family,[2] clearly indicates that Sanguinetti had stopped replying to hers some time before. "Given his situation, my Uncle decided to move on", recalls James Gordon.[3]

He went on to tell Vaughn that he had studied Freud and met Freud's daughter in New York. This led to an enigmatic self-description. "Three quarters of my personality is submerged. I am what I am. I am only what people think I am." Sanguinetti was essentially giving Vaughn an elaborate version of "I'll tell you more when I know you better", which he would never do.

In 1965, he was called to the Bar in Hong Kong.[4] Back in his London days in "digs" with the Massias brothers when they had played at moots, it was Sanguinetti who had always been the barrister. This vision of himself had been dimmed by dutiful application to making an assured living which being a Crown counsel and a magistrate provided. By now, he had come to see that his temperament could not be bounded by official employment. He needed the more open emotional spaces of the Bar. He was one of those fortunate among men who could not duck his destiny.

He was a sparking, tough litigator who was more than willing to fight, and he could intimidate opposing counsel and hostile witnesses because he had a shrewdness about people. He had a different trial style, with plenty of theatrics, and was admired for its creativity. He had abundant self-confidence which lead him to rely on his quick wit and capacious memory in which he carried his unusually large knowledge of case law. He simply stood up and asked great questions, yet behind that were hours spent in voracious reading, preparing his cases. He had a special ability to communicate in a simple, concise manner to the jury because he knew what they could cope with.

Judge David Leonard[5] recalls Sanguinetti appearing before him when he was a magistrate in North Kowloon, a court busy with young men accused of triad society membership. This was from 1977 when Sanguinetti was well into his stride.[6] "The prosecution invariably depended on police evidence of 'verbals'…together with written confessions allegedly made by the defendants. These…were only admissible if made voluntarily", explained Leonard. "Albert was a past master at demolishing police evidence and getting acquittals. His flamboyant and dramatic style of advocacy, backed by deep knowledge of the relevant legal authorities, was very effective."

He had an aptitude for language and a flair for interpreting the possible meanings of words, and from the very beginning of his career as a criminal defence barrister, he was unabashed at proposing the most extraordinarily pedantic definitions to get a client off. In the winding up of the Canton Trust Bank on 21 May 1965 in the Supreme Court,[7] he proposed to Judge Alan Huggins[8] that though the ordinance directed the Financial Secretary to "take steps to present a petition", this did not mean that he was expressly authorised to present a petition himself. Unsurprisingly, this went nowhere. Neither did he in an appeal on behalf of a waiter of a food stall, or dai pai dong,[9] where he drew a distinction between an arrest that was lawful and one that was justified. The officer had the technically legal right to arrest the appellant, but because he could not justify it to him, he could not take him to the police station in due execution of his duty, so the appellant could resist him.

Quite often, he won these semantic jousts. For example, in appealing against the conviction of a client, Cheng Chung Yat, against a drugs conviction,[10] Sanguinetti not only got his client off but forced the Court to make an interpretation of section 47(1) of the Dangerous Drugs Ordinance 1969 by performing a wonderful sematic ballet around the meanings of "whatsoever" and "anything".

Naturally, judges came to be wary when Sanguinetti was in front of them. In a trial of an expatriate man for rape in 1970,[11] in which Sanguinetti later got his client acquitted, Chief Justice Ivo Rigby had reached the point in his summing up about distress as a corroboration when he looked out and said, from expectation, "and I see Mr Sanguinetti with his finger on a passage from Archbold".[12] With similar resigned good humour, Rigby coped with Sanguinetti's appeal against sentence on behalf of a policeman convicted of extorting money with menaces. At the end of the judgement which rejected it, he observed: "Mr Sanguinetti has said all that could possibly be said."[13] Sanguinetti had indeed said all that was needed because, in trials and appeals, he did not rely on single lines of exquisitely toned argument but brought to bear every possible point of explanation and mitigation supported by a battery of authorities. This is often called "scattershot", but this description barely does justice to the thought that Sanguinetti put into it.

To judges whom he considered to be falling short or plain lazy, he could be withering with question statements dipped in sarcasm and mocking with feigned acceptance. On 25 March 1972, for instance, he was in an appeal that involved a breach of Judges' Rules.[14] The judge attempted to pack Sanguinetti away by saying that "Mr Sanguinetti had proceeded to go through the Judges' Rules at great length". At the end of the judgement, Sanguinetti jumped in:

Sanguinetti:	Has your Lordship made any findings about any breach of the Judge' Rules in connection with the case of Mr Justice Huggins that I have quoted yesterday or are you just leaving it at that?
Court:	As I say. Mr Sanguinetti, this was a long ruling already and I have considered all the breaches which you have brought to my attention.
Sanguinetti:	… but you haven't found specifically which breach of the Judges' Rules, the old ones or the new ones.
Court:	No but I am satisfied, as I said, there were.
Sanguinetti:	Without specifying…
Court:	… without specifying.
Sanguinetti:	… without specifying whether there were twelve or — whatever — or one, but you are satisfied. Thank you very much.
Court:	Well, I can go through the record, Mr Sanguinetti, and point them out if you wish.
Sanguinetti:	No, no, I have already said what is the usual procedure in Mr Justice Huggins — and the Prager case, but I don't think your lordship can now give them after giving your ruling.
Court:	As, I say, I am satisfied that there were breaches of the Judges' Rules.

> Sanguinetti: There were.
>   Court: Yes.
> Sanguinetti: Without specifying which rule and without saying how many of them. Thank you.[15]

Sanguinetti's cleverness was not always on the side of the angels. He appeared before the Court of Appeal for one of two transport officials found guilty of issuing a certificate of roadworthiness to an unfit vehicle. He and counsel for the other appellant had their Lordships in what they admitted was agony over proof of conspiracy, and the client, who appeared to be as guilty as sin, had his conviction set aside.[16] More usually though, his efforts were on behalf of if not always the purely innocent then certainly the hard done by. In February 1970, a minibus driver was awarded HK$7,000 after being beaten up by a sergeant in the Kwun Tong police station.[17] In March, Au Yeung Ming had his caning set aside in an appeal by Sanguinetti,[18] who also had established through the judgement that the offender and counsel should receive a copy of any probation report—a procedure that he was most keen on and which was far from clear in Hong Kong.

Sanguinetti's disapproval of other lawyers could occasionally be theatrical. One display of this was early in his practice, in July 1965, against Max Lucas, who had a fearsome reputation for pursuing prosecutions to the bitter end. They were appearing before Judge T.L. Yang, who was again to be caught up in a Sanguinetti temper burst. He was defending two employees who were on a charge of aiding and abetting the forging of tally sheets.[19] Judge Yang remembers that Sanguinetti and Lucas got into very heated arguments in court and he decided to adjourn so they could calm down. Ten minutes later, he re-entered unannounced to be greeted by a tableau of Sanguinetti with a chair raised over the head of Lucas and Lucas raising his arms in self-protection. Yang quickly backed out of the courtroom and a few minutes later went back in again, this time with the precaution of having himself announced. He found decorum had been suddenly restored. The case proceeded. Sanguinetti's trademark cross-examination completely destroyed the Crown witness' evidence, and his clients were found not guilty.

Although fury against Lucas abated, implacably unforgiven was Miles Jackson-Lipkin, whom Sanguinetti generally referred to as "Lipstick". Jackson-Lipkin was a successful barrister who took silk and fought and wrote well when it came to judicial reform. Unfortunately, though the son of a respected Jewish doctor in Liverpool named Dr Jack Lipkin, he had *folie de grandeur*, of which his adapted name is a clue. He wore a bowler hat, pin stripes, and a button hole in Hong Kong and a mandarin's cheongsam in London, which might have sneakingly appealed to Sanguinetti, and he was obsessed with heraldry and antecedent, as was Sanguinetti.

There was something of the rival performer in Jackson-Lipkin which Sanguinetti may have recognised and not liked, and the sort of technicalities he raised in court annoyed Sanguinetti as being inconsequential. So, whenever Sanguinetti was appearing against Jackson-Lipkin, he always included in his list of authorities handed in to the judge a case in which Jackson-Lipkin had been severely criticised by the English Appeal Court, even though that case had no relevance to the one in hand.[20]

However, where Sanguinetti's occasional exaggerations were colourful renderings of a distant past, Jackson-Lipkin's were dangerously close to his present and a nemesis awaited him. What began by improperly flying a flag on his car and wearing questionable naval decorations at mess functions in the headquarters of British forces led to the discovery of an altered birth date and a false account of his war service and decorations in the 1983 and 1984 editions of the *International Who's Who*.[21] Jackson-Lipkin hurriedly resigned from the Bench but reappeared, again in ignominy, 20 years later when he and his wife received prison sentences for receiving years of Hong Kong social security payments and public housing based on false declarations of income.[22]

Released from the constraints of Crown employment, Sanguinetti began to take up the freedom to comment and apply pressure in public. In May 1965, he sent a compellingly concise letter to the *Hong Kong Standard* about a case in which eleven people were sentenced to from three to seven years, after legal aid was refused and they had had no representation.[23] He quoted Mr Justice Darling on the state of affairs in England in 1900: "The Law, like the Ritz, is open to everyone."

On November 27, he wrote to the acting Deputy Director of Public Prosecutions about procedures on witness statements and the attitude of the Crown Law Office.[24] He told him of a Chinese female defendant who gave a Chinese statement to an Inspector who then translated it into English. She did not know this, had not and could not have read it, and yet it was admitted into evidence without two countersignatures. He said that fewer solicitors were taking legal aid cases and barristers were not being assigned. Some defendants were being brought to trial without knowing the evidence against them. There was a pressing need for legal aid in district and magistrates' courts, something Sanguinetti would spend over a decade crying out for.[25]

He flexed his muscles at the executive branch of the government in a talk to the United Nations Association in the City Hall lecture room on 16 December 1965. He punched at several targets. He told them that the government paid lip service to the rule of law. He attacked the General Warrants Ordinance, which he said had been chucked out of the window in England in the eighteenth century, saying that they should do away with any emergency power, unless it was serving the reasons it was first legislated for. He also stressed that the Legislative Council should debate affairs which were current, like the recent case of prisoners in detention without trial who went on a hunger strike. The Association certainly got its money's worth for one evening.

On 4 October 1967, he was the guest speaker at a Lions Club meeting and two weeks later at the Harvard Club, which hoped he would come back again. On New Year's Day in January 1968, he was accredited as the Far East correspondent of the Gibraltar Broadcasting Corporation. There is no record of any discussion about the professional status of a barrister as a foreign correspondent or of any actual broadcasts for that matter, but they surely would have been worth listening to. He did go on air, in his own right, on the local TV programme "Meet the Press" in February 1970. A spin off from this was published in an article in the *South China Morning Post* on 28 February 1970,[26] which specified Sanguinetti's proposals for revealing the Crown's case to the defence, for juries in district courts, and, to a lesser degree, magistrates' courts, and not all judges being appointed from the local Bar. Barristers Ming Hua, Henry Litton, Brook Bernacchi, Peter Chan, and John Rear (of the University of Hong Kong) later gave varying degrees of support to the proposals. These issues, which were close to Sanguinetti's heart, were gaining traction.

He learned early on about putting his reputation for pugnacious reasoning in alliance with the press to corner and embarrass authority. A small matter of arrogance which would have struck a symphony of chords among the reading public prompted him on 18 October 1966 to write and take issue with a surcharge for late payment of a water bill under a waterworks bill amendment. The deadline date chosen was arbitrary, not predictable, and only 9 days in advance, he said. This obviously panicked the Water Department. The "Tiger Talk" column in the *Hong Kong Standard* was clearly primed by Sanguinetti. He once even described himself as a contributor to the newspaper. The column reported that the government was trying to wriggle out of this situation by now refusing payment of demanded surcharges. The writer depicts a conversation with a civil service friend: " 'Is the matter going to be explained to the public', Mo looked at me. 'Are you serious?' "

His reputation at the Bar itself was also growing. On 17 November, aspiring young lawyer, R.C. Tang, wrote from London asking for pupillage in Sanguinetti's chambers.[27] Years later, Sanguinetti noted on the letter that Tang was "now a judge of appeal".

His celebrity amongst working-class groups was beginning too. On 18 December 1965, the Chinese press reported that the leaders of the Hong Kong/Kowloon Hawkers Association had gone to Kai Tak airport to formally see Sanguinetti off on his leave on "an Indian airline" to Bangkok, Bombay, and Rome on his way for Christmas in Gibraltar.[28] This was a significant public show of respect for his efforts in "defending and fighting for the interests of hawkers". It must have been a noisy and satisfying event for Sanguinetti in full public view in front of the screens which separated the concourse from the departures area in the old airport. With them, and adding her voice, was the famed social crusader Mrs Elsie Elliott,[29] who was soon to become a comrade in arms.

His appearance when in court eschewed the starched black and white presentation of the usual barrister which distinguishes them from the population. He replaced it with eccentricities of dress and style which marked him out from other counsel, the common man, and everybody else. He wore patterned shirts, Cuban heels, jewellery, and a monocle. As his hair thinned away, he wore, to quote Judge David Leonard, "a blatantly cheap and obvious wig of unnatural hue, often displaced and worn at a rakish angle".[30] On top of that would go his barrister's wig askew in another direction, battered and given careless or little attention, in the tradition of the seasoned practitioner. The gown would be scruffy, and the crocodile skin briefcase he carried was shiny from wear.

All this was stylistically self-conscious for effect, and he loved sending himself up, says Leonard. His theatrical behaviour in court, including his use of language, could be entertaining or discomfiting, but it was a way of navigating the case and setting his position. Leonard went on:

> In the Magistrates' Court when he was doing badly I was "Your Worship"… When he thought I was with him, I became "Your

Honour". In the District Court when he was doing badly he called me "Your Worship". If he was not sure of his position, I was "Your Honour", and when he thought I was with him I would be "Your Lordship". In the High Court he signaled his displeasure by calling me "Your Honour" and I think on the occasion of a triumph in that venue he may even have addressed me as "Your Majesty".

Sanguinetti's courtroom antics were pillars of his popular reputation. Before the Court of Appeal with the Chief Justice Sir Geoffrey Briggs and Sir Alan Huggins sitting, Sanguinetti submitted that you could not have a conspiracy between husband and wife alone, but Sir Alan Huggins doubted this. Sanguinetti put both hands over his heart, feigning a seizure in disbelief, and then, in a music hall gag about not knowing where his heart was, he hammily shifted both hands to the other side of his chest and continued the seizure. He had little time for Briggs as a lawyer, although he did invite Sanguinetti to dinner, and it was this invitation that he was supposed to have declined using Oscar Wilde's infamous quip "due to a subsequent engagement".[31]

Huggins, on the other hand, Sanguinetti greatly admired. The respect they shared for each other made them strange bedfellows. Huggins was a man of traditional religious beliefs which could cause him to appear somewhat stern. He was an honorary life governor of the British and Foreign Bible Society, president of the YMCA, and a diocesan reader for Hong Kong and Macau. Sanguinetti was by now a lapsed Catholic who would know more about the insides of a dance hall than the YMCA. Huggins was, at first, impressed by the Hong Kong police's success in maintaining law and order on the streets. He was shocked when his former neighbour in Kowloon, the deputy district police commander Peter Godber, was extradited from Britain and jailed for four years on bribery charges. It was then that he came under the guidance of Sanguinetti. Huggins's obituary in *The Telegraph* said that his "eyes were eventually opened to the realities of police corruption by his close friend Alberto Sanguinetti", who kept him informed of all that bubbled below the colony's surface.[32]

It was again in front of Briggs and Huggins that Sanguinetti pulled a stunt that people not only in legal circles but those who have nothing to do with the law and had never met Sanguinetti still speak of. The Court was not being sympathetic to his argument, so Sanguinetti dropped some law books on the floor and went down on his knees to get them. After some time, Briggs asked him what he was doing down there. Sanguinetti's head popped out from under the table, and he responded: "I am simply searching for justice my lord."[33]

No one knows if this was quite the full script. Some remember the story with different judges, but Brian McElney believes Briggs and Huggins were indeed the judges involved. The time and place have also never been quoted. Some versions have no details at all—apparently all you need is Sanguinetti, a judge, and a table and you have the recipe for an urban legend.

Wigs turned out to be usefully topical for Sanguinetti in the case of Franklin Ming Dong Tsu's firm, R&D Products, which made wigs of human hair for export chiefly to the United States.[34] Only China and Indonesia had human hair of the right type for wigs, but since the Korean War, the United States had banned the importation of goods made in China, including its wigs. Therefore, wigs bound for the United States needed certificates of origin from the Hong Kong authorities of the raw materials and place of manufacture.

The US Consulate in Hong Kong monitored the ban and noticed a wide discrepancy between the official export figures from 1964 to 1965 for hair from Indonesia to Hong Kong and Indonesian hair declared to be in wigs manufactured in Hong Kong going to the United States. Pressure was brought to bear on the Commerce and Industry Department to clamp down on what appeared to be flagrant violations of the rules. There was a raid on Mr Tsu's factory, where a large quantity of invoices for Chinese hair purchases was found.

Mr Tsu was accused of making declarations that were false and that he had used Chinese hair to make the wigs for the

United States. Sanguinetti was instructed to defend him in the Causeway Bay Magistrates' Court. The case was important. Conviction would have virtually closed Hong Kong's human hair wig industry overnight. During the trial, he displayed his usual and ruthless command of the rules of evidence. Whenever an invoice for Chinese hair was produced by the prosecution, he objected to it unless the person who had issued it was called. The magistrate agreed with him, which was correct as the law then stood. Of course, the issuer of the invoice was in China and quite unavailable. After three days of vainly trying to get one invoice accepted in evidence, the Crown dropped all charges against Mr Tsu,[35] who, on his way out of court, observed how pleasant it was to do business in a place where the rule of law was so strong.

Hong Kong's human hair industry was saved until Chinese hair was soon and speedily replaced by wigs made of Kanekalon, which became a huge industry in Hong Kong and, thanks to Sanguinetti, added not only to his own wig collection but those of many Hollywood stars of the late 1960s and 1970s. In the early 1990s, he decided to upgrade from his wig of unnatural hue (as the fascinated Judge Leonard described it) to an expensive "rug" from Vidal Sassoon in London with a judicious selection of plausible white hairs interwoven.

Sanguinetti's father, Alberto (seated on the right),
and uncle, John Garcia (standing on the right).

Sanguinetti (far right) as an altar boy at Christian Brothers Preparatory
School in Gibraltar in 1936.

Walking in London, circa 1950: (left to right) Imoss, Willie Piccone, Sanguinetti, John Alcantara, and Louis Triay.

Sanguinetti in his room at London House in 1952.

Sanguinetti (left) out with Nairobi Society, circa 1953.

Sanguinetti and two high society women leaving a lavish Nairobi club.

Sanguinetti (right) talking to Sir Richard Woodley,
Mayor of Nairobi (left), circa 1953.

Caricatures of Sanguinetti given to him in 1955
when he was in Gibraltar.

Sanguinetti (front row, left) with all of Gibraltar's barristers in 1957.

Sanguinetti (second from the right) with Sir Joshua Hassan,
Mayor of Gibraltar (left), and Abraham Serfaty (right).

Sanguinetti filling his pipe and strolling with Chief Justice Flaxman.

Sanguinetti as the acting Attorney General of Gibraltar just before leaving
for Hong Kong in September 1958.

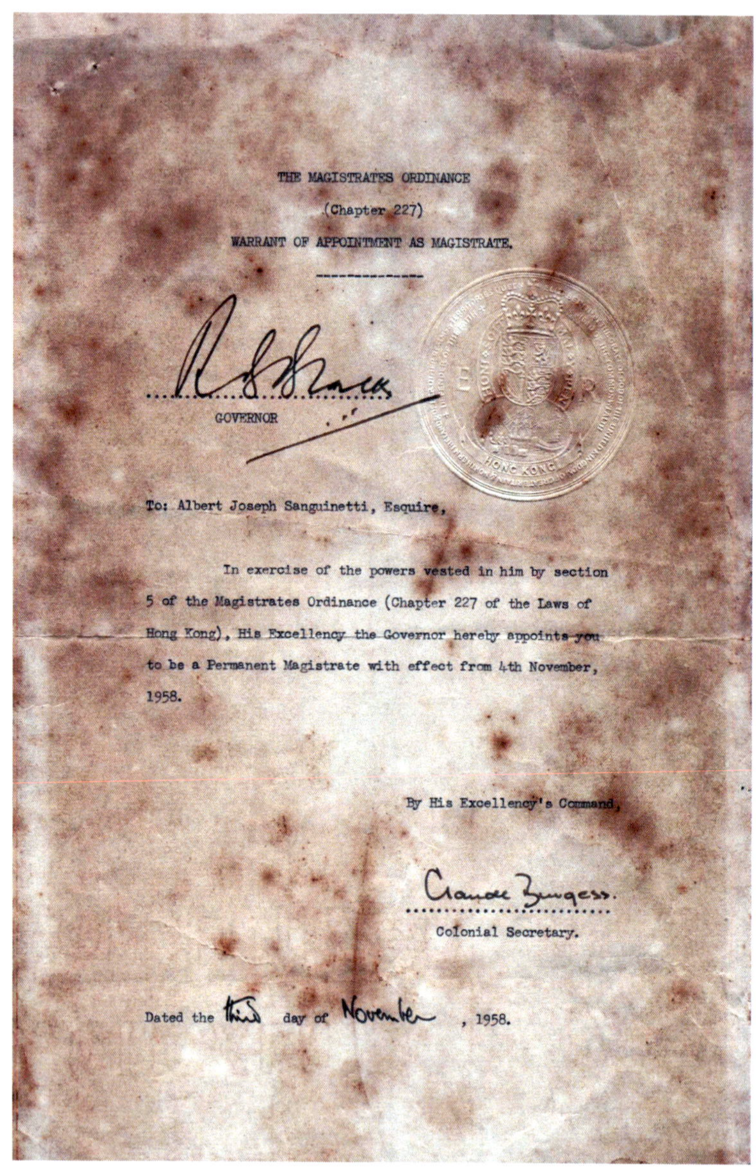

THE MAGISTRATES ORDINANCE

(Chapter 227)

WARRANT OF APPOINTMENT AS MAGISTRATE.

GOVERNOR

To: Albert Joseph Sanguinetti, Esquire,

In exercise of the powers vested in him by section 5 of the Magistrates Ordinance (Chapter 227 of the Laws of Hong Kong), His Excellency the Governor hereby appoints you to be a Permanent Magistrate with effect from 4th November, 1958.

By His Excellency's Command,

Colonial Secretary.

Dated the third day of November, 1958.

Sanguinetti's Warrant of Appointment as Magistrate in Hong Kong, dated 3 November 1958.

Sanguinetti with Princess Pari Arfa of Iran (left) in 1959.

Sanguinetti (left) and Judge Jennings (right) in 1959.

Sanguinetti bowing and taking the hand of Countess de Robiano of Belgium at a social event in Hong Kong in 1959.

Sanguinetti in discussion with Lady Hogan, Chief Justice Hogan's wife, in 1962.

Sanguinetti (front row, second from the right) in a group photo of Hong Kong's legal professionals in April 1969.

Sanguinetti in discussion with Han Suyin, author of *A Many-Splendoured Thing* and other works, at a reception held by the Xinhua News Agency at the Mandarin Hotel in February 1970.

Sanguinetti in his chambers in 1974.

Sanguinetti photographed at High Waterway Commune outside Canton in
October 1975 while on a tour of China sponsored by
the Xinhua News Agency.

Sanguinetti with Gladys Li taking Silk in 1990.

Sanguinetti (left) next to Adrian Huggins when he took Silk in 1991. Sir Alan (right) was a long-time friend of Sanguinetti's and a fellow member of the Hong Kong judiciary.

Sanguinetti with Anson Chan Fang On Sang (left), Elsie Tu (middle), and Elsie Leung Oi Se (right). Anson Chan was Hong Kong's Chief Secretary (1993–2001), while Elsie Leung served as the Secretary for Justice (1997–2005).

CHAPTER EIGHT

Riot and Reform

While Sanguinetti's name was widely known in courtrooms and legal chambers, the first five years of his private practice also brought him straight to the public's attention, primarily through one of the most highly publicised enquiries that Hong Kong ever held. The enquiry focused on one of the most serious threats to the colony's survival. Sanguinetti's part in the proceedings was assured by the beginning of a strategic partnership and friendship with the crusading worrier of the colonial government, Mrs Elsie Elliott.

Expatriates, chiefly British, filled the higher ranks of the government. The inspectorate of police was also largely recruited from the United Kingdom. Most expatriates had no idea of the pervasiveness of corruption or how it had corroded their own ranks and would not face that until Senior Superintendent Peter Godber fled the colony in 1973 after charges of bribery.[1] As a magistrate, Sanguinetti had developed suspicions about the way the police operated. Elsie Elliott was an elected member of the Urban Council, a directly elected body responsible for municipal services on Hong Kong Island and in Kowloon, and she held clinics to hear complaints by members of the public. She took up many of their causes and was convinced that corruption was widespread, notoriously so in the police force and government. She had, with barrister and fellow Urban Council member Brook Bernacchi, compiled a report on corruption and dangerous drugs for the Reform

Club, a gathering of elite liberal minds which was the nearest Hong Kong had to a political party. Confrontation between expatriate liberal conscience and the colonial government was about to be set.

The controversy was kicked off when the Star Ferry Company applied to open a new ferry service from Kowloon pier to Wan Chai. As part of this, the company had agreed not to apply for a fare increase on its main Kowloon–Central route for at least a year. However, it applied for a 50 percent increase to its first-class fare within months, and the Transport Advisory Committee approved this in March, with Elliott as the one dissenting member. She was dissatisfied with the breach of the Company's undertaking and soon made her views public and started a petition.

On 4 April 1966, 25-year-old So Sau-chung sat down in the Star Ferry pier terminal in Central in a black jacket with "Hail Elsie. Join hunger strike to block fare increases" written on the back. He was later joined by another young man, Lo Kei. The following day, So was arrested for obstruction. A young unemployed Eurasian, Brian Raggensack, gathered a group of supporters to carry on. Warned against staging demonstrations by both Elliott and Bernacchi, the group nevertheless went to the ferry terminus in Kowloon, and hundreds came into the streets, sparking rioting by youths who set fire to shops and attacked police stations. This went on for four days.

A dim view of Hong Kong at the time might see half a million in squatter huts, poor working conditions, disparities in wealth, and official corruption. Yet manufacturing was booming, prosperity was increasing, and a huge expansion in housing and social services was underway. The arrested youths were not particularly poor. They had no interest in riding on the top deck of a Star Ferry. When asked about their motives, they said they were angry, frustrated, or did it for kicks. The problem was social more than purely economic.[2]

A "Kowloon Disturbances Commission of Inquiry" under the chairmanship of Chief Justice Sir Michael Hogan was hastily convened. Elliott, in her crusade against corruption in

Hong Kong, had gone to England in the second half of April to lobby members of parliament and ministers on the state of affairs in Hong Kong. Before she left, she wrote to Sanguinetti on 13 April 1966.

Dear Mr Sanguinetti,

My instinct and information both suggest that a witch-hunt is on concerning the riots, and before long there will be a slaughter of the innocent;…I want to put this short report in your hands first, before it happens.

I have been informed…that the ruffians who entered into the peaceful demonstrations and turned them into riots were "ah feis" from black societies, appointed by corrupt police, with the intention of forcing them afterwards to prove that I had paid them to do it…The motive is not far to seek if this is true: recently I have been reporting police and black societies in that area for corruption and drug rackets. I knew they were planning revenge…the demonstrations offered them the chance they were waiting for. The information came second-hand from a decent policeman related to someone who knows me.

I heard from Dr. Bell that the original hunger-striker has admitted that he was paid to do it, but I feel sure that this is a rumour; he struck me as being genuine, but I do not know him so cannot judge too well. What I do know is that some of those accused of "inciting a riot" were not arrested until several days later; their arrest must have depended on hearsay rather than their having been caught in the act.

What kind of world do we live in?…If I am accused, will you defend me and send the case to Justice please? Meanwhile I must try to save the innocents, if I can find out who is innocent, which is difficult.

Sincerely, Elsie

Several lawyers who saw the letter thought Elliott was, in the words of Sanguinetti in a private and confidential memo to the local committee of the International Commission of Jurists (ICJ) on 5 September, "fanciful, frivolous and ridiculous".[3] However, *The Star* newspaper, never slow to sniff the prospect of malfeasance, ran an article in mid-April saying Elliott would probably be made a scapegoat. Sanguinetti kept the letter. He was later criticised by the Commission of Inquiry for not revealing it to the police, a neither confidential nor prudent course, given its content.

On 18 May 1966, allegations were made to the Commission against Elliott by Raggensack, now one of the Commission's witnesses. He said through counsel representing the government, Mr Rea, that he had heard Elliott had paid Lo Kei, who had now been arrested for rioting, HK$5,000 to participate in the riot and would pay HK$20 to anyone who damaged windows or a bus.

On 20 May, on the instructions of Brian Tisdall of Johnson, Stokes & Master, Sanguinetti appeared before the Commission of Inquiry on a watching brief for Elsie Elliott for a fee of HK$1, which was never claimed or paid, an anecdotal tidbit between them for years. Thus began a collaboration made in the heaven rejected by both; Sanguinetti as a lapsed Catholic and Elliott as a disillusioned evangelical missionary.

Sanguinetti laboured to be given the statements to the police by Lo Kei, Lee Tak Yee, and others (all of whom had been questioned for four to five hours on several occasions) to demonstrate the lengths to which the police had gone to implicate Elliott. The police counsel made this difficult, presenting the transcripts only minutes before proceedings, causing vigorous complaint from Sanguinetti which was widely reported in the press. Lo Kei denied under oath the truth of his statement to the police, and Sanguinetti insisted that substance for the allegations of a plot existed.[4]

Elliott volunteered to give evidence to the Commission, which she did well and without hesitation for five days under cross-examination by counsel for the Commission and for the police as well as questioning by Sanguinetti, except that she refused to name her officer informer of the police plot. According to Tisdall, she wavered in this, offering to give evidence "in camera", which she felt would provide enough privacy in the proceedings to allow her to give a name. However, there was a threat of suicide from her informer if she did, so she stuck to silence. Sanguinetti said in his memo that it was not correct to say that Elliott did not substantiate the police plot because she refused to name her informer. "That was a red herring to conceal the real matters in issue, the real difficulties and embarrassing position the police force found itself in losing face."[5] The result was that Elliott was found to be in contempt. The Commission adjourned overnight to consider whether to imprison or fine her, which she would have refused to pay. It was feared that those courses might lead to further disturbances, so the Commission announced it would send her to the bar of public opinion "for censure".

The Commission prevented Sanguinetti and Tisdall from going any further. Existing witnesses could not be recalled. Further witnesses were not called. The Commission could have subpoenaed two people who might have disclosed the informer's name but did not do so. The Commission refused to let Sanguinetti ask any further questions or to probe further into the alleged plot and refused to recall Raggensack for cross-examination.

Only the Commission could call witnesses; hearsay upon hearsay evidence, opinions, and leading questions were all allowed, and despite protest after protest, rulings unfair to Elliott were made. Eventually, Hogan asked Sanguinetti and Tisdall to consider why they were even still there. This lit a scriptural fuse in Sanguinetti. From a large bible brought into the court, he read a passage from St Paul's First Epistle to the Corinthians:

> But let a man examine himself, and so let him eat of that bread and drink of that cup. For he that eateth and drinketh unworthily, eateth and drinketh damnation to himself … For if we would judge ourselves, we should not be judged.[6]

He slammed the book shut, swept it under his arm, and strode out with his solicitor and his client.

The newspapers had a glorious time trying to find the "bar of public opinion" and laughed at the Commission's wording. The following year, Elsie Elliott polled the highest number of Urban Council votes ever, a clear judgement on her from public opinion. In June 1967, the "Tiger Talk" column in the *Hong Kong Standard*, doubtless by Tisdall, published a ditty to be sung by the defeated candidates:

> Send me to the bar Mike, send me to the bar
> Tell them to condemn me, spread it far and wide
> She got all the votes Mike, ain't that most bizarre?

The Commission's final report led to the setting up of city district offices which, eventually, were of some good, but for the most part, the report discovered little and deduced less. It was accepted as a government cover-up and received with indifference. The establishment seemed to be letting it blow over, but the Maoist riots were only a year away. Sanguinetti expressed some final thoughts in his memo. If the government thought there was no substance to Elliott having paid rioters, what was the purpose in adducing and prompting such evidence? "I decline to give [it] now but it is certainly not difficult to ascertain. There is evidence to suggest that Raggensack was at some time a police informer." He added a note seven years later: "The Bar Association never even held an inquiry. Ko Lei subsequently committed suicide." So Sau-chung became a Buddhist monk, and Brian Raggensack was last heard of running a bar in Wan Chai in the 1970s.

To Elsie Elliott's mind, much of the misfortune that befell the ordinary man and woman in the law was due to complicity between the police and the triads. Sanguinetti was not far behind her in that thinking, but the nature of his profession meant that it was necessary to be if not complicit at least as helpful as legally possible to clients who were, unless one was to suspend disbelief to the level of simple-mindedness, most certainly fully fledged and busy triads. He defended a number of cases which consisted of confessions, and Sanguinetti performed his expert cross-examination, often producing an obscure authority on points, which got the confessions excluded and regularly led to his client's acquittal.

Friends in low places showed gratitude. In one case, two policemen, Ip Chiu and Tsui Shu Hung, were convicted of accepting HK$2,000 as an advantage under the Prevention of Bribery Ordinance. The police officers were off duty at the time, and Sanguinetti submitted that they had been convicted on the wrong charge. It should have been blackmail. The Court allowed the appeal, and the policemen literally wept with relief. The outraged Crown appealed the case all the way to the Privy Council but got nowhere. As interesting as the amorally correct result was, the defendants' gift to Sanguinetti of a framed plaque made of gold inscribed with open handcuffs in a surround of five golden bats was awkward—or should have been. Apparently this is a strong triad society symbol, and Sanguinetti hung it in his chambers. He always affected not to have understood the triad allusions in the five bats, but for someone with an eye for detail and an interest in heraldry, this seems unlikely. People like Sanguinetti who pursue criminal justice are often visited by scoundrels, and those of his clients who fell into this category would have recognised it immediately. The bats would have been a stamp of approval and, thus, good for business.

He could never put a similar stamp of approval on Chief Justice Hogan. The feud continued and, again, in a car park. Sanguinetti had been convicted of parking somewhere close to Hogan's space at the Supreme Court, which is doubtless where Sanguinetti would like to have taken the case, but he was appealing it now in the High Court. He had been difficult from the start, insisting on appearing for himself as a layman and not a barrister. "Don't call me Mr. Sanguinetti! Call me Sanguinetti, like you would a common accused", he roared to the Bench. The irresistible headline was his assertion that he had been "tricked" into giving evidence against himself.

He could not be charged with stopping his car at that place because he was not in the car when the policeman saw it, so he could not see him stopping it. Technically, he had parked too close to a zebra crossing on Jackson Road. Given the changes in the landscape around Central since then, it would take a long memory to recall how this coincided with the Chief Justice's space but the HK$20 fine was upheld.

Warfare with Hogan continued into October 1967. Sanguinetti was accused of not taking any assigned criminal legal aid cases for two years, and Hogan was assumed to have put the Registrar up to this. It was actually a quite childish sparring since it was of no great importance or threat to either side. Yet Sanguinetti shot off a question to the Lord Chancellor of England. When in conflict with the colonial authorities, he was fond of asking the views of improbably high authorities in England who were the font of the system and of greater pedigree, even though they barely condescended to answer, let alone intervene. The local Bar Association wrapped it up eventually on 3 April 1968. Why would Mr Sanguinetti have to take assigned cases? In 1965, he had taken one assignment from the Deputy Registrar without knowing there was a roster or that his name would be put on it. The Bar believed that taking cases was voluntary and that even if his refusal was some technical breach, it was not professional misconduct.

A more amicable event occurred in September 1966 when Jeremy Thorpe, a friend from Sanguinetti's London student days, paid an official visit to Hong Kong as leader of the Liberal Party. This was extrovert calling unto extrovert. Much was done by Sanguinetti to smooth Thorpe's time along on that visit. Appreciation was expressed in a letter beginning "Alberto, cher Alberto" from the plane back to London. Sanguinetti was clearly fond of the Thorpes. A letter from Thorpe in 1973 expresses his gratitude to Sanguinetti for his gift of jade horses, which were now on two mantelpieces at his home. He had already met Thorpe's second wife, Marian, who had divorced the Queen's cousin, the Earl of Harewood, to marry him. "Do come and see us", they implored.[7] Then, down many sad roads later for Thorpe, he wrote to Sanguinetti on 16 March 1994 as "Jeremy Thorpe Assocs. Development Consultants" about finding a manufacturer for prototype see-through laminated trays, decorated with the banknotes of royal dependencies. The Queen and the Queen Mother had already been given one each of these insipid items. Cheery desperation rings through—"Can cher Alberto help?"[8] There is no record of a reply.

In an interview Sanguinetti in 1970,[9] Rob Snow of the Hong Kong Christian Industrial Committee observed that "Mr Sanguinetti drew on his pipe with tired eyes". He also indicated that Sanguinetti had told him that "British justice here…is all appearance and no substance". To Snow he also lamented the paucity of legal aid: "I believe that every defendant facing a serious charge which may involve the loss of liberty…should have the right to counsel even in the lower courts, wherever the Crown is legally represented." He then expressed to him a concern that a man needed to know legal techniques: "He needs to know how to cross-examine. If he doesn't cross-examine, he has no ground for appeal. In a Hong Kong court, a person with money is in a better position than a worker." Sanguinetti was forever on the lookout for that worker, no matter where. For example, on 19 June 1966,[10] he rattled off a letter to James Norman, Commissioner of Prisons, about how he had happened to be coming out of the toilet after visiting a client in Victoria prison and spotted a newly admitted prisoner being interrogated for drug possession in the prison yard. Someone nearby claimed that a policeman had sold them to him. Norman easily swatted that off by saying the assertion had been investigated and had no substance, yet it showed how dangerous it was to have the sharp senses of Sanguinetti wandering loose. In the coming months, his powers of observation were used on a bigger stage.

The Cultural Revolution was launched in 1966 in Mainland China by Mao Tse-tung to preserve Chinese communism in the spirit of perpetual revolution by purging itself and society of remnants of capitalism and traditionalism. It spilled into Hong Kong through labour disputes between factory owners and pro-communist trade unions, which sparked into violence in a plastic flower factory in San Po Kong in May 1967. The disturbances involved dramatic demonstrations, street riots, violent border clashes, intimidation, bombings, and the deaths of around 140 people. Temperamentally and professionally, Sanguinetti found it impossible not to be involved.

In his files, he kept a clipping from an English language version of the pro-Beijing *Ta Kung Pao* newspaper dated 2 August 1967,[11] in which an "anti-colonial Englishman" writes on corrupt practices and speaks of "Government Misinformation Services", "David Trench so-called governor", and makes an attack on the "Attorney General", written in quotation marks to make sure that no legitimacy was recognised. There is no suggestion that the writer was Sanguinetti, however. His respect for the offices of the law precluded this—not to mention, that it would have been better written if it had been from him. Even so, many of the political sentiments could have been his—or Elsie Elliott's.

Sanguinetti was clearly not a communist, unless his love of liberty was an elaborately contrived cover. He did though admire the People's Republic, and it would be wise not to be too critical of this from the advantage of hindsight. The vast mismanagement and callousness of the series of "campaigns" conducted by the Communist Party from 1949 were not widely understood in the early 1960s. Sanguinetti would have known that the new China was not a model of democracy, but it mattered to him in two ways. It was a contradiction of the colonialism which he paradoxically prospered under and condemned, and it represented the Chinese people standing up, a people he had developed a great respect for. This sentiment was noticed and ever remembered by the Party.

He had made a good friend in barrister Percy Chen, who was originally from a high ranking Kuomintang family but who later moved his allegiance to the Communists. As well as being a founding member of the Hong Kong Bar Association, Chen was a prominent pro-Beijing voice, a member of the Hong Kong and Kowloon Committee for Anti-Hong Kong British Persecution Struggle during the riots, and later a member of the Chinese People's Political Consultative Committee. Chen even asked Sanguinetti to act for the People's Republic if there were moves to confiscate its property located mid-way up the Peak. He agreed, though no such moves were made, and his services were not required.[12] He was regarded by the People's Republic of China as representing the Italian community in Hong Kong—which Sanguinetti wryly, if not quite accurately, pointed out consisted entirely of Catholic priests and nuns.

It was for the Church that he did act in court under the Emergency Regulations. The Diocesan Bishop Lorenzo Bianchi asked Sanguinetti to defend two church workers. He found, to his surprise, that the proceedings were to be held "in camera". He immediately protested, pointing out to the magistrate that it was illegal to hold the proceedings in camera and that he had "to perform in public". The magistrate agreed and adjourned the proceedings for two hours. When the court re-convened the entire public gallery was filled to capacity, but with members of the disciplined services, and there was no room for members of the public. He thus performed before an audience of policemen and prison wardens.

Perhaps Sanguinetti's most significant contribution to the law under the stress of disorder was not so much in the courts as monitoring them as a member of the Hong Kong branch of the ICJ, otherwise known as "Justice". In 1962, he became involved in setting up this branch. It had a long gestation period after its initial meeting. A draft constitution was prepared in 1963 with these aims:

1. To uphold and strengthen the principles of the rule of law in Hong Kong; and
2. To assist the International Commission of Jurists as and when requested in giving help to peoples to whom the Rule

of Law is denied and in giving advice and encouragement
to those who are seeking to secure the fundamental liberties
of the individual.

Unfortunately, the group's secretary left Hong Kong before
the constitution was adopted. It was not revived until 1965
when, on 17 April 1965, Sanguinetti, McElney, Huggins, and
others discussed the revival of the movement. It was decided
that a meeting should be convened by Mr Justice Huggins in
his chambers on 3 May 1965. Brian Tisdall, Sanguinetti, and
McElney attended this meeting. As far as it was possible for an
English solicitor with one of the city's most prestigious firms
to be so, Brian Tisdall was a social activist. A tall man with
forceful good cheer and a strong sense of social justice and
legal duty, he was a frequent collaborator with Sanguinetti in
politically high profile actions and a usefully biting contributor
to the *Hong Kong Standard*.

At the meeting, the constitution was agreed for submission
to the Register of Societies, and an executive committee was
appointed.[13] The Hong Kong branch of Justice was formally
approved in August 1965. Sean McBride, secretary general
of the ICJ, visited Hong Kong on the 23rd of that month,
and a tea party was held at the Royal Hong Kong Jockey
Club. It was a group of lawyers that would always be ahead
of its time. In 1969, Hong Kong Justice set up a committee
to look into the use of an ombudsman. The office was finally
created 20 years later.[14]

The first thing Justice did was to deliver a report on
the desirability of legal aid in Hong Kong; the report was
published in February 1966. Sanguinetti and most of the
members of Justice wrote to the government asking for the
second and third readings of the Commissions of Enquiry Bill
to be postponed to allow for observations and comments on it.
The newspapers welcomed the Bar and Justice's criticisms and
hoped that the government would take it into account.

Justice commented on the Legal Aid Bill in October 1966,
which only covered legal aid in civil cases. Sanguinetti believed

priority should have been given to legal aid in criminal cases, particularly in the District Court where sentencing powers were then being increased.[15] He also wrote separately to Amnesty International on 24 May 1967 regarding the convictions arising out of the Cultural Revolution anti-colonial riots and drew attention to the draconian sentences being imposed by courts where legal aid was not given. There were no juries in the district courts or magistrates' courts, though five-year sentences could be imposed in the district courts and up to three-year sentences could be imposed in the magistrates' courts. Various Emergency Powers ordinances were then in force which could permit imprisonment indefinitely without trial. Sanguinetti was particularly concerned that these ordinances meant that the rule of law and individual freedoms were nothing more than a theoretical right. He pointed out that heavy pressures could be brought on those on the Bench by means of, inter alia, "acting appointments". He stated that "there may be reprisals on me for giving you this information".[16]

On 1 June 1967, Amnesty expressed gratitude to Sanguinetti for the report and asked him to hold a watching brief for them on the riots. He carried out this commission with rigour. He reported on 5 June 1967 that some heavy sentencing for breaches of curfew had been quashed on appeal. There were also rumours of deportations of 24 nationalists and three communists. The three communists had asked to be (and were) deported to Taiwan. The courts themselves had become targets for demonstrators. He seemed to think that some of the Communist Party propaganda on brutality had substance.[17] Reliable sources told of people forced to swallow brass Mao badges. Barrister Martin Lee also heard allegations of brutality from clients. Some 12 people were said to be in the hospital from it. Changing topic, but equally alarming, he reported that 20 South Vietnamese refugees had been deported to Saigon and shot on the pier upon arrival.

Sanguinetti regularly sent the details of individual cases to Amnesty for their information and assessment for intervention. These were mostly during the riots but were not limited to this. However, they never found a sustainable individual case to act on or general injustice that was persistently widespread enough. This did not discourage Sanguinetti. What worried him was not the violence of the disturbances as much the conduct of the law under the pressure of the Emergency. He went around the courts, observing, and enquiring and on occasion even advising other counsel.

One of the cases Sanguinetti sat in on was on 3 July at the North Kowloon Magistracy and involved 17 defendants charged with unlawful assembly. The proceedings were to last several days. "One day for me was enough", Sanguinetti wrote.[18] There was "monstrous, scandalous behaviour" by the magistrate. The defendants were unrepresented. "None of these wretched people were given pencil and paper to record evidence against them." The magistrate recorded everything except his "howling" at the defendants. Their questions to prosecution witnesses under cross-examination were not recorded. They could not frame questions properly which made the Bench furious and began to worry the defendants. Sanguinetti even told two Crown counsels that the defendants were actually challenging the evidence, but that if this was not recorded, it would prove fatal on appeal. All of them got 18 months to two years in prison.

He painted a gloomy picture of the atmosphere in a letter to Stephanie Grant of Amnesty on 21 July 1967.[19] In this, he described a case where three police officers had been indicted for murder and malicious wounding with intent—inside a magistracy—and only after great pressure had been brought to bear. They were defended by a leading silk. Sanguinetti said that he could predict they would not be convicted on the major charge at least and that he could do so was depressing, saying:

> Some of the trials are literally a mockery of justice. In some courts principles of justice are upheld. In others, not so few, the proceedings are a farce and a travesty … one would never expect to find this state of affairs in a place where the Union Jack flies.

In another letter to Grant while she was in Denmark on 31 July 1967,[20] he says that he was

> prepared to dedicate some time (though I risk being framed up for passing information to you) in ascertaining … certain matters such as the spiriting away of a Mandarin film star and the treasurer of Chinese Chamber, and the number of times courts sit in camera.

He indicated that he would try to interview some of the prisoners, "but I need official status as your correspondent". In the same letter, he recommends that she "contact HRH Prince Peter in Copenhagen for his views on the political situation. He is an old friend of mine and may have useful information and contacts." What contribution a Greek prince, anthropologist, and Tibetan specialist had to make, apart from an opportunity for Sanguinetti to name drop, is not clear.

To *The Star* newspaper, on the same day, he sent a letter about the Emergency Regulations. He mentioned no details but made clear his deep reservations under a fig leaf of optimism, stating:

> Naturally one does not want to be governed by extraordinary laws which are alien to the Common Law of England. Personally I have an abhorrence for them … I must confess that it is not for me to say whether or not in present circumstances, this legislation is necessary and if so, to what extent. I can only hope that, in their practical application, the high standards of British justice will prevail.[21]

It took some courage to be critical of these regulations, however obliquely. As the violence worsened, the majority of the population stood with the government, and any criticism of measures that were defeating it would be unpopular or even measured as treacherous. Yet Sanguinetti brought to this situation his memories of similar regulations in Kenya, the harshness with which they were applied, and the deterioration in protection which the law was supposed to give, even to colonial subjects. He was not alone in his doubts.

Justice objected to the Emergency Regulations in a letter to the Chief Justice on 16 August 1967 on sentences of up to ten years with no defence, no jury, and no prior knowledge of the prosecution's case for the defendant.[22] Ian McCallum, the secretary of Justice, also wrote to the Colonial Secretary about this and the powers of detention on 3 August 1967.[23] He stressed that the regulations

> undermine the true position of the rule of law as understood in all free and democratic societies. Power of detention had been given to the Colonial Secretary and increased criminal jurisdiction was given to the District Court. The government has adopted the attitude that the present irresponsible and undesirable elements in the Colony must be fought at their own level.[24]

Consider how valiantly out of step with popular and official opinion against the rioters this must have been when the bus bombings began.

Sanguinetti added a dash of realism. Probably nothing would result from Justice's letter to the Colonial Secretary except that caution may be taken by those responsible when they know that there are some people "keeping an eye" on the situation.

Later that same year, Justice voiced a deep objection to the consolidating Public Order Ordinance published in October 1967 and enacted in November. It appears to have been the most consistently controversial ordinance on the statute books up to that time. The Justice Chairman's Report of 1968 complained that it had been rushed into law and was "one of the worst ordinances ever drafted". A detailed report about the ordinance was submitted to the Attorney General. Sanguinetti also submitted the report to Lord Shepherd, the Foreign and Commonwealth Minister of State, while they were both in Gibraltar in February 1968. It was an ambitious pitch. They did not meet.

The Hong Kong government made gestures in the form of a discretionary legal aid proposal for emergency cases in the District Court. Sanguinetti sent press cuttings about this to Stephanie Grant at Amnesty on 4 September 1967.[25] He described the proposal as "a sham".

While he enjoyed such advocating, it was being on his feet in court that Sanguinetti brought most joy to the distressed, the maltreated, and even, in some cases, the foolish. This is exemplified by the case of the curfew and a necklace, whereby one evening during the disturbances, a youth found himself with three friends outdoors away from his flat at the start of the 10 p.m. curfew. Rather than rush home and risk getting caught that way, they all hid and slept in a parked lorry where they were discovered and arrested anyway. The mother was a former amah and asked for help from her previous employers, the family of Haking Wong, the camera and optics manufacturer and developer. Oswald Cheung, QC, represented the youth who pleaded guilty and was put on probation for a short period with no conviction recorded. During his probation, the foolish boy snatched a necklace in the lift of their apartment block and was conclusively robbed of an escape because the lift got stuck. The youth's mother became a nervous wreck. The plan was for her and the boy to join her husband who had begun a successful business in New York. Her hopes and dreams were again in jeopardy—the youth was due to be interviewed for his US visa, and a conviction would be the end of that. On the recommendation of Ignatius Wong, Sanguinetti was instructed to appear, plead guilty, and mitigate, without getting reported in the press court pages.

Sanguinetti was crafty. He got the case fixed at the end of the list before Judge Stewart Collier in the Hong Kong District Court, part of the Supreme Court building, at a time when all court reporters would have already left for the day. He knew from experience that Collier was a particularly understanding judge. His plea, explaining all the circumstances, was successful, and the judge gave the youth a further chance on probation with no conviction recorded. The boy got his visa and went with his mother to New York as planned. The newspapers never got the story. Happily, the boy developed no interest in jewellery theft. He studied hard, married, had children, and was a boon to the family business. Victories such as these, though of great personal value to client and lawyer, did not answer the basic injustices which perpetually worried Sanguinetti.

Besides monitoring the 1967 disturbances, Sanguinetti also performed two services for Amnesty International which involved overseas investigations. In November 1972, he went to South Korea on behalf of both Amnesty and Justice about the appeal by Soh Sung, a Japanese-born South Korean student, who had been sentenced to death for spying.

This was a different South Korea from that of today. There was a National Assembly and elections were held, but it invariably and unanimously voted in Park Chung Hee as President and he controlled it. This was called the Yushin system of Korean-style democracy which was, in fact, a dictatorship, so spying could cover a lot of ground, including sending adverse criticism of the economic social or political situation in South Korea to North Korea, which is what Soh was accused of. Amnesty actually asked Sanguinetti where he thought the line lay between spying and conscience. He said that in England "spying" meant learning and handing secrets to the enemy, while "treason" was giving comfort to the Queen's enemies. The line could lie anywhere.

Soh had been in custody since April 1971 and had attempted suicide, suffered horrific burns, and had signed a confession with his big toe print while in hospital. He was in no fit state to make a confession, but Sanguinetti confirmed that the appeal had been conducted in an exemplary manner. He also reported that members of Amnesty and Christian church leaders who had been held under house arrest were released while he was there, almost certainly because of the international interest in the case. The appeal was dismissed in December 1972, but Soh's sentence was commuted to life imprisonment as a result of all the pressure from international agencies and Amnesty's involvement.

Sanguinetti's long report to Amnesty had a confidential annexe which said that, although the government was keen to appear democratic, this was not the case in practice, and, in his opinion, a virtual reign of terror was being conducted by government agencies such as their Central Intelligence Agency. He reported details of meetings with supporters and activists involved, including Catholic and Protestant clergy.[26]

In Seoul, he stayed in the cheerily named Hotel Poon Jug. His expenses were 16,300 won for three days, and he spared them expenses of a fourth day, calling it "a contribution to ICJ and Amnesty".[27] His efforts were appreciated. On 7 December 1972, he received a letter of thanks from Niall McDermott, secretary of the ICJ, and on 12 December, Martin Ennals, secretary general of Amnesty, told him that his "difficult mission" taken up at such short notice had been "more than justified".[28] The Report, without the annexe, was sent to President Park. His success in having the sentence commuted was only picked up in Hong Kong by the *South China Morning Post* and *Ming Pao*.[29]

In dictatorships, there can be implications for defence lawyers. Soh Sung's lawyer, Dr Seughum Hahn, who Sanguinetti had dealt with on his trip, had been jailed for 18 months but had been given early release. He was an expert on the state's anti-communism law and national security law. This was clearly a dangerous commodity for the Park regime, so after his release, he was not allowed to practice. Sanguinetti showed support and they corresponded. On 24 January 1976, Seughum Hahn wrote to Sanguinetti: "It takes no time for the intellectual to be acquainted with each other. I appreciate your favours that you gave me in my unhappy days. Despite the coldness of winter, the pine tree keeps green."[30]

At an inglorious moment in British diplomatic history, Sanguinetti attempted to help Amnesty from outside Hong Kong. He was on holiday in Gibraltar in August 1972 when there was an attempted assassination of King Hassan II in Morocco by air force officers in an attack on the king's plane as he returned from France.[31] The attempt failed, and two senior officers fled to Gibraltar, one of them Lieutenant Colonel Mohamed Amekrane who was a leading conspirator. Sanguinetti volunteered any information he could find to Amnesty and to Justice, and approached the British Foreign Office's man on the Rock, Raymond Bray. It was too late. The British government had come to a speedy deal with Morocco, and the pair had been sent back with indecent haste. Amekrane was later executed, despite an assurance to the British that he would not be.[32] There was nothing further to be done, but on 20 August, the *Gibraltar Sunday Telegraph* reported that Sanguinetti had been in Gibraltar making enquiries at the request of Amnesty.[33] Sanguinetti no doubt enjoyed the flash of publicity, but he was also concerned that he seemed to have appointed himself as an Amnesty representative. He was apologetic to them, but they laid no blame on him for the over imaginative local reporter who would not have had a story of coup and assassination to work on very often.[34]

Good works like these did not distract Sanguinetti from taking cases involving the gore of crime and making interesting laws out of them. In July 1973, four men were accused of burning down the home of an associate in a revenge attack for not having served one of them a cup of tea properly (but other psychotic offences one presumes festered under that). In the fire, the man's aunt and his eight-year-old daughter perished. The publicity was intense.[35] Sanguinetti originally acted for one of them, Cheng Pak, at first instance, and he was acquitted because it was proved that he was in Macau at the time.[36] The other defendants were convicted principally from evidence from Cheng Pak's concubine. They appealed and Sanguinetti, having done well for one of them, along with Henry Litton, later a Judge of the Court of Final Appeal, acted on the appeal.

The chief ground of the appeal was that the evidence of Cheng Pak's concubine Wong Shuk Han should not have been admitted into evidence because she was a secondary wife and therefore not a competent or compellable witness.[37] The full Court consisting of Justices Huggins, McMullin, and Pickering reviewed the law and the status of a concubine in Hong Kong. The result was a long judgement delivered by Mr Justice Pickering which held that a concubine is a secondary wife and is not a competent or compellable witness, therefore her evidence was inadmissible. The appeal was allowed unanimously.[38] This was the first time the point in question had been decided and made legal history, although, from a lay observer's point of view, the side of the angels was scored against. Sanguinetti would have relished the victory in law, nonetheless.

He already had experience with the subject of Chinese customary marriage. Back in 1959, as a magistrate, he had heard a case over child maintenance payments which had gone to appeal. In his magistrate's statement of findings on the marital status between Au Hung Fat and Lam Lai Lah,[39] Sanguinetti said that Au had gone through a form of Chinese wedding ceremony and had lived with Lam. Therefore, she was not a concubine, and he could not use that as a reason for not paying support to their children. In October 1966, Sanguinetti petitioned for a woman seeking to divorce her adulterous husband.[40] Both of Han Chinese descent, they had been married in the People's Republic of China after Article 1 of the Marriage Law had been enacted, specifying "that all marriages celebrated thereunder are monogamous".[41] However, questions of jurisdiction (both parties residing in Hong Kong at the time of the case) and the view that marriages in China are potentially polygamous, brought the case to trial in Judge Rigby's court. He held in favour of the petition for divorce.[42]

As well as having a sense for Qing dynasty marital law, which would now have feminists frothing, Sanguinetti had a feeling for forgery which also broke new ground in local law. He had a client, in 1968, who had forged the stamps used to pay National Insurance contributions in the United Kingdom.[43] The offence of forgery is highly technical, and Sanguinetti succeeded in getting his client acquitted on the grounds that the law in Hong Kong had not made forging these stamps a criminal offence. The Attorney General appealed on a point of law, and the

Court upheld the acquittal on this point. In another forgery case which Sanguinetti took to appeal involving the use of a photocopy of a forgery, it was held that a photocopy is not itself a forgery, so there was no offence.[44]

Not so much forgery as a misrepresentation sprang right out of Sanguinetti's passion for heredity. On 12 November 1976, he represented a Macanese man named Alfredo Marques D'Oliveira who had been charged in the District Court before Judge Stewart Collier with selling forged travellers cheques and instruments for forgery to a detective.[45] Sanguinetti was instructed to salvage what he could with a plea in mitigation. He told the Court that the defendant had been in Hong Kong over 30 years and had a clean record. Sanguinetti went on to say that he thought the defendant was more stupid than criminal. Then, firing from every direction, as was usual, he mused aloud on the defendant's distinguished name and, with a theatrical sigh that could be heard a room away, he said: "Ah, but what is in a name these days?" The judge indicated that a name was still of considerable importance in his opinion. This opened the heavens, and Sanguinetti rained down many wonderful observations on the splendours of the name of D'Oliveira, so high among the noblest of the Iberian Peninsula and how this scion of a great family had fallen so low. His client was totally bemused, but the plea was successful, and a very lenient sentence was imposed of one year's imprisonment, suspended for a year. In fact, the man was completely Chinese with not a drop of Portuguese blood in him, and the glorious name had been given to him by a mischievous clerk at a Macau orphanage. Sanguinetti was most disappointed when the man visited him at his chambers not to thank him, but rather to ask how he might go about getting a coat of arms.

CHAPTER NINE

Hard Work and High Points

By the middle of 1974, Sanguinetti had been at the private Bar for almost ten years. His reputation for quick-wittedness, cross-examination, knowledge of precedents, and a scathing flair against rigidity and indifference had put him in high demand. His association with Elsie Elliott in 1966 and his persistent championing of the cause of the poor defendant over legal aid and the conduct of prosecution cases had identified this eccentric Latin barrister with the common man. The underprivileged trusted him with their affairs. He collected honorary positions with organisations which might be expected to square off against the establishment. He was already legal adviser to the hawkers. On 12 December 1973, the Government Schools Non-Graduate Teachers Union invited him to join their Board of Advisors. In May 1980, he became the honorary legal adviser to the Hong Kong Federation of Students and, shortly after, to the Hong Kong and Kowloon Inhabitants' Association.[1] The coming ten years were to be the most intense of his life.

His work for Amnesty in South Korea had not been forgotten. In June 1974, 119 people disembarking a South Vietnamese vessel arriving in Hong Kong were taken into custody as illegal immigrants.[2] These were the beginnings of a situation in which Sanguinetti would again act in his unofficial representative capacity for Amnesty International.

The refugees included women and children, as well as men liable to be drafted by the South Vietnamese government into the ongoing war against North Vietnam. The war was supposed to have ended with the Paris Peace Accords of 1972, and the South was now devoid of US support.[3] The South's fight was turning into an accelerated retreat under a fatally misconceived strategy by President Nguyen Van Thieu. South Vietnam asked the Hong Kong authorities to send all the refugees back and was prepared to send a chartered plane for them.[4] Approximately 5,000 to 6,000 ethnic Chinese from South Vietnam were estimated to have already entered Hong Kong illegally, and a news report indicates that of the 1,561 of these immigrants who had been arrested during this time only 20 had been deported back to Vietnam.[5] Both governments knew there was a people-smuggling racket in operation, and they wanted to break it up. This captured boat load was their first breakthrough. One youngster among the 119 was found to have been born in Hong Kong and had the right to remain, while the remaining 118 faced return. However, there was serious concern that the refugees would be killed when they got there.[6] Amnesty International made representations to the Foreign Office which indicated likely asylum from several countries. Amnesty also pleaded with the Hong Kong authorities to postpone the deportation.[7]

This was all to no avail. In the early hours of 17 June, the refugees were forced to board the chartered plane. There were combative scenes at Kai Tak airport, and approximately 200 relatives and friends tried to prevent their deportation.[8] A total of 33 people were arrested and several injured in a fracas, including three policemen. Those arrested were all granted an absolute discharge with no conviction recorded. Two charged with assaulting the police were released on bail, one of them fled Hong Kong and the other was fined HK$200. Eleven journalists were fined small amounts. Sympathy in Hong Kong was not widespread. Derek Davies in his column "Traveller's Tales" in the *Far Eastern Economic Review* said the refugees should go back. He then asked why Amnesty was so silent about refugees being handed back to Maoist China every day.

The Hong Kong authorities said they had assurances that the Vietnamese refugees would be fairly treated,[9] but there was scepticism over this. Newspaper reports said they were sent to the notorious Con Son prison.[10] There were also reports of torture, that 14 had died including two children, that draft dodgers had been sent to the front lines with no training and thus to almost certain death, and that 62 were tried secretly, eight of whom had died in Con Son. This was all denied by the South Vietnamese Consul in Hong Kong. Then, a South Vietnamese official was discovered saying that no undertakings had been given to Hong Kong. On 26 June, Sanguinetti, as "the Colony representative of Amnesty International" was quoted in the *South China Morning Post* calling the events "an act of barbarism".[11] He went on to say: "Any country with decency or shame would release the refugees at once." The Consul General redoubled his denial of any issues.

Amidst all the uncertainty, Amnesty International asked Sanguinetti to go to South Vietnam as their official representative to investigate the fate of the 118 deportees. This was a considerable call on him. Unlike the trip to Seoul which was, if nothing else, secure, Saigon was the capital of a dissolving country, a casket of corruption, and a field of violence. Yet still he went, from 8 to 10 August 1974. He broke his journey in Bangkok where he received assistance with visas from the British Embassy.[12] In Saigon, he stayed at the Caravelle, in Room 605, and took all his meals there. The British Embassy arranged access to the minister in charge. The minister confirmed that initially the 118 had been sent to the Con Son prison but had been removed a few days later to a prison in the Saigon region. Only 40 had been released on bail. All would soon be put on trial. However, he told Sanguinetti that no independent observer had interviewed any of the detainees, and no names of the detainees had been recorded by the Hong Kong authorities or were supplied to him.

Sanguinetti observed, acidly: "Even cattle are shipped with some kind of documentation." It was the most important discovery he made in his investigation. Hong Kong had not bothered to take the names of the people present on the halted ship. They just turned them around and sent them back. It may have reminded him of the early hawker cases he heard on the Bench and the en masse guilty pleas. The South Vietnamese had no idea who they were receiving, not initially, anyway. The possibilities for substitutions and disappearances were boundless. So, in the subsequent trial of the 118, plus the 63 involved in the people-smuggling racket (where sentences ranged from 6–12 months, and 15 people were acquitted and two minors excused prosecution), who was to know who was who? The 50 defence lawyers buzzing around the court and the British embassy officials all claimed not to have heard a squeak of complaint. Lord Goronwy-Roberts, Foreign Office Minister of State, asked Amnesty to acknowledge that Saigon's undertakings had been kept. Given what Sanguinetti had uncovered, they refused.

Sanguinetti left Saigon before the trial. He paid the last day's hotel expenses himself, again as a contribution to Amnesty's efforts. He wrote his report[13] characteristically by hand, drafted on notepaper from four hotels: the Suriwongse, the Dusit Thani, and the Amarin in Bangkok, and the Dinasen in Rome. It was more likely he was drawing on a stationery collection rather than the fruits of just one trip, and he signed off the document in the peace of Fuchal, Madeira, with the conclusion that, given the lawless instability of South Vietnam, any certainty was impossible.

Sanguinetti had, however, helped establish certainty in Hong Kong. Amnesty International corresponded with the Governor who was on leave in the United Kingdom during this time. With a generous helping of disingenuousness, Governor Murray MacLehose explained that, when out of the colony, he had no right to interfere with the decisions of the acting Governor but gave a directive that, in future, illegal immigrants would be treated as individuals.[14] This meant that, no matter what else they would suffer, not one of the 200,000 Vietnamese to come over to Hong Kong in the following years could be completely forgotten.[15]

The episode ends on the sort of personal note which Sanguinetti cherished. Two of the refugees sent back were the wife and daughter of a Vietnamese resident in Hong Kong, Liew Yet Jan. They were released by the Vietnamese authorities on 23 July 1974, and the Director of Immigration indicated that he would permit them legal entry to Hong Kong if they applied through the British embassy. Mr Liew wrote to Sanguinetti expressing his profound thanks for what he had accomplished.[16]

Sanguinetti's empathy for the common man was laudable, yet when it came to Mainland China, it transmuted into an enthusiasm for collectivism which rooted for state success, put liberty on hold, and cocked a snook at the colonialists. In October 1975, the Xinhua News Agency invited him to join a carefully selected tour group to China.[17] It was clearly out of gratitude for being an admirer, supporter, and friend of Percy Chen, the pro-Beijing barrister and Chinese People's Political Consultative Conference member, through whom he was asked for legal help by the People's Republic of China in 1967. At Chen's funeral in 2004, Sanguinetti would be one of the pall bearers.

The tour group was a collection of minds to be influenced, such as Robert Hutcheon, editor-in-chief of the *South China Morning Post*, and, a harder sell, Brian Barron of the BBC. These were still politically turbulent times. Mao was yet to die, and it would be another year before the Gang of Four, the radical group seeking to continue the Cultural Revolution, were removed.[18] Yet none of this appeared on the surface. Sanguinetti wrote a series of articles about the tour in *The Star*. In his essay "Modern Miracle", written for the paper on 30 October 1975,[19] he wrote in admiration of the Communist state's determination, unity of purpose, and its ingenuity. He noted the rarity of policemen, that they did not carry guns, and that there was little or no major crime, primarily because of education rather than heavy sentencing. Corruption had been eliminated. There was a lively nightlife with queues outside theatres. He was struck by the much vaunted Huadong commune near Canton. To read this now, with all the benefits of hindsight, is to wince a little, knowing about the collapse of order in which there had been no policemen, how a crime was the wrong ideology, and sentencing was by political meeting, that there had been no education for a decade, and people had been eliminated along with the corruption. That there were theatres to sit in again would have been a relief. When he returned to Gibraltar the following year for a two-month summer sojourn, he repeated these impressions to the local *Panorama* magazine in a lengthy article.[20]

However, Sanguinetti was not the only one to be impressed. Over at the *South China Morning Post*, Hutcheon was turning out optimistic accounts of his trip too. After the end of the Cultural Revolution, many, particularly in Hong Kong, were looking on the brightest of bright sides in China. On the death of Chou En Lai on 8 January 1976, Sanguinetti, enjoying his association with the new China, shot off a letter of condolence to the Xinhua News Agency in Hong Kong, the de facto Mainland government presence in the territory. A fulsome reply came from the director, Liang Wei Lin: "Your condolences give us much comfort at a time when we still feel profound grief at the tremendous loss of the great proletarian revolutionary of the Chinese people and an outstanding communist fighter."[21] In 1984, Sanguinetti submitted a signed support of the Joint Declaration.[22] On Tiananmen, his papers at least are silent, but by the 1990s, he seems to have felt that whatever Governor Chris Patten and his reforming policy might be attempting in Hong Kong, China was what was best for the people.

Even though he had concern for the ordinary Hong Konger, Sanguinetti still had fun with "high" society or what passed for it in Hong Kong. This could be one of the sequined events held by Brenda and Kai-bong Chau, the wealthy couple with the famed matching gold and pink Rolls Royces and the design sense of vaudeville.[23] They held a Chinese costume ball in December 1975.[24] "Fit for royalty", trumpeted a social columnist in the *Hong Kong Standard*, even if real royalty would have had to be dragged there by their coach horses. The Chaus had, instead, barons of business, including property developers Timothy Kwok and Cecil Chao,[25] as well as Sanguinetti who wore an antique jade piece plus an elaborate nail guard on his little finger. He already had the furniture of an imperial concubine so this device may well have been in admiration for the Empress Dowager Ci'xi who reputedly had six inch long nails.

In 1976, Sanguinetti's beloved uncle and benefactor John Garcia died at the age of 91 and left in his will to Sanguinetti his major property holdings in Gibraltar. All the revenue from this came to Sanguinetti. However, this benefaction was in the form of a life interest because Garcia knew that Sanguinetti had no plans to marry, and he wanted, ultimately, to keep his property held within the family.[26]

Before Uncle John's death, no matter where else he visited in his travels, Sanguinetti returned to Gibraltar annually. He got together with his good friends from his childhood days — Willie Piccone, J.E. Triay, Paco Galliano, John Gaggero, Louis Andlaw, Guy Stagnetto, and more. He gave talks and displayed some of his antiques collection. They came to his talks not as a bored indulgence of an old friend but with enthusiasm. Sanguinetti's nephew, James Gordon, says that he was frequently told by friends in Gibraltar that, from an early age, Sanguinetti spoke of places and historical events he had only read about as though he had been present, with an immense amount of detail, and as if he knew personally all the members of the historical cast. They all referred back to a talk on Pompeii in 1964 which had deeply impressed them. When, on the following annual visit, he could not give a talk, there was great disappointment. The antiques display was another annual ritual in which boxes were opened at a hidden location to show some of his friends his collection and objects that had been added. They would be adored for a few minutes and then put back for another year.

He was quite a sight on Main Street, Gibraltar, choosing a style which drew attention for not being quite in keeping with the location — as he had in Kenya. He selected exotic tropical outfits for his promenade which had entertaining contradictions — exotically patterned silk shorts with a Panama hat and a sliver handle walking stick. His childhood friend Mesod Massias, Raphael's brother, said that when he greeted you "he was always jovial friendly, with his educated ways and his flashy, showy, elegant style of dress, but his smile never left his character".[27]

However, with the passing of his Uncle John, so died the last of the elderly members of the family. The attraction of Gibraltar lessened for some years, and Japan, in which he had developed a great interest, became the more regular call. This is not surprising considering he had been collecting Japanese art from the late 1950s. Sanguinetti developed a genuine passion for the country and culture. He became an active member of the Japan Society of Hong Kong and was its president from 1965 to 1970 as well as one of the vice-presidents after that until his death. The society owned and operated the Hong Kong Japanese Club on the 38th floor at 500 Hennessy Road. This was where Sanguinetti entertained his best friends and was well looked after by the staff. He made a point of attending all the meetings of the Japan Society of Hong Kong if he was in Hong Kong and physically able to do so. He was later decorated by the Emperor of Japan with an Order of the Sacred Treasure 4th Class (there are six classes) for his services to Hong Kong-Japanese relations.[28] It is one of the more widely given honours in Japan and does include foreigners, but not that readily.

Sanguinetti went to Japan regularly during the two or three months when the summer humidity in Hong Kong was at its most oppressive. He made Japan economical for himself by staying in small Japanese-style inns, or *ryokan*. He went to the department stores and ate from the peculiarly generous food samplings the Japanese offer there. He could eat breakfast in the Eastern Orthodox Church in Ochanomizuy so long as he prayed (or at least seemed to) with them.[29]

A Gibraltarian friend who knew Sanguinetti has also referred to his "economy gene", a streak of parsimony in him which cannot be ignored, not least because he acknowledged it himself, with self-denigrating humour. Brian McElney presented him with a book one Christmas on the theme of Scrooge describing ways of living well and not spending money.[30] His response was: "This book is useless. I could add another two thousand ways." His old Gibraltar friends loved him because of and despite this and were guarded about criticising it. The streak was obviously evident at the peanuts parties Sanguinetti held in his days as acting Attorney General in Gibraltar, which were regarded as a delightful eccentricity. It may have widened in him after the Hong Kong government salary was given up and the uncertainties of private practice were faced. Even when any financial worries were removed by the Garcia benefaction, this money consciousness remained.

It was not frugality, per se. He loved and bought items of beauty, dressed well, and travelled. It was not meanness. He was unboundedly generous towards people in effort, time, and affection that went beyond money. He was simply cautious about spending the very cash in his pocket. Was this inherited from his father? At the risk of applying cod psychology, did he have an innate fear of running out of money? Was that carelessly spent dollar, that unguarded excess dime, the thin end of the wedge to poverty? Though his family enjoyed comfort in his childhood, was the Rock a fortress that bred a hoarding instinct, a constant stocking and preserving against attack? What should not be underestimated is the sudden threat to his sense of security delivered by the war and then his seeing on his early travels the sudden deprivations of others.

This instinct was most pronounced towards food. He garnered as much of it as he could when it was free, as in a cocktail party or a Japanese department store display, or when the deal allowed for an unlimited supply, as in a buffet. His attitude was in some ways no different to that of many people suddenly faced with tasty food passing freely before them. Yet often for Sanguinetti, it took on the features of a campaign. Some of them were very amusing, some were as curious as they were funny, and some were unsettling in their scale.

He did do his fair share of entertaining. He gave small drinks parties at his Hong Kong government quarters both at Tower Court and Mount Nicholson. McElney recalls one evening at Tower Court when his servant, newly off Lamma Island, hunted in the fridge for small eats and offered sausage shaped white objects with cocktail sticks stuck in. These were actually nose suppositories Sanguinetti had just brought back from Europe where he had caught a cold. Alerted by the unplanned appearance of food, Sanguinetti grasped the plate before any were bitten into. David Leonard was once entertained by Sanguinetti in his apartment for a splendid view of the New Year's Eve fireworks. This vantage point was a regular treat he gave to his good friends. The amah served the fruits of his travels—small squares of chocolate that are left on hotel pillows and drinks miniatures served on airplanes.

Rather in the manner of the penniless student, at cocktail parties, he ate enough to make dinner unnecessary. His tendency to pick choice pieces of cheese or charcuterie off a buffet table and put them into a doggie bag had his friends' eyes rolling and waiters trying to look the other way. David Leonard, who marvelled at Sanguinetti's creativity as a buffet bandit, was amazed how, at the Furama Hotel buffet, he returned to their table with the entire platter of salmon and enjoyed their reaction to his effrontery as much as the food. In a strategy unsettling in its extent, Sanguinetti invited a group to an all-you-can-eat buffet lunch in the Dusit Thani Hotel at which lobsters were the big draw. He booked every table in the restaurant and only released them when his table had had their fill of the lobsters.[31]

He was always happy when others could share the benefit of his cheek. In a sort of reversed generosity, if there was a large gathering and the hosts were old friends, he might invite friends of his own to accompany him. Justice Alan Huggins's son Adrian, also a QC, remembered meeting Sanguinetti on his way to a party. Adrian was with his brother straight off a plane from Paris, with a full beard and looking scruffy. Sanguinetti took them to the party and, in a masterstroke, introduced his brother to the host as a palaeontology professor from the Sorbonne.

He delighted in receiving visitors from home and being received by him in Hong Kong was always worthy of a mention in the papers back in Gibraltar. A 13 December 1978 report in the social column of *The Telegraph* pictures him at the Mandarin Hotel hosting Paco and Lourdes Galliano along with Hong Kong Gibraltar expatriate Lydia Armstrong, the same Lydia who gave him hospitality in Nairobi and seemed destined to track him around the globe. His Gibraltar visitors went back with excellent impressions, not all of which were mediated by Sanguinetti himself. Louis Andlaw recalls being with him in Hong Kong in 1976 when Sanguinetti stumbled and fell while crossing tram tracks. Before Louis could help him to his feet, several Chinese had already crowded around to assist him. One of them told Andlaw that Sanguinetti was "the best lawyer in Hong Kong".

When Sanguinetti decided to show visitors the sights, they were not necessarily ones that would have been endorsed by the Tourist Association. For instance, he organised a trip for his friend, Count Serge de Robiano, the Belgian Consul General in Hong Kong, to view the ballet Swan Lake at the Lai Chi Kok Amusement Park. According to Brian McElney, the show was disappointing, and they went on to visit the Kowloon Walled City, a peculiar contrast, but de Robiano had expressed a wish to see it. Some form of police escort was arranged. That notwithstanding, opium and heroin were being sold and consumed openly, there were gambling dens and divans with several people smoking on couches, on one of which there seemed to be a dead body. There were also dozens of dental and medical shops where unregistered doctors and dentists practiced, and dog meat was being offered for sale in markets and food stalls.

In a similarly dark expedition, Sanguinetti took Elsie Elliott on an outing to a drug market in Ma San in Causeway Bay. In a January 1971 booklet on corruption, she wrote:

> I visited this drug market with a friend. We saw drug addicts by the dozen smoking heroin: they were leaning over lamps in huts, or holding their silver paper containing the drug outside in the gutters, while stalls sold to any who wanted to buy. Such a scene of filth and degradation it would be hard to surpass. It had been the same several years earlier when my friend visited it.[32]

To surprise Elliott with degradation took some doing. Sanguinetti clearly found the market an arresting stop for friends and visitors.

After his achievements overseas for Amnesty, Sanguinetti continued to attract publicity from the courts. In its early stages, in February and March 1976, he was a key counsel in a case which attracted huge public attention to the arrogance of the police and the potential for acquiescence in the lower courts. A police detective named Au Pui Kuen shot and killed a man, Lai Hon Shing, and seriously injured a passerby.[33] The policeman claimed that Lai was robbing him and that he was justified in shooting him. In fact, in a crowded street in Mong Kok, Au had driven his BMW too carelessly around a corner and brushed against Lai. The humble Lai, probably in very clear terms, told the "Ah Sir"[34] that he should drive more carefully. With his girlfriend beside him, status was at stake for Au. He got out of the car and, after an altercation that involved some pushing and shoving, he pulled out his gun and shot Lai dead as he was running away from the drawn weapon. Several bullets were fired, one of which hit the passerby.[35]

At the Coroner's Inquiry, which lasted from 2 February to 20 May 1976, Sanguinetti represented the Lai family. He made a battery of jury objections and straightaway questioned why Brian Caird, a Crown counsel who often represented the police in cases against them, should be acting as the coroner's officer.[36] Later, when Caird addressed the coroner, Sanguinetti objected that he could only ask questions. Relations between the two counsels curdled from the start.

During the course of the trial, Sanguinetti requested to see a witness's statement to the police. The witness objected. Caird also objected, saying the coroner would inform him of any discrepancies. While adamant that he should be allowed to view such evidence, Sanguinetti faced bringing proceedings to a halt, so he suspended that application, reserving the right to revive it at any time.[37]

Evidence from a witness in the case named Fong Bun had all the characteristics of being set up by the police in Sanguinetti's eyes.[38] He demanded to see the police notebook carrying a statement given three days after the offence, when the witness just happened to be in the Mong Kok station with his brother who was being blackmailed. This was a troubled and troublesome cast of characters. Caird asked: "How many books does Mr Sanguinetti want?" "Only Fong's—at the moment", he replied.[39]

There was now a furious row over an adjournment of the cross-examination of Fong. At this point, Sanguinetti and Caird were told to calm down by Coroner Li. "I have a duty. I am a spokesman of the deceased", declared Sanguinetti.[40] Eventually, Sanguinetti browbeat out of him the details of another witness whom Fong said he would never disclose and largely discredited Fong's own account.[41]

Another witness named Kwok also objected to his witness statement to the police being seen.[42] He had heard someone shout "robbery" and saw one man being held while two others attacked him. Cross-examined by Sanguinetti, he could not tell the Court how the man had been held. He did not know what was said. He could not testify to there being a car. He was on his way to the Victoria Theatre to see a 9:30 p.m. movie. He did not know the name of the street where the theatre was, even though he had been there many times. He also could not say approximately how long it took to walk there. He had not seen the film because he decided it did not look that good after seeing the movie advertisements outside. He had not known the film was showing before he got there, and he had not thought of going to a cinema nearer his workplace. He went home by bus and did not know how long that took him.[43]

Based on the witness's lack of details, Sanguinetti took to using the word "false" in the cross-examination.[44] Caird naturally objected. In response, Sanguinetti declared: "I shall withdraw because no useful purpose can be served by being here with all these interruptions from Mr Caird." A feature of Sanguinetti's cross-examinations was that he did not like them being interrupted, as though a work in progress was being interfered with. Caird said he was just trying to be helpful, resulting in Sanguinetti responding: "I am conducting the cross-examination and the choice is mine, and I am not going to be corrected as to the words I choose."[45]

Sanguinetti also strongly objected to the anonymity being allowed for Au's girlfriend. Au was a married man. Later, Sanguinetti made her cry on the stand. He apologised but without much enthusiasm, quoting that it was his duty.[46] The eventual verdict was "excusable homicide", and Au walked free.[47] Such was the public outcry at this and so strong the belief that the homicide was not excusable that Attorney General John Hobley decided to prosecute Au for murder in a trial before Mr Justice Li from 20 to 30 September 1976. He was found guilty, but the Court of Appeal quashed the conviction in January 1977 on the grounds of misdirection by the trial judge and ordered a retrial.[48] Whether the Court of Appeal was right to order a retrial went to the Privy Council, which, on 4 December, declined to intervene. The Privy Council's opinion now constitutes the guidelines in respect of when a retrial should be ordered. Au was re-tried and was eventually found guilty of manslaughter and sentenced to five years in prison.

The only further involvement Sanguinetti had after the inquest was indirectly, to help Graham Jenkins of *The Star* draft a letter to the Attorney General over information he was in possession of and on *sub judices* circumstances.[49] He did this from 6 Gavino's Passage, Gibraltar, on 26 July 1976, during his return following the death of his uncle.

Ian MacCallum of Wilkinson Grist, Solicitors, wrote to Sanguinetti about the trial on 1 October 1976:

> The conviction of Au Pui Kuen must be attributed mainly to your efforts at the death inquiry. Without your resolute cross-examination of the various witnesses, I am sure that no criminal proceedings would ever have commenced against Au and the community must therefore be grateful to you for ensuring that justice has been done in this matter.[50]

On 22 December 1976, Sanguinetti received a letter of fulsome thanks from a pupil, Cheng Huan, who wrote: "Words cannot express how grateful I am for all the kindness, understanding generosity and that I learned so much intellectually and morally."[51] This was typical of the appreciation many young lawyers had for Sanguinetti's guidance. Cheng Huan went on to be a lawyer well known for his wit, skill, and effervescence, and he eventually took silk as did other Sanguinetti protégés.

Barristers of over ten years' experience at the Bar could apply to the Chief Justice to be appointed a Queen's counsel, who wears a silk robe and waistcoat—hence the expression "taking silk". The actual regalia must have amused Sanguinetti, who was no stranger to florid presentation. He kept on file the minutes of a meeting of judges in October 1980, which must have been secretly slipped to him, about some new Crown Court robes that were being displayed for them. The style of the minute shouts out the authorship of Chief Justice Denys Roberts, who states: "The gown was elegantly modeled by 'Judge X' whose complexion showed to advantage the purple trimming and interchangeable purple and red shoulder sashes."

Sanguinetti's principal objection to taking silk was that a colonial QC was a second-class QC. He could only act as such within Hong Kong. Unlike an English QC, it was not recognised everywhere the Queen's writ ran. However, a QC always appeared with a member of the junior Bar, who by tradition, was paid a fee based on a percentage of the QC's fee. Although this increased the overall cost of the case, the junior barrister learned much from understudying the QC. It was eventually pointed out to Sanguinetti that his refusal to apply for silk meant he was reducing the available work of other junior barristers at the criminal junior Bar. This was a call to duty which he responded to with true and typical generosity. It did not change his mind about taking silk, but from about 1980, he never appeared in court without another member of the junior Bar with him, and this was how it went until he ceased practice. Such was his fame anyway, that he was able to charge as much as any QC. On one occasion, an unscrupulous solicitor's clerk tried to pass off another barrister of more modest capability as the famous Albert Sanguinetti. The real one did not know whether to be furious or flattered.

Being a junior barrister receiving help from Sanguinetti was a blessing for many a young lawyer. Lawrence Lok recalled being helped by him on a case which turned out to be his first major victory after being at the Bar for only two years.[52] In *Chan Kwong v The Queen*,[53] a large quantity of drugs had been found on a ship called the Lu Chiang in 1982. The judge was Frank Addison. Several members of the crew had been charged. Sanguinetti was acting for the shore contact of the alleged drug smugglers, while Lok was acting for the chief purser on the ship. "In cross-examination, it appeared likely that the prosecutor had interviewed the witness and the Judge prevented me from investigating that fact further", Lok told

Sanguinetti, who immediately referred to a statement by Joe Duffy, a Crown prosecutor, indicating that it is improper for a prosecutor to interview a prosecution witness.[54]

When the case resumed, Sanguinetti immediately picked a fight with the judge, saying Lok should not have been stopped asking questions on this, based on Duffy's statement and other authorities to the same effect. The judge conceded he had been wrong, and Lok was allowed to continue his cross-examination on the point.

Most of the evidence against the chief purser, Lok's client, was in a confession statement of an accomplice, let in after a *voir dire*, a trial within a trial to test whether or not a statement is legitimate. The accomplice's evidence under oath and cross-examination was different to what he had said on the *voir dire*. At lunchtime, Sanguinetti invited Lok back to his chambers where, over mozzarella cheese and watermelon seeds which came out of a doggie bag, he drew Lok's attention to the case of *R v Watson*,[55] which said that where the witness's evidence on the *voir dire* and on oath in the trial differ, the judge can and normally would exclude the statement. Lok subsequently drew the judge's attention to this, the judge excluded the statement, and the case against his client collapsed. Such help given by a senior member of the Bar to a junior member was in keeping with the best traditions of the Bar, traditions which Sanguinetti valued above all else.

This value also explains a very tough line he took with a young barrister who he had been informed was touting for business on his own by taking one of Sanguinetti's former clients (a woman he met while acting as a junior for Sanguinetti) out for coffee. Sanguinetti threatened to report the barrister to the Bar Council unless he explained himself. He said in his letter:

> I should like to point out to you that the sole purpose of reporting the matter is to uphold the ethical standing of the Bar, particularly at a time when so many hard-working barristers are

struggling to make a living…without infringing on the Bar's ethical code. I and many others in the profession feel that ethics must be sustained and maintained.

He notes on the letter that he did not proceed but that the young barrister was subsequently "convicted on another matter and served a term of imprisonment".

As a senior member of the junior Bar, Sanguinetti met up with an old friend in court in spring of 1977. He appeared before Judge Simon Li to curb the use of executive power. Li had granted a man bail of HK$500,000 and surety of a further HK$500,000 on 22 April. The police had then alerted the Inland Revenue Department (IRD) to substantial trading by the defendant, and they immediately raised a tax claim for HK$450,000 and a further claim on his wife of HK$45,000 in addition to requesting that their bankers freeze their funds until the tax was paid.

Sanguinetti applied for a reduction in the amount of the bail to HK$250,000. Li required the Crown to explain itself. The police said that it was standard procedure to inform the IRD, and the IRD, in turn, dodged behind its right to secrecy. Judge Li expressed his shock at a collusion designed to frustrate the granting of bail. He held that it was a cardinal principle of justice that bail conditions should not amount to a total negation of bail, and if negation came from improper exercise of executive power, then it was the Court's duty to correct it. The application for a bail reduction was granted.

Sanguinetti was a wizard at detecting flaws not just in evidence but in procedure—down to a wrong description, a forgotten process, or the seemingly slightest difference of words. In a 1976 case,[56] he made a successful appeal for two defendants convicted of attempted bribery of an expatriate policeman on the grounds that since the policeman's record keeping was so unreliable, so too was the conviction.[57]

In another case, one of Sanguinetti's clients got drunk when dining with his family and fell into a brawl with policemen. In an appeal against conviction,[58] Sanguinetti demonstrated that the magistrate had changed the wording of the charge, albeit insignificantly, but had not called back the defendant to tell him. Later, in a case that made it into the *Hong Kong Law Review* of 1975,[59] he got a conviction quashed for three defendants for conspiracy to defraud by playing "heavenly swindle" dice. The original conviction may have been influenced by "expert testimony" on the heavenly swindle from a man who was not truly an expert. It was the man's answer to just one question that undid his status.

In front of Justices Briggs, Huggins, and McMullin in 1974,[60] he got his client's murder conviction down to ten years for manslaughter because the trial judge's summing up did not make it plain to the jury that the prosecution must prove provocation. To give a client a surprisingly happy new year on 2 January 1975,[61] Sanguinetti got his conviction and sentence for blackmail, theft, and wounding quashed by Mr Justice Leonard because the criminal trial had been adjourned for three months, involving daily reports to the police station by the client. Adjournment indefinitely made conviction unsatisfactory. It was one of a basket of grounds which Sanguinetti threw at Leonard, but just this one sufficed.

Later that same year, a *South China Morning Post* article on 18 April reports that Sanguinetti also managed to stop a murder prosecution in its tracks.[62] His client was a Pakistani prison guard who had killed an inmate. The report quotes "legal arguments" from Sanguinetti. They must have been surprising and clinching because the Crown folded its tent, offered no evidence, and everyone, including the prison guard, went home.

Sanguinetti's benefit to hawkers as a sympathetic magistrate continued during his time the private Bar. For example, he conducted a clutch of appeals in hawker cases before Mr Justice Leonard in December 1977.[63] These give a sense of how crushing life at the bottom could be in a society where pressure was oppressively downwards. The original sentences were excessively harsh, and unjust fines and confiscations had been ordered. One case involved a 19-year-old boy who was fined a total of HK$4,300 for hawking without a licence and for obstruction. A rubber chop was used saying "Defendant: I plead guilty. Nothing to say" with the fine amount inserted by the magistrate.[64] The spirit of the en masses guilty pleas seems to have lived on.

A 65-year-old woman faced a similar charge of HK$3,700 but was unable to pay part of the fine and was sentenced to six weeks in jail in default.[65] She applied for bail pending appeal, and this was fixed at more than the balance of the fine so was, in effect, a denial of bail. Another judge ordered her release on nominal bail, but by that time, she had been in jail for 15 days already. Judge Leonard concluded that she had suffered enough, cancelled the fine, and ordered her release. The confiscation order again involved items which were not within the terms of the power of forfeiture which only extended to items seized as equipment used in connection with the hawking offence. Things such as a radio, a television set, three cooking pots, two electric fans, a photograph, three refrigerators, and three sets of mahjong tiles which the judge held were all household goods were ordered returned to the hawker together with the HK$1,500 partial fine she had already paid.

Similarly, Lam Chau Kwai was fined HK$500 for hawking without a license and operating a cooked food stall.[66] He was assisted by his schoolgirl daughter and her friend, who were both also fined HK$500 each, while Lam Chau Kwai was fined HK$2,000 for obstruction. An order was also made to forfeit all exhibits with no reasons given for the forfeiture. These exhibits included a sum of cash and two refrigerators. Following Sanguinetti's appeal, Judge Leonard reduced the fines for hawking without a licence to HK$250 for Lam Chau Kwai and HK$25 for each of the other defendants, and on the obstruction charge to HK$400 and HK$5 each, respectively. There was no power to forfeit cash, and he allowed the appeal in regard to the cash and ordered the return of the refrigerators.[67]

In March 1978 in the High Court, Sanguinetti got sentences of nine hawkers radically reduced. The judge actually called the sentencing magistrate "vindicative".[68] Sanguinetti's sympathy was not limited to hawkers though. There were also two simple cases of putting a young life back on track around the same time. In the first of these, in March 1978, a student stole a tin of sardines and a pair of gloves.[69] What kind of plan led to that concoction was difficult to see. The magistrate gave him a suspended sentence. Sanguinetti posed a sympathetic case before the Chief Justice himself: Could not the Court spare him any harm and not record a conviction? Could it not view this as a momentary lapse by a dutiful hard-working lad studying well at the Polytechnic? The Court agreed, and the student went out to a fresh start.[70]

In the second case, on 25 May 1978, Sanguinetti conducted an appeal in the High Court against the conviction of a 15-year-old boy for blackmailing a man for HK$300.[71] The magistrate, he contended, had a mistaken view of the evidence. The boy's conviction, plus a conviction for bike theft three years before, meant that he had been sent to Castle Peak Boys Home. Sanguinetti persuaded the judge to alter the probation order as well as to set aside the sentence so the boy could start fresh.[72] This again appears to have been the work of Magistrate Bowran in Kwun Tong. "Is he the right sort of man to be dispensing justice?" asked *The Star*.[73]

In that same month, a report was published of a joint investigation Sanguinetti conducted with Elsie Elliott. From this, his interpretation of the findings, his understanding of what he was seeing, and a heaven sent opportunity for these to gain a hold on the conduct of the law in Hong Kong could be said to have been his greatest achievement.

CHAPTER TEN

Two Reports

Tom Garner, was an unusual man. He was a former British army sergeant who became Commissioner of Prisons in Hong Kong. He imposed strict discipline and yet had a profound belief in rehabilitation over punishment. He transformed an old colonial jail system into a modern Correctional Services Department. He was born in Liverpool and had known only soldiering and then the prison service, yet he knew Sanguinetti because both were members and sometime chairman of the Japan Society of Hong Kong. He was a uniformed civil servant, yet he took the initiative to invite, of all people, Elsie Elliott and Albert Sanguinetti to go into his prisons—any of them—in secret and review how the penal system in Hong Kong was operating.[1]

So came about the Elliott-Sanguinetti Report on the Prisons and Legal System in Hong Kong in May 1978.[2] A key element of this report's title is the addition of "Legal System". The prison system came out of the exercise looking well, as Garner must have calculated, but what the investigators were told inside it, interpreted by Sanguinetti, had an unexpectedly strong knock on effect to the legal system.

During March and April of 1978, Elliott and Sanguinetti visited 18 penal institutions in Hong Kong. The main points made in their report were that, though its intention had been just to see how penal institutions were working, other matters arose unexpectedly which could not be ignored and had wider ramifications. Generally, the vast majority of prisoners admitted their guilt, but many of them said they were wrongly charged or "framed-up".

The Criminal Investigation Department was criticised in particular for routinely failing to comply with the requirements of section 51 of the Police Force Ordinance, which specifies that "[e]very person taken into custody…be forthwith delivered into the custody of the officer in charge of a police station or a police officer authorized in that behalf by the Commissioner".[3] They were instead holding persons arrested for hours and extracting confessions before complying with these requirements. If officers had complied with the Ordinance, then any misconduct by the department would have become known throughout the uniform branch.

The favourite charges used for framing included loitering, small possession, and triad accusations including possessing triad poems, which would sometimes be dictated by policemen with a lyrical flair. Some of the ways charges were framed, such as "waiting for an opportunity to commit an offence", were absurd. People with previous convictions were most likely to be framed up.

The purposes of frame-ups were several. There was pressure on the police force to produce good arrest statistics. There was also all manner of corruption driving them, including covering for triads under police protection. The report quoted a detailed confession to robbery in a cinema from a man who was in another prison at the time. Another case was quoted in which compensation on appeal was granted for a conviction on a false statement brought under duress leading to a damaged spinal cord.

Among the prisoners, fault was found with magistrates' courts in particular. There was a laissez-faire attitude. There was bullying by magistrates reinforced by pressure from the Criminal Investigation Department outside the courtroom, and there was very little help coming from solicitors whose time was money. There were complaints of injustices in the magistrates' courts, especially from San Po Kong, referred to the Attorney

General's Department, most of which were entirely ignored. There was a crying need for legal aid to be extended here.

It also became apparent that non-violent offenders were being sent to centres for violent offenders. Sanguinetti got one such inmate out, 22-year-old Choi Yui-Leung, who had been sentenced to Ma Po Ping Detention Centre[4] for being a member of a triad society and possessing triad poems to which charges he had pleaded guilty. He was the only inmate there for a non-violent crime. Sanguinetti obtained a review of sentence, and Choi was put on probation for 18 months.

In these lowly circumstances, the legal profession was charging enormous fees for ineffective services. Most lawyers charged HK$3,000–$4,000, and few would even consider taking on a case for less than HK$1,000. Expatriate lawyers were only approachable through an interpreter and were not met with before the hearing. Some magistrates had the opinion that it would be better for a defendant not to have a lawyer at all than to have some of the incompetents who appeared before them. With the exception of a handful of barristers, well-established members of the profession were not interested in these cases and left them to juniors.

Elliott's detailed comments were mostly about the prisons which, for the most part, were approved of. She was, however, depressed by the Siu Lam psychiatric facility, Tai Lam girls' prison, and Stanley prison's death row. Generally, prison staff were conscientious people who got involved with the inmates. She saw a regime of work and reform rather than pure punishment. Drug rehabilitation units on the islands earned special praise.[5]

The final Elliott-Sanguinetti report was revealed at a press conference in the Hong Kong Press Club on 9 May.[6] The Hong Kong press fell upon it. The *South China Morning Post*, for example, ran an article quoting large excerpts of the report,[7] while other newspapers in Hong Kong and London ran headlines alluding to widespread abuses in Hong Kong's legal system. The report was sent to the Governor with a forthright summary of the findings and recommendations. Initially,

Governor MacLehose asked for details about the prisoners who had been framed. Elliott and Sanguinetti declined because they were confidential. No permission had been given to share the information, and they feared details would be passed on to the police—suggesting the Governor was potentially a stool pigeon. Elliott said that she would talk about the details if she and MacLehose could meet alone[8]—a huddle difficult to imagine.

At the press conference, Henry Litton, the Bar chairman, said that the government had had plenty of warning about "some deep seated ill in the administration of criminal justice". The Bar suggested that improving the administration of justice in the lower courts required a more professional handling of the prosecution case during trial and the provision of legal aid for the defence.

It can fairly be said that a direct result of the Elliott-Sanguinetti Report was the creation in that same year of the Duty Lawyer Scheme, administered by the Law Society and Bar Association of Hong Kong but funded by the Hong Kong government. Moreover, legal aid for chiefly victimless crimes in the magistrates' courts came a mere four months after the report was released, and legal aid for defendants in many criminal cases in the District Court was provided at about the same time. The government never admitted cause and effect in these provisions.

Initially, the Duty Lawyer Scheme operated only in three magistracies (North Kowloon, San Po Kong, and Causeway Bay) and covered only six offences:

- Membership of, professing to be, or acting as a member of an unlawful society (section 20(2), Societies Ordinance);
- Loitering (section 160(1–3), Crimes Ordinance);
- Unlawful possession (section 30, Summary Offences Ordinance);
- Going equipped for stealing (section 27, Theft Ordinance);
- Obstructing a police officer, assaulting a police officer, and resisting arrest (section 36(b), Offences Against the Person Ordinance); and
- Possession of dangerous drugs (section 8, Dangerous Drugs Ordinance).

In 1981, the number of offences covered was extended to include three more offences:

- Possession of offensive weapons (section 33, Public Order Ordinance);
- Possession of dangerous drugs for unlawful trafficking (section 7, Dangerous Drugs Ordinance); and
- Possession of equipment or apparatus fit and intended for the consumption of dangerous drugs (section 36, Dangerous Drugs Ordinance).

These offences are the very ones in which injustices had been identified in the Elliott-Sanguinetti report.

In 1980, 4,062 defendants benefitted from the Scheme with a 57 percent acquittal rate. This increased to 7,371 defendants in 1981 with a 64 percent acquittal rate. Liaison Officers were appointed in each magistracy where the Scheme operated to help with interviewing clients, interpretation, and logistics. In April 1983, the Scheme was extended to cover all the remaining magistracies and the Juvenile Court as well as all offences involving juveniles. The Duty Lawyer Scheme report for 1982 found the widespread disquiet both within the legal profession and among the public at large about unlawful possession and loitering prosecutions to be thoroughly justified. The Scheme's acquittal rates for these offences were extremely high, but it considered the possibility of miscarriages of justice in these offences still a strong one, particularly when mentally ill defendants were involved. The mental ability of the defendant was a worry brought to the attention of the Attorney General, who directed that prosecution be dropped in such cases.

By 2009, the Scheme had shouldered 3,053 cases with 36,991 defendants helped by over the 1,000 lawyers participating in the Scheme covering over 300 different offences. The report for that year shows that of the 6,107 cases in which "not guilty" pleas were entered and maintained, acquittal was achieved in 4,608. The Scheme has been regarded as an outstanding success. This alone would be a proud legacy for Sanguinetti.

Another direct result of the Elliott-Sanguinetti report was a re-organisation of the Attorney General's Department with the appointment for the first time of a Crown prosecutor in the rank of Law Officer; notwithstanding his official designation, this position was styled almost from the outset as Director of Public Prosecutions. The appointment of a Crown prosecutor led to a marked increase in the professionalism of prosecutions in all of Hong Kong's courts over the subsequent years.

Tom Garner wrote to Sanguinetti on 1 May 1978: "Thanks and appreciation to you for the interest you take. It is people like you, who in Hong Kong are all too few and far between, that give such encouragement to the work of the department."[9] He did, however, criticise Elliott for

> back pedaling at the last moment in praise of the work of the department … no prison service in the world would allow a series of visits to take place as we have done in HK and the fact that Mrs Elliott did not fully acknowledge this is a matter of great disappointment to us all.

In 1983, Sanguinetti received honorary life membership in the Correctional Services Department Office. It was this good standing he was in with the department which must have led to one of his most treasured wig anecdotes. He was invited take the salute at the department's officers passing out parade. As he stood on the rostrum and lifted his hat in salute to the colour, the wig came off with it and shot across the parade ground. It was returned to him by the officer of the parade, on the tip of his ceremonial sword. Depending on the vigour with which he was telling the tale, he would sometimes include the detail that the band was playing selections from *The Mikado*.[10]

Following the report's triumph, an event took place which shook Sanguinetti. His flat on Gloucester Road, Wan Chai, had been broken into back in 1977,[11] and on 20 November 1983, it was burgled again. Approximately HK$43,000 worth of jade items was stolen this time. The burglary had happened while he was out entertaining his old friends Paco and Lourdes Galliano, who were visiting from Gibraltar, at the nearby Excelsior Hotel. He came home to find his front door had been opened without any sign of force. The burglar evidently had a key. Sanguinetti may have been the victim of the company he kept, or the help he was trying to give. Suspicion fell on one Mario Wong, who had been doing work for him in the apartment and who had been referred by a former triad friend and one-time client. In a peculiar gesture meaning to signify good faith, Wong and his wife returned a gift Sanguinetti had given them. The police investigated, but no grounds for a prosecution were found.

Mr Justice T.L. Yang wrote to say he was "heartbroken" to hear about the loss of the valuables. Sanguinetti was now deeply discouraged. During the 1967 troubles, as a precaution against a total collapse of order and a Chinese takeover, he had shipped a significant number of valuable items he had bought in Asia back to Gibraltar. Now, according to fellow collector Brian McElney, he stopped collecting in Hong Kong altogether. The pieces he had left, he took great care of. A friend from later in his life tells of how, before he went on a trip, he took days to pack his antiques into a chest which was then tightly secured, and how he took days to take them out and display them again when he came back.

The burglary prompted Sanguinetti's friends, in particular Wendy and John Mao, to urge him to cease renting and buy his own flat, one which was more secure. The Maos helped him find a unit on the 17th floor of Elizabeth House on Gloucester Road, Wan Chai, which had a fine view of the harbour, the Yacht Club, and the flyover into the Cross Harbour Tunnel. He purchased it on 15 April 1979 and was to live there for the rest of his life.

After these events, Sanguinetti took a break in Bangkok which, alongside other favoured spots, had become and was to remain his default retreat. It was also a stop he often made to break the long journey back to Gibraltar and was the last place he travelled to before he died. It was in Bangkok that he put on an exhibition of his occasional and potentially suicidal combats with motor traffic. He was being featured in the January 1979 edition of *Blackwood's* magazine, in John Haylock's article titled "Bangkok re-visited". The "Edward" referred to in the piece is undoubtedly Sanguinetti. Why he was referred to under a pseudonym is not clear, but perhaps he requested it. Haylock describes "Edward" crossing Bangkok's congested streets, where crawling traffic can suddenly make a dangerous surge of speed, using his rolled umbrella like the lance of a horseless picador to tame the cars, some of which shaved him as closely as would a bull in the ring. Yet "Edward" arrived unscathed on the other side.

One Christmas, Sanguinetti was hosted in Bangkok by a man whose niece he had represented in the District Court in the early 1970s when dangerous drugs had been found in a suitcase lent to her but, according to his successful defence, packed by someone else.[12] The uncle's house had a vast swimming pool, life-sized statues of race horses in bronze, and the general ambience of *Miami Vice*.[13] To take a short side trip to Kuala Lumpur, Sanguinetti borrowed a small suitcase from the uncle and history looked set to repeat itself. At Kuala Lumpur airport, the suitcase became the centre of attention for an excited customs sniffer dog, which Sanguinetti patted and cooed "Nice doggie". The case was opened, and a sizable chunk of Parma ham fell out—Sanguinetti had doggie bagged the ham at a buffet dinner the night before to save on lunch in Malaysia.

The new decade saw the avenging duo of Elliott and Sanguinetti formed up again in the summer of 1980 for the Commission of Inquiry into the death of Inspector John MacLennan, chaired by Mr Justice Yang. Inspector MacLennan was to be arrested on the morning of 15 January 1980 on eight counts of gross indecency. An arrest party went to his quarters in Ho Man Tin. There was no answer to the bell, and they had to break down the door. They found MacLennan's body with five bullet wounds in it and his police 0.38 service revolver lying nearby.

Keen, impulsive, instinctively conservative, bombastic in drink, and noisily interested in girls, MacLennan was, on the surface, representative of many of his colleagues. Under this façade, exposure to the novel beauties of Asian men seems to have triggered his gay side. The way he handled this hurt him almost as much as the revolver. He either fumbled the wrong man or breathed in the thin rancid air of Tsim Sha Tsui male prostitution.

Hong Kong's colonial overlay had created a curiously poisonous hypocrisy over sex and a particularly antiquated homophobia in which white people getting off the plane from Britain turned the ethical clock back to the 1930s. Expatriate officials similarly struck by the charms of Chinese youth had managed to avoid exposure, and MacLennan could have navigated occasional, if sometimes tense, relationships through the murk had it not been for naivety on his part and a collision of circumstances.

In August 1978, a libidinous solicitor, John Richard Duffy, was charged with homosexual offences with underage Chinese boys and was imprisoned for three years. Peeved that he had not received a lighter sentence for having cooperated, he revealed that he had a long list of senior officials with the same tastes as him. This did Duffy no good in terms of his sentence, but it sent an electric charge through the Attorney General's Department. A section of the Criminal Investigation Division was tasked with investigating homosexual prostitution and the procurement and exploitation of youths. This became known as the Special Investigation Unit. It was tasked with targeting procurers and paedophiles but also consenting adults, if a charge could be made to stick, with particular emphasis on government lawyers and policemen. However, if the target was a very senior official, the Attorney General would personally decide whether or not to let it pass, in the public interest. These guidelines were known internally as "the Charter".

At about the same time, MacLennan was upsetting his superiors in the force by complaining about lingering corruption in his Yuen Long station and rather artlessly taking young men back to his quarters. He was given notice of dismissal, without reason, and he appealed this decision. As part of this appeal, he was helped by two judges and an unofficial member of the Legislative Council. Probably not thoroughly understanding who she was, MacLennan was persuaded to let Elsie Elliott write to the Governor. The ignorant self-harm in that choice is almost painful to consider in hindsight. Elliott's access to Governor MacLehose was immediate. His agreement was fair, calculating, and fast. The long-held detestation of Elliott by many powerful police officers was now laid on MacLennan as a betrayer of the force. He was reinstated, but his career was in ruins.

Thus, when the Special Investigation Unit, keen to show they could police their own queers, needed a scapegoat, there was MacLennan, a proven traitor and certainly of no seniority to trouble the Attorney General. Setting up MacLennan was sordid, shallow, and clumsy, involving defective personalities, both police and prostitute, and took up as much time of the Inquiry as did whether MacLennan committed suicide or was killed. The original coroner's jury had left a disturbing open verdict. Within days of his death, Elliott alleged that MacLennan had been the victim of a "high powered police frame up".[14] She said he was one of three police officers, who had all been framed, whom she had brought to the attention of the Attorney General three weeks before MacLennan's death. She called for an inquiry, earning herself a place in the box as a hostile witness.

This assured Sanguinetti's place in the courtroom too. Originally Elliott had wanted him to represent the MacLennan family but that was recoiled from by the government who said they would appoint their own barrister, so Sanguinetti represented her instead. Broadcaster and fellow campaigner Aileen Bridgewater described the pair as "Hercules Poirot with Miss Marple".[15] The case had so many aspects that engaged

Sanguinetti: corruption, sexual hypocrisy, police hounding of an underdog, and exemptions for senior colonials. He described "the Charter" as "discrimination", saying that it "has a sinister and dangerous smell about it".[16] Simply constructed, this highly flavoured imagery was some of Sanguinetti at his understated best.

The proceedings were the stage of one of Sanguinetti's flashes of temper, which gave no quarter to persons or place. During a cross-examination, two counsel fatally interrupted Sanguinetti who whipped round on them as though errant boys and spat out: "When I want advice from you two, I will ask for it."[17]

The Inquiry was not a success for his client. The Commissioner's report said that Elliott was undoubtedly sincere and confident in her beliefs, stressing that her great sense of justice and her compassion were not in dispute, but that not everything she said was correct or supported by the facts. He found that she had a tendency to exaggerate and use emotive and extravagant language to state opinions or make inferences as fact, as well as to interpret simple and straightforward facts in the most sinister light. It was a fair but harsh criticism from T.L. Yang who was to speak relatively mildly of others in the report. Elliott's allegations of a frame-up or persecution were rejected.

Yang held that the death was suicide. The Commissioner of Police, various officers, and Attorney General John Griffiths came in for relatively minor criticism, but no actual blame was apportioned. Nevertheless, all parties disliked the report. Yang was accused of a whitewash and having been pressured by the Governor. Sanguinetti was deeply disappointed in Yang. Their enduring friendship went under severe strain as a result, and Sanguinetti did not speak to him for some time. The ice was broken only when Yang crossed the room to speak to him one day in the Hong Kong Club and said how life was too short for this. Sanguinetti accepted this olive branch, and they embraced.

Sanguinetti had the peculiar distinction of asking the last question of the last witness of the Inquiry. It was on the subject of disputed witness statements and posed to another lawyer, Joe Duffy.[18] The transcript states:

Sanguinetti:	No, I'm asking you whether these statements contained certain practices.
Duffy:	They contained descriptions of sexual perversions. Yes.
Sanguinetti:	Perversions …
Duffy:	Yes.[19]

This exchange and the MacLennan scandal in general are described in the book *A Death in Hong Kong*.[20] The author, Nigel Collett, feels that the transcript of the proceedings is "redolent with the tone of contempt in Sanguinetti's voice". Interestingly, the book introduces the transcript by saying: "It was fitting, perhaps, that the last question to be posed at the inquiry was put by a homosexual barrister on the topic of homosexuality."[21] If Collett had said that of him at the time, Sanguinetti would have sued him, which is exactly what he did to the *Tin Tin Daily News* in May 1980 for two articles they published on the 10th and 11th of that month, allegedly identifying him as a homosexual. The case was one of small town coincidence and scruffy journalism. A member of Sanguinetti's chambers who had previously been his pupil was caught by patrolling policemen in an act of gross indecency in a Wan Chai alley with a Korean man. In the news articles, the "wretched" Korean was named, while the barrister was not. However, his address was given and with it the crucial devious detail that this lawyer had only recently been tied and gagged by robbers in his own home — an event which had received some press coverage, in English as well as Chinese, and conclusively identified him. Allegations, light on proof, flowed on from this. The barrister, said the paper, had switched his sexual affections to the Korean from others, including his pupil master. Sanguinetti had been the barrister's only pupil master in Hong Kong. Sanguinetti saw the report as libelling him and accusing him of breaking the law and breaching professional ethics. He brought an action against the *Tin Tin Daily News*.[22]

There was at first some question of whether the original Chinese term — approximately "professional teacher" — could be translated into "pupil master". In advice sought from his friends Alan Huggins and Kemal Bokhary,[23] they explained that they believed he had been defamed. Now, although Sanguinetti was famed for his skills as a criminal law barrister, his capabilities in civil law were considerable. Bokhary would later say: "Having worked with him in advising on many defamation cases, I saw at first-hand how his mastery of the facts was always accompanied by his mastery of the intricacies of defamation law."[24] It is not surprising, therefore, that Sanguinetti was particularly rigorous in his homework in this matter and went beyond their advice. An abiding respect for the London Bar led him to get an opinion from Charles Gray, who specialised in defamation and went on to be a judge of the Queen's Bench Division. Gray agreed he had been defamed but believed that colleagues and friends who read Chinese would have to give evidence and that Sanguinetti himself would have to go into the witness box. Gray's opinion ended in a calm tone: "Settle." The people who would have seen the articles and could identify him were very few. There would be inevitable embarrassment and wider publicity in going to trial and giving evidence, while the damages were unlikely to be exemplary. Sanguinetti settled for HK$60,000 plus costs and a published apology from the paper.[25]

To many of his friends and his broader public, Sanguinetti was not discursive on the subject of his personal relationships. There were few verifiable attachments to women, and the references to beautiful women he was friendly with were rarely more than conversational flirtations with the person he was talking to. He could be socially captivating with women who were nobility or those to whom he thought honour was due. He would take the hand, make a low bow, and kiss it, all in the speedy assurance of a fashion long ago and left now only to royals among themselves. He has been captured in this pose with Princess Peter of Greece and Denmark, who used to visit Hong Kong and whom he counted a friend, and with the Princess de Liege, later the Queen of Belgium, at a City Hall reception.[26] He could hold such ladies in rapt attention, leaning forward slightly, his wide eyes sparkling into theirs with intense interest, his right hand upwards and off, holding a cigarette in a holder, and his left hand held down and flayed out behind—a courtly posture, indeed.

However, while chivalrous, these actions could not be considered courtly love. Sanguinetti refused all attempts by friends at matchmaking. His family also seems to have had some insight into his personal life—his Uncle John at least knew perfectly well that Sanguinetti would never marry, as highlighted by the provisions he made in his will so his property would stay in the family. In Hong Kong, it was understood by those who knew better and guessed at by those who did not know quite so well, that he was gay. Collett took this as a fact. Similarly, David Leonard wrote outright that "Albert was openly homosexual; an ageing queen" and then moved on without further remark.[27] However, Leonard was probably wrong about "openly". Sanguinetti was of a generation where a man in the public eye could be effete, camp, or in ways exhibitionist without any inference of homosexuality being drawn. If the man was respected for his position and did not scare the horses, then these traits would be accepted as endearing eccentricities, and although an observer might say "queer" to himself, the thought would remain a buried one. In such a setting, a gay man of Sanguinetti's stature in Hong Kong would be open about his true feelings only in a very closed and trusted circle, if at all, or he would go abroad.

In this way, it is possible that Sanguinetti enjoyed travelling on many levels. In Japan, he had a devoted friend from Minami-Gyōtoku named Hidetoshi Kuga, commonly called Hiromu,[28] who showed him many of the sights of Japan and helped him collect Japanese antiques. On one occasion, Hiromu accompanied him to the United Kingdom, and he also holidayed with him several times in Bangkok, including on the occasion of the magazine article in 1979, which also features Hiromu and was perhaps why Sanguinetti decided to be "Edward".

There were likely other relationships but with little evidence of intimacy. At least this was the case until an attachment seems to have blossomed with a Hong Kong Chinese civil servant. This happy and comfortable relationship developed over the last ten years of Sanguinetti's life, during which time they saw each other often and holidayed together. This lover is quite sure that Sanguinetti felt no embarrassment over who he was. He recalls one evening in the street on a Bangkok holiday when Sanguinetti was approached by a young woman offering sex. "Good heavens, no my dear!" he told her and several others within earshot, "I'm gay."

CHAPTER ELEVEN

The Golden Years

The Elliott-Sanguinetti Report and the MacLennan case ushered in the golden years of Sanguinetti's professional life. On 9 October 1980, Sanguinetti received an invitation from Chief Justice Denys Roberts to become a temporary deputy District Court judge.[1] To a raconteur with a wicked sense of irony, there could not have been a greater gift. After the pain involved in ridding itself of him 16 years before, the judiciary, in a fit of administrative amnesia, was asking him to come back, albeit as a stop gap in a temporary position, which was exactly the status that Sanguinetti excoriated.

Of course, he declined. The principle was glaring and as a successful barrister with a private income, who needed it? Yet here was an anecdote supply that could not stop giving. On 17 November 1981, a second invitation was sent to him to be a temporary deputy District Court judge at HK$1,500 a day. The Registrar suggested that it could be HK$2,000 but no promises—he clearly did not have the hang of Sanguinetti on this subject. Evidence that the department may have lost all grip on its own history came with a third offer in 1985, this time for a quick six-week holiday filler in the manner of a supply teacher, at a daily fee of HK$2,500. On the letter,[2] Sanguinetti has written "Declined AGAIN". What Sanguinetti would invariably add to this note when telling the tale was "In the public interest!", mimicking the official wording of his long ago retirement letter.

A return to the Bench was not in his future but he was curious about what might be. Thus, he once more, in 1984 at age 61, had his fortune told.[3] There need not have been too much intent in this. In Hong Kong, in the precincts of a temple or the doorways of an older neighbourhood, fortune tellers were easily come across. This one told him that, between the ages of 63 and 67, he should not travel east of Hong Kong and that he should retire at age 68. Further, he was also told that he should expect to die at 77, though life might be prolonged 15 years by happy events. So, for the last ten years of his life, he stuck with the age of 77 and kept his real age a serious secret, guarded not very strongly by black hair dye.

In addition to his blackened hair, he also developed a signature, almost ecclesiastic look. He wore a very substantial antique signet ring of spinach green jade with the family crest engraved with gold. Sometimes he wore a maroon or purple shirt without a tie and always a jade Buddha set in gold. Although the intention is unlikely, the impression that he was a senior Catholic priest could have been easily given to the not too attentive. This would have been ironic since Sanguinetti lost his cradle faith at an early stage.

Ignoring the fortune teller in one matter, he travelled for various holidays to Bacolod in the Philippines from the late 1980s through to 2004, sometimes for Christmas and Holy Week. He stayed at the Sea Breeze Hotel in the centre of town where he was well looked after and where the hotel proprietors, who took to him, organised a car with a driver to get him around. This was a cheerful lodging where he was clearly held in warm regard. In January 2000, they sent him a Valentine's Day card: "Dear Judge Sanguinetti…with our heartfelt gratitude for your generosity and thoughtfulness." It was signed by the whole staff, including Nilo the driver, Rex the cook, and Steven the new bell boy.

Another frequent hotel guest was his fellow Hong Kong barrister Michael Bunting. Bunting tells of a morning after Sanguinetti's meticulous toilette and breakfast, when he strolled out and spent some time listening to a priest haranguing a crowd in Spanish on a religious topic. When the priest was done, Sanguinetti, unable to bear it and fluent in Spanish, mounted the rostrum and corrected the man's religious and historical mistakes.

Though Sanguinetti was repelled by much of its doctrine, from papal infallibility to the forbiddance of condoms, he was fascinated by the history of the Church and possessed an encyclopaedic knowledge and shelves full of books on it.[4] The paradox is neither surprising nor unusual in people with intellectual curiosity, aesthetic sense, and childhood exposure to the disciplines of the liturgy. In Sanguinetti's case, it led to amusing conflict when he saw this beloved liturgy, in which he did not actually believe, misused. Not even the mass was spared his critiques. On one occasion, he acted as one of the 12 apostles for the Holy Thursday ceremony and let the priests wash his feet in imitation of Christ's humility. He was the only foreigner involved, the other 11 being poor but worthy locals, but this did not prevent him from firmly correcting the priests over their performance of the ceremony. Sanguinetti may have barely set foot in a church for years but his memory of the detail from his time as an altar boy at St Mary the Crowned was quite unfaded.

Another Bacolod event where he faked with aplomb at two levels was a beauty contest which he was invited to judge with the Bishop of Bacolod. This should properly have been a case of the blind leading the blind, but Sanguinetti professed to be a lover of the creation's beauty in all its forms.

Sanguinetti's equanimity and deftness over the sins of the flesh, as they appeared in court, brought him work acting both at first instance and on appeal. He became an expert in the technicalities of the offences involved and succeeded in many appeals. His appointment as honorary legal adviser of the Dance Hall Owners Association was another acknowledgement of appreciation coming from the shadows of working-class life, and it was a significant position since dance halls were synonymous with a multitude of fun and games which had little to do with the waltz or the two step.

If lewd acts were performed in a dance hall on more than one occasion, and they often were, the dance hall could be held to be keeping a vice establishment and the manager could be charged with enabling such acts. There had to be evidence of both. To prove "keeping", several lewd acts had to take place over a period of time, and generally the police evidence, lazily, only covered one. Sanguinetti took the 1985 case of Law Cheuk Hung and Chuk Kam Wing, who were convicted of managing a vice establishment and not a dance hall, to appeal,[5] and it was allowed. The judge said that the magistrate may have thought it looked like a vice establishment and acted like one, but that it fulfilled all the requirements of a dance hall, even if no one was dancing. What had happened was that two policemen had both gone in on one occasion, but separately, and just one of the two dance hostesses had behaved lewdly to just one of the officers.

In the case of Li Kin Wai and Chan Wing Sam in June 1985,[6] Sanguinetti was not so lucky. There was no dance hall registration, and Mr Justice de Basto was not buying Sanguinetti's scattershot argument that one of the women involved was a "mistress" since the room was so dark that the parties could not even identify each other. In one case he dealt with,[7] the licensing authority had revoked the dance hall licence on the grounds that Sanguinetti's client was not in control of the premises. However, this decision was made without giving his client a chance to dispute the allegation. Sanguinetti got the ruling overturned on the legal principle that both sides should be heard before a decision is made, a principle that came as a surprise to the government licensing authority, which changed its procedure thereafter. He held his Dance Hall Owners Association appointment with considerable pride.

Sanguinetti knew much about the legality of brothels too. He proved to the Court of Appeal on 16 February 1978[8] that Yiu Ka-chi could not have been operating the Golden Lion bar in Wan Chai as a brothel even though four lucky auxiliary policemen went in, took four girls out, and had sex with them in a hotel. If no intercourse is going on in the bar, then the bar does not qualify as a brothel. On 22 November 1988, a conviction for managing a vice establishment was also quashed[9]—the prosecution could only prove that one woman was being lewd and you need to prove that there were at least two. Sanguinetti was good on rates and frequency of lewdness.

He proudly displayed his good work to Adrian Huggins. Huggins, by then a QC, was appearing with Sanguinetti on an appeal involving an alleged indecent exhibition.[10] The appeal was successful on technical grounds, and Sanguinetti took Huggins a few days later to see the show at the venue in question. Huggins was left in no doubt that it was indeed an indecent show.

There was no such success for *Discovery* magazine, which was prosecuted for an obscene article in 1984. During the trial, which received some local media coverage,[11] Sanguinetti quoted Mr Justice Staple in a case in England where the judge, with comprehensive eloquence, stated:

> Approaching the matter which—let us face it—throughout the ages has been one of absorbing interest to men and women, you get two schools of thought poles apart and in between those two extremes, you have a variety of opinion and thought. At one extreme, you get the conception illustrated in some of the teachings of the medieval church, that sex is a sin; that the whole thing is dirty; that it was a mistake from beginning to end and the less said about it the better; let it be covered up and let us pretend it does not exist. At the other extreme, you get the line of thought which says that nothing but mischief results from this policy of secrecy and covering up, that the whole thing is just as much a part of God's universe as anything else, and the proper approach to the matter is one of frankness, plain speaking and the avoidance of any sort of pretence. Somewhere between these two poles the average, decent, well-meaning man or woman takes his or her stand.[12]

Sanguinetti added to this a heresy which would have sent the Bishop of Bacolod into fits. "If sex is a sin", he declared to the Western Court magistrate, M.W. Fung, "it was the great creator of life who made a mistake, not you or I". Mr Wong clearly took his stand somewhere else, and the magazine was fined HK$500.

Two years before this, Sanguinetti tried hard for a postman named Szeto Yuk Man in an appeal on 14 May 1982[13] where he clearly thought that an unspoken sexual factor underlay an injustice. When Szeto's home was raided, apart from some opened parcels with unfranked stamps on them, police found gay pictures and videos. Szeto was processed roughly, which included an unacceptable delay in being brought to a magistrate. These, at least, were the grounds for dismissal Sanguinetti presented at the appeal, but it was not allowed.

He was as outspoken on sex as he was on the law and politics, and he could afford to be. He was interviewed in Gray's Inn's *Graya* magazine in 1986 as part of an article on the Inn's members who lived in Hong Kong.[14] It described him as having 22 years in private practice, 30 years in Hong Kong, and maturity in career and reputation.

> He is retired but does cases that appeal to him … When someone has been badly treated or an injustice is done, he is first to step in. He has a passion for justice. He is fearless and dreads no one. He is of independent means, which may help to preserve this attitude.

His attitude towards the establishment was as socially accommodating as it always had been when he was invited into its midst for food and drink, although there is one barb attributed to him at Chief Justice Ivo Rigby's retirement party when he is supposed to have told the poor man that he had stayed in office too long. In the telling of this anecdote, this remark has been sometimes transposed to Michael Hogan's farewell, though Sanguinetti would have been as welcome there as a witch at a christening.

Sanguinetti was particularly happy if a function had connections with Mainland China. A picture of him with the entire grey-suited establishment, including the Governor, Sir Edward Youde, was featured in *The Tatler* on 18 December 1985 in their coverage of a cocktail reception hosted by Ji Peng Fei of the Xinhua News Agency at the Hilton Hotel. He must have been high on Xinhua's guest list by now. High Court judge and later the Ombudsman Arthur Garcia wrote to Sanguinetti on 9 July 1985, saying he and his wife's invitation to join a group to Beijing was "due entirely to your kind intervention with Xin Hua".[15]

He just was as comfortable with aristocrats as with communists and probably enjoyed himself more. When he met the Princess de Liege (later the Queen of Belgium) at City Hall, Count de Robiano (the Belgian Consul General) introduced him to her husband, the Prince and heir to the throne. In a note written on a press clipping of the event, Sanguinetti referred to him as "Another Albert…Now king since 1995".[16]

In addition to the Iranian princess, he managed to have a queen on his calling list. On his way to Gibraltar he usually made side trips into Europe which could include Greece, France, and England. He would also stop for a few days in Madrid, and when there, he made a point of taking tea with Queen Geraldine of the Albanians, the widow of the deposed King Zog.[17] A Hungarian-American who spent only a year in Albania as queen and 60 years in exile, she was highly sociable so it is not surprising that a charming Sanguinetti met and made friends with her.

Sanguinetti's calling list of high-profile friends and acquaintances naturally took him to high-quality establishments, and he was an occasional patron of higher-class hotels—but only on certain, apparently discounted, conditions. The assistant to the general manager of the Imperial Hotel Tokyo sent him a letter on Christmas Day of 1972 in response to Sanguinetti's requests for a discount.[18]

Topped and tailed by the usual Japanese courtesies, there is this message. One cannot be sure if the satire is intentional.

> VERDICT. The Imperial no longer offers any flat discount.

> SENTENCE. Best we can offer is special Winter Package Plan available to hotel employee's family and friends.

Sanguinetti probably did view himself as a "family and friend", particularly as he regularly spent many months on holiday in Japan. Day-to-day Japanese eccentricities bemused and delighted him. He was once caught jaywalking and was handed a ticket. This did not impose a fine but required him to go to an "apology bureau" where he had to bow and apologise to an official. The bureau was in a far district of Tokyo, and it took him the whole morning travelling to make the apology, which was a punishment in itself. He vowed never again to jaywalk in Japan. His theatricals with an umbrella in the traffic would have been unthinkable.

He would often wear his monocle while in the country, for effect no doubt because the Japanese thought he could only afford one glass, which greatly amused him. Another of his favourite pastimes was to sit for hours in one of the Western-style coffee shops that sell excellent cakes and play classical music and are perfect locations for people watching.[19]

Sanguinetti liked introducing his Hong Kong friends to his Japanese world. Charles Yeung, a solicitor who was a chairman of the Japan Society and whose wife was Japanese, remembers that Sanguinetti used to make a point of attending the numerous local festivals known as "Matsuri" held in and around Tokyo throughout the summer almost on a weekly basis. Moreover, in August 1987, he met Chief Justice Sir T.L. Yang and his wife, Barbara, at Narita airport in Tokyo and took them to the Narita-San temple nearby as well as to lunch at a pleasant club.[20] This was obviously after they had reconciled their friendship following their falling out over Yang's handling of the MacLennan case.

Sanguinetti's relationship with Yang, who was also a fellow member of Gray's Inn, stretched back to his beginnings in Hong Kong when they were both on the Bench and where Yang remained. Sanguinetti, while obviously not always in agreement with Yang's rulings, was fond of the man and keenly supportive of him in his role as the first Chinese Chief Justice. Yang, in turn, seems to have found Sanguinetti a consoling confidant. It was said of Yang that, along with his reforms and innovations during office, he was too sensitive and accommodating. Sanguinetti was a shoulder to cry on outside the more regular circle of colleagues. On 12 May 1986, for instance, Yang wrote to him: "Talking with you the other evening and over the phone just now cheered me a little for you help me to see things in perspective. And, for the moment at least, piece of mind was restored."[21]

Later, on 8 October 1989, Yang wrote to him distraught. In a clear out, he had unwittingly destroyed confidential papers of Sanguinetti's which he was in possession of. "What to do now?" he asked. "So very sorry." Many papers must have passed between them. Yang sent Sanguinetti articles he had read and written as well as addresses he had given, even one at a girls' school speech day.

A despairing letter about Yang's state of mind was sent from the Chief Justice's chambers on 4 February 1993:

> I feel so useless and helpless. Thanking you for books sent. I can only read very light stuff as a form of escapism. I can't face anything that is sad or confrontational. It is almost a paranoia…Have we placed ourselves in a position of those who cannot emigrate?[22]

Sanguinetti had underlined the last sentence.

In general, Sanguinetti saw judges as the obligatory high priests of the law, and when they were good, he admired them. When they were not, he scorned them for failing the faith. Peter Wesley-Smith of the University of Hong Kong compiled a table of all the judges and magistrates who had been appointed between 1950 and 1990. Sanguinetti had a copy of this and made a pencilled note on the fate of nearly every one. He was or had been on good terms with many of them. Judges like Yang, Huggins, and even Denys Roberts, who wrote a warm letter of thanks for Sanguinetti's congratulations on his appointment as Chief Justice,[23] admired or enjoyed Sanguinetti. A particularly jovial friendship existed between him and Mr Justice Pickering. When Pickering was moving chambers in May 1978, he sent Sanguinetti a parcel.[24] The note read:

> Mr Justice Pickering presents his compliments to Mr Albert Sanguinetti and regrets … that he is unable to offer free storage space for the enclosed much travelled feline objet d'art; much travelled because clearly at one time it got plastered (in Paris). At the same time Mr Justice Pickering takes the opportunity to present the enclosed feathered example of the taxidermist's art which has so long been the subject of envy and admiration on Mr Sanguinetti's part.

Sanguinetti not only had his stuffed cat returned but was now lumbered with a stuffed bird. He replied:

> Seriously injured though that cat may have been by the ravages of time, plastered as he is by foreign elements, he does indeed prove the proverbial nine lives. If only blind Justice herself, tottering precariously from her perch, also had another life. … This bird and that cat, each prominently positioned to catch the writer's gimlet eye each working day, will be continual reminders of Mr Justice Pickering's warm heart and animal loving good nature.

Good relations may have been obtained with individuals, but Sanguinetti never let that get in the way of a principle, particularly when it came to judges taking advantage, and particularly the Chief Justice. In a letter to the *South China Morning Post* on 8 May 1976,[25] Sanguinetti was critical of extensions to judicial service being not automatic but conditional upon "good behaviour". Except, he pointed out, that this did not apply to the Chief Justice. Why not? Was he not but *primus inter pares?*

Similarly, in April 1988, an admission was made by the judiciary to a technical error in having extended the term of Sir Denys Roberts as Chief Justice without using the Letters Patent. In an article in the *South China Morning Post* on 15 April, an eminent lawyer, not named but with the fingerprints of Sanguinetti all over him, said: "It was a blatant breach of the law, showing complete disregard for legal procedure … The Chief Justice is the head of the judiciary, he ought to know the law." [26]

He also opposed extending the retirement age of the Supreme Court, and he wrote to Denis Chang of the Bar Council about it. He said that in 1976 the Letters Patent had been amended to increase the retirement age from 62 to 65 in great secrecy. The government had said that this would encourage the local Bar to join the judiciary. Nobody had been consulted,[27] and the change did little to increase judiciary membership. Judges in that position, he said, earned too much for too long. He pointed out that they enjoyed full pensions from their High Court retirement at age 55 plus the salary of Supreme Court office. Stayers-on would block promotion prospects for junior judges and discourage the local Bar. He went on to make some scathing generalisations about keeping on old men for too long. He believed that Supreme Court work was too exacting. The arteries of the mind harden. Sympathy and imagination atrophy. Quickness of apprehension perceptibly slow down. Continued and concentrated attention becomes fatiguing. Old men get garrulous. They become out of touch as generations pass them by.

He recalled Lord Westbury, former Lord Chancellor of England, asking Sir William Merle why he had not attended a Privy Council session. "I'm too old deaf and stupid", Merle replied. "That is no excuse", said Westbury. "Lord Chelmsford and I are both every old, Napier is very deaf and Colvill is very stupid. Yet the four of us make an excellent tribunal."

Sanguinetti concluded with scripture and sarcasm: "Some may think that destroying angel, senility, passes by Supreme Court judges as the other destroying angel passed by the Israelites at the first Passover. With a little luck, the office may become hereditary."

One of the strongest objections Sanguinetti had to the ways judicial appointments were generated was the Hong Kong habit of appointing members of the Attorney General's Department to the Bench. A remarkable succession of Directors of Public Prosecutions found their way on, but when it became what seemed like the turn of Jim Findlay, QC, the Judicial Services Committee recommendation was that he should not be confirmed in the post, even though he had been sitting as a deputy for some months. Then came a report in the *South China Morning Post* on 22 March 1990 that a Court of Appeal judge had written to the Governor to get this decision reversed and that other judges were behind him.[28] Sanguinetti was outraged over the ethics of this. He went into immediate alliance again with Elsie Elliott (now Elsie Tu) who, similarly disturbed, had put down a Legislative Council question about back door approaches by some judges. It was not very well written though, and he assisted her in amending it.[29] After submission, they thought of a further amendment, but it did not get opened in the Legislative Council members' office in time to be accepted. Perhaps Sanguinetti had transferred his courtroom elegance to the less sensitive setting of the debating chamber—not that debates in the Council of that period were very frisky. The question was called vague and convoluted by Jim Biddulph in his "From the Gallery" column in the *South China Morning Post*.[30] He wrote: "Government officials had no problems dancing around it." Findlay was sent back, disappointed, to his government office, but he finally got the job in 1994. The system has a way of outwaiting even its most tenacious critics.

Though he harried the judiciary, judges came to him when they needed him. Sanguinetti's old university friend Mr Justice Simon Li got him to defend him on a careless driving charge in North Kowloon in 1984. He had experienced some difficulty changing lanes in Hung Hom, making stop-start movements at a 90 degree angle to the fast oncoming traffic. The police constable at the scene seems to have been a little flustered, possibly because he recognised the offender, and did not record the conversation or measure the skid marks of a taxi that had to brake to avoid collision with Li. Facing Sanguinetti, he was dead meat, and Judge Li walked. Similarly, Judge Feenstra engaged Sanguinetti for his wife, who had managed to land upside down in her car on Ting Kwok Road, Tai Po. There were absolutely no witnesses to this, but, as a good judge's wife, she reported it to the police anyway, including that she had hit a pedestrian, who disappeared from the scene and forever. Since there were no witnesses and no body, Mrs Feenstra walked away from any charges too.

It was indeed good to have a friend in Sanguinetti, and Wendy Mao had made him one since he first arrived in Hong Kong. She invited him to parties and drove him to the airport when he travelled. She also played an instrumental role in helping him find a new flat to buy after his home had been burgled in 1983 and even helped him move. She later asked him to represent her son who was in deep trouble because of the crash of the family's finance company, Dollar Credit, which now had a deficit of around US$163 million. A massive cheque kiting scam from September 1977 to September 1982 circulated cheques with the total face value of US$21.7 billion, and Willie Yu, the company's managing director, had fled Hong Kong. Many of the cheques were signed by Wendy Mao's son John, leaving him holding a smoking gun.

However, Sanguinetti persuaded the Commercial Crimes Bureau and prosecutor Warrick Reid that Mao had played only a minor part, had not personally profited, and knew little of what had been going on. He convinced the investigators that Willie Yu was the major figure. Mao cooperated with the Bureau, but the Crown was determined to have someone pay and prosecuted him. He pleaded guilty. That he was only a minor player was accepted by the prosecutor Warrick Reid, but that and Sanguinetti's plea during mitigation had little impact.

Because of the huge sums involved, the judge sentenced him to three years and this was upheld on appeal.[31] The judgement described Sanguinetti's plea as "long and eloquent … suffice it to say that everything that could be said on his behalf was very well put, if I may say so, by counsel".

Willie Yu eventually came back to Hong Kong and was subsequently arrested and charged with the same scam. Again, Warwick Reid was the prosecutor, while Yu was defended by Oscar Lai. To Sanguinetti's surprise, Reid minimised Yu's role and laid the blame elsewhere. Yu went down for only four years. Sanguinetti thought this *volte-face* by Reid was suspect. He was not surprised when Reid was later investigated for corruption and left Hong Kong for China with a fake passport. From China, Reid moved to the Philippines. The Independent Commission Against Corruption (ICAC)[32] persuaded the Philippines to deport him not to his native country of New Zealand but to Hong Kong. He was arrested on his return, and convicted and imprisoned on corruption charges. Yu's lawyer, Oscar Lai, also served a jail sentence later on. Sanguinetti found a bit of humour in this as he had joined the Oriental Club in London because it had reciprocity with the Hong Kong Club and allowed him to use it for 20 days a year—the club's membership included Oscar Lai and Ronald Li, the former head of the Far East Stock Exchange, also in jail. Sanguinetti quipped: "I have now joined the jailbirds."

During these years, Sanguinetti found alliances with Elsie Tu against the police irresistible. In a 1988 case,[33] they went into battle with the Commissioner over the unsympathetic figure of Senior Inspector David Fernyhough, who was prosecuting a case in the District Court involving resisting a police officer.[34] The case itself was sidelined by an incident in an interview room where the defence solicitor snidely suggested that "Asia's finest" could not operate a tape recorder properly. Fernyhough lost his temper, shouted "fuck off", and threw a roll of tape and mobile phone (which would have been shoe-sized in those days) at the lawyer in the witness room of police station, all of which was caught on the interview tape.

During Sanguinetti's cross-examination for the defence at the trial, Fernyhough, possibly a man who thought everything could be "winged", blithely denied using foul language and claimed the assault never happened, even though the tape was played twice in court.[35] Sanguinetti's destruction of Fernyhough was economical and ruthless, but the defendants were still found guilty. The case was taken to appeal, but it was not allowed — the Court did not agree that the policeman had committed perjury and said the assault was "very technical". Tu, prompted by Sanguinetti, swung in to harass the Assistant Solicitor General, but nothing came of it. Sanguinetti's view was that Fernyhough's behaviour was collateral damage to a conviction because it depended on the policeman being credible in everything he said. He was supported in this by a *New Gazette* "Law Bulletin" article in August 1991.[36] They then asked the Commissioner of Police what disciplinary punishment had been given to Fernyhough. The police replied that he had pleaded guilty to bringing the police force into disrepute and had been given "a caution, suspended". However, the trial judge had written to the Commissioner saying that Fernyhough had been "severely provoked" and that Sanguinetti's cross-examination had been "severe and testing".[37]

When you consider the Sanguinetti and Tu alliance, the attack on someone like Fernyhough sprang from two distinct crusades — Sanguinetti was conducting a war against colonialism, while Tu was fighting a class war, a working-class woman against the British bourgeoisie. Fernyhough may not have come from an exalted social background, but he was an agent of both targets. He was later promoted to chief inspector, an event Sanguinetti ruefully noted in his case files.

During his last ten years in practice, Sanguinetti tended to specialise in criminal appeals, where he was well known for raising every conceivable point because, as he said, he did not know which of the points he raised would be the most attractive to the appeal judge. Generally, one point or another stuck, and he had an excellent record of success. A tally of the judgements suggests, broadly, a 70 percent win rate.

Judge Eric Barnes commented that when Sanguinetti was involved in a case you knew his client was in good hands and that the Court would not be misled. In one case, the Appeal Court president repeatedly asked Sanguinetti how much longer he would be on his submissions. In the end, he said he might take five minutes, five hours, or five days, with his voice rising, or he might even take five years with these constant interruptions. He was not interrupted again.

There was one appeal case in which Sanguinetti had one very telling argument, and it got him into the law books. In the late 1980s, Tam Chung Sing, a founding board member of the electronics manufacturer Conic,[38] was prosecuted on charges of conspiracy to defraud involving substantial sums of money. There were two separate trials.[39] Sanguinetti was not involved in the first trial, but Thomas Lu in his chambers was, and he advised Lu behind the scenes. The defendant was convicted after a lengthy hearing, and an appeal was lodged, one of the grounds of which was that one juror had fallen asleep during the trial.

The second trial, involving very similar facts to the first, came on before the appeal of the first judgement was heard. During the course of the second trial, evidence was given of the conviction in the first trial, now under appeal. This evidence was very prejudicial to the defendant who was speculated to have been found guilty. Sanguinetti was then instructed to appeal the second judgement, the glaring ground for the appeal being that the result of the first judgement, still under appeal, should not have been allowed into evidence at all. The Appeal Court agreed that the conviction in the first trial should never have been allowed into evidence while it was under appeal. This point had, surprisingly, never been decided before so the decision entered the law books not only in Hong Kong but in England too as an important precedent. The appeal of the first judgement was also allowed, and the Crown did not ask for a retrial. For all that, the defendant died of cancer a few months later.

Scattershot tactics remained Sanguinetti's normal technique for appeals, but they unfortunately did not always hit the target. In the case of Wu Tung Lam,[40] convicted of a jewellery robbery, Sanguinetti made an appeal on 26 April 1984 based on 15 grounds but to no avail. For Lo Kwong-hing and Li Pak, who were convicted of trafficking, the appeal in January 1980[41] that the conviction was "unsafe and unsatisfactory" on 12 grounds did not work, and both the conviction and sentence were upheld.

An appeal against a sentence in April 1994 on behalf of Chan Kwok-hing, who had been caught bribing Television and Entertainment Licensing Affairs licensing officers in an ICAC sting,[42] demonstrates the range of grounds Sanguinetti could offer in one case. In front of Justices Penlington, Nazareth, and Litton, he explained that his client was a divorcee responsible for three children. He needed to keep paying back a business loan. He had bad health. The charge was a stale one, having taken three years to bring. However, his main claim was that the defence did not take the initiative, and the 12-month starting point was wrong as a sentencing guideline. Their Lordships were unmoved by this accumulation of woes.

He had good days, too, particularly when he was walking all over incompetent police work. He got Yeung Pui Yuk's conviction for criminal damage quashed on 10 October 1987 because of police conduct.[43] Sanguinetti laid in blow after blow. They had kicked and beaten Yeung so artlessly, they had left marks. Because of these, they could not show him in public. They had taken six days to charge him, prevented him from seeing a solicitor, breached procedure, and made up stories, including that they were "too busy" to charge him.

While Sanguinetti had his moments in the jurisprudence spotlight, his body of work, even in the Court of Appeal, generally involved using the law as it stood, as artfully as he could, to take the cause of the ordinary accused as far as it could go. It is worth giving light to just some of these accused, not all of them virtuous, but then Sanguinetti knew that justice was owed to rascals too — and he had long ago taken "Angel" out of his name.

On 28 October 1988, he got one month deducted from the sentence of a Taiwanese merchant[44] who had travelled into Hong Kong on a false passport, erroneously out of stress, said Sanguinetti, caused by his high blood pressure, even though he had gone in and out the same way four times before.

Similarly, with Sanguinetti's help, factory owners had a conviction for interfering with electricity meters quashed with costs on 16 June 1988.[45] In the same month, a Sha Tin construction site robber got his four and a half year sentence reduced by one year[46] because, pleaded Sanguinetti, he was a family man of previously good character and a loving father. Appeal against conviction stood no chance, but a year less in prison is a long time.

Sanguinetti got a bunch of housing estate decorators off a blackmail conviction on 22 February 1992[47] because the trial judge had rather hurriedly concluded what they were up to and that they were triads and had interjected his view into the cross-examination argument. Sanguinetti probably agreed with the trial judge's conclusions entirely, but the judge had stepped down into the arena, opening the gates to an appeal. So did a magistrate trying a man for obstructing a police officer. At the appeal on 24 April 1992,[48] Sanguinetti pointed out, fatally for the Crown, that the original charge had left out the word "wilfully", leaving it defective. The magistrate had not addressed his mind to it and changed it. It was skill rather than innocence that was triumphing, but there was a job to be done.

As there was with the errant moneylender on 7 April 1993, who was willing to buy himself out of a three-month jail sentence.[49] Judge Michael Wong in the High Court caught Sanguinetti's drift when he explained to the Court that the appellant was capable of paying a HK$30,000 fine, triple the original one. The trivial sentence was suspended for two years in favour of the fine booty.

He took another client as far as he could go in a hearing of the Court of Appeal in October of 1987.[50] The client, Mak

Yuet-hang, one of the factory owners mentioned above who was acquitted of interfering with meters and represented still by Sanguinetti, wanted costs against the Crown which she said had not been awarded by the District Court. The Court of Appeal initially awarded them but was required through a conflicting judgement in another court to review itself. The Court had a lot of sympathy for Mak's position as put by Sanguinetti but could not now find their way to grant costs. Nevertheless, special leave was given by the Privy Council for Sanguinetti's client to appeal. The Crown heard alarm bells in this and settled an amount with her. The petition was withdrawn.

Not all of his cases had happy endings. Poor Cheung Hong-yeung did not have a good beginning to his 1993 when appealing against a trafficking conviction.[51] On 15 January, Justices Silke, Power, and Macdougall in separately written judgements by different routes of deduction all came to the same conclusion. The appeal was not allowed. Parole notwithstanding, Cheung would be seeing in the new year in prison up to 2003.

On 31 March 1992, Sanguinetti made himself available pro bono for a man accused of assaulting a police officer.[52] Pro bono work was something he did throughout his career and was a mark of generosity and a professional obligation. He said he could not represent Mr Siu Tat Wah, the accused, in magistrates' court, but he would pass the case to the Duty Lawyer Scheme, who would get him counsel. He also said he would give his informal advice, and if there was a need to go to appeal, then he would represent him there, for free. This was a clear example of his preference in his last working years for doing only appeals, opinions, and mitigations.

This case must have gone well for Siu as he sent Sanguinetti greeting cards afterwards.[53] One, in April 1992, is from him and his family and is full of white cats. "We will remember you forever", it says. Another appeared in July of that year showing a child-like rendering of a green field and birds flying, under a big lemon sun. On it is written: "You said things would work out … and they have." If anything proved the rightness of free legal representation to Sanguinetti, this would.

CHAPTER TWELVE

Retirement

In an interview for the Hong Kong Bar Association's 50th anniversary publication in 2000,[1] Sanguinetti said that people often advised him to "mind his own business". His reply to this would typically be: "That is precisely what I am doing." He stated that he subscribed to the view of the classical Greeks when they said: "We do not say that he who minds his own business has a place in our community; we say that he has no place in our community at all." Everybody's business was held to be one's business. "This philosophy adds spice to life and one cannot die of ennui", he concluded. It was an approach he had maintained all his working life, and it would continue to be a theme of his retirement. It is interesting that an October 2008 *Economist* obituary of the solitary and austere Singapore opposition politician J.B. Yeretnam is clipped into Sanguinetti's personal files.[2] They were so similar in spirit and tenacity if widely apart in style. "We met several times in SG and HK", Sanguinetti wrote on the clipping, and it seems hardly surprising. All of Singapore's business had been Yeretnam's business as so much of Hong Kong's had been Sanguinetti's, and to the consternation of both governments.

Sanguinetti slowed down and declined work as most ageing people must, but such a temperament in a profession like his never really retires. If an actual date is required for when he stopped accepting briefs, it would be March 1995, which is when his account book records that he ceased paying rent for his chambers in Swire House and paid only a fee for a correspondence address. Thereafter, there are no more entries. His commitment to the law, to social issues, and to individuals for whom he felt fondness or compassion continued, however.

In his report of 22 February 1993 on the Lan Kwai Fong disaster,[3] Mr Justice Kemal Bokhary, Permanent Judge of the Court of Final Appeal, acknowledged the advice he had received. Individuals he mentions are Mr Justice Kempster and "Mr AJJ Sanguinetti, a distinguished member of the Bar whose independent and inquiring way of thinking is always of value to anyone conducting an independent inquiry with whom he shares his ideas".

Bokhary first met Sanguinetti when he was a pupil and Sanguinetti's chambers were along the corridor.

> My first impression of him never changed although it grew. He passionately believed in justice, was determined to see that the law was administered justly, had the ability to carry through that determination and would do so without losing his sense of fun.[4]

Bokhary and Sanguinetti became friends from the start. It was one of the closest friendships of Sanguinetti's life, extending to Bokhary's wife, and their daughters, to whom he became "Uncle Albert". "He was more like one of the family than a friend", says Bokhary. As his career moved into civil work, he saw less of Sanguinetti in court than in earlier years, but he did lead him once, in a case before the Court of Appeal. "The script contained no speaking part for Albert, but even from a seated position he managed to make a valuable point in an aside audible throughout the courtroom." He also supported Sanguinetti in his claim of defamation by the *Tin Tin Daily News*.[5]

A man of compassion and moral courage, with a sense of fun and even a touch of constructive mischievousness at times is how Bokhary characterised Sanguinetti. He goes on to say: "If Albert was addicted to anything, it was extravaganza. And some might say that if he was allergic to anything, it was extravagance. But they are the ones who do not know of his generosity." This is firmly along the same lines of the judgements that were made by his oldest friends from that long ago youth in Gibraltar.

It was very shortly after he stopped court work that a case done years before for a client with strong Communist Party connections became fuel to a fire that ran through the press. In 1978, Sanguinetti acted for Tsang Hin Chi, the founder of Goldlion Holdings Limited, when he appealed against his sentence for possession of goods to which a false trademark had been applied. The magistrate had sentenced Tsang to fines totalling HK$22,000 and two months in prison. On appeal, the total fines were increased to HK$200,000 and the immediate sentence of imprisonment was varied to a suspended term of four months. He had also been fined in 1971 for a similar offence.

When Goldlion went public in September 1992, the prospectus had not mentioned either conviction, although the 1978 conviction had been disclosed to the Stock Exchange. Tsang was also a non-executive director of Denway Investment Limited, another company that went public in February 1993. The report for that flotation also failed to mention the convictions. By now, Tsang was a deputy to the National People's Congress, the only one from Hong Kong to sit on its Standing Committee and one of the most prominent supporters of Beijing in Hong Kong, so when this came to the notice of the press, there was a burning interest.

Sanguinetti was prevailed upon to write to the Stock Exchange explaining that he had been Tsang's counsel in the 1978 conviction. This was, he said, not a serious offence, and, from his experience as a barrister and magistrate at the time, it was a common one in the 1960s and 1970s when the garment industry was growing quickly. The argument that "everyone was doing it" was not one of Sanguinetti's most powerful mitigations, but it was unofficial and helpful to the parties who looked to him. Tsang resigned from Denway, but carried on in his own firm and as a National People's

Congress member until 2004. He was also a member of the Preparatory Committee for the post-1997 Legislative Council and Chief Executive elections and a vociferous critic of the pro-democracy position thereafter. His reputation within the establishment did not suffer. Tsang was awarded the Grand Bauhinia Medal in 1997.

Sanguinetti's letter for Tsang may have been a broad brush gesture, but the years never diminished his taste for legal research and detail. In 1996, at the Foreign Correspondents' Club, Sanguinetti was a member of a panel discussion on the role of the Attorney General. This informal evening session, upon which nothing of any real import rested, is an example of his fastidiousness. He studied seven long papers and speeches supplied by the Director of Public Prosecutions. He read articles from the *Hong Kong Law Journal*, extracts from papers on Commonwealth law, two book chapters, and a Legislative Council discussion paper. He also sought the views of the Attorney General of Gibraltar.

He was again called upon by Justice in 2002 to take part in a series of legal seminars, at the Foreign Correspondents' Club, on "Expectations from Judges", "Article 23", and, his topic, "The Accountability System". Taking part with him were Solicitor General Robert Allcock, barrister and politician Alan Leong, law professors Johannes Chan and Michael Davis, Judge Kemal Bokhary, and the Roman Catholic Bishop of Hong Kong, Joseph Zen. These were certainly not occasions for a mind that was in retirement.

Similarly, Sanguinetti was still asked to professional and social functions with regularity because his status in both worlds was high and his entertainment value as a raconteur and observer was peerless. In 1993, Mr Justice Simon Li invited him to a dinner for 40 attendees being held for the visiting English Chief Justice and Law Lords. The Chief Justice invited him to the Opening of the Legal Year ceremony, every year, and to a talk by Lord Woolf, the former Chief Justice of England, in March 2006.[6] There were only 24 VIP guests at this event, and Sanguinetti was seated among them. David Li, chairman of the Bank of East Asia, wrote to him personally thanking him for attending the Bank's 80th anniversary celebration. This may be as much to do with the good business he gave them over the years as his celebrity.

The Chinese press also never forgot him. He is prominent, for example, in their colour photo layouts showing the great and the good attending Sir Oswald Cheung's funeral. While unforgettable, Sanguinetti himself did forget those he met sometimes. There is a press clipping in his files reporting a speech made by John Negreponte, US Deputy Secretary of State, in September 2008 in Hong Kong.[7] Sanguinetti wrote on it: "He inquired about me — I do not remember him."

The most momentous event in his retirement came right at its beginning. On 9 October 1995, he received a letter from Gladys Li, then chairman of the Bar Council, telling him that by unanimous decision, it wished to propose at the Association's Annual General Meeting "that life membership be conferred upon you in recognition of your contribution to the Bar, of your professional standing and the high esteem in which you are held by all".[8] On 13 October, Sanguinetti accepted, saying: "I myself feel that I have done little of matters outstanding to deserve such an exclusive honour. After mature heart searching…I accept. If I did not consent, it would appear presumptuous, vain and arrogant." He knew the distinction between that and great modesty.

Life membership of the Hong Kong Bar Association is conferred on those who have rendered outstanding service to the Bar or to the administration of justice in Hong Kong. The proposal to confer the honour must be made by at least seven members of the Hong Kong Bar of whom at least three have to be Queen's counsel or senior counsel. This proposal of life membership for Sanguinetti was granted by unanimous resolution on 31 May 1996. Only three people had ever been given such recognition up to that time: Leo D'Almada, Patrick Yu, and Leslie Wright (who was famed for living in the Hilton Hotel for 30 years and, for his last few, in the Ritz Carlton). The renowned Patrick Yu had always declined to take silk on much the same grounds as Sanguinetti. Leo D'Almada, the first life member, had died earlier that year. Now there were to be five. Along with Sanguinetti, Brook Bernacchi, QC, and Sir Oswald Cheung, QC, were admitted. Bernacchi passed away only weeks afterwards.

Letters of congratulation flowed in, including one from Jacqueline Leong, QC, in which she said:

> The Bar, more than any other institution, genuinely nurtures and shapes its future generations by the example of its senior members. Your outstanding professional skills are, of course, legendary. But your most lasting legacy to the Bar will be your wicked sense of humour, your merciless lacerating asides and your rapier-like wit—all of which combine to make you easily its most waggish member, as well as one of the livelier and more fascinating characters in town.[9]

Leong chose to highlight Sanguinetti the performer, the character who would always add verbal colour to a courtroom or a cocktail party. During his lifetime, these were essentials of his image, and long after his passing, they will remain so, but they have also hidden somewhat the seriousness of the man. His knowledge of jurisprudence was immense, his reading into subjects unstoppable, his attention to detail unflinching, and his dedication to the law and making it available to the common man intense.

Gladys Li, SC, in a speech at the Faculty of Law graduation ceremony at the University of Hong Kong on 1 November 2008,[10] tells of how Sanguinetti had come to her the day before with an envelope containing three clippings of moments in his life. Perhaps he viewed them as the most important expressions of his philosophy, and, with some presentiment, he wanted her to have them. This was a dear gift, for in ten months he was dead.

One of these clippings was the landmark speech he made in Gibraltar as acting Attorney General, one was of a speech in December 1965 on "Human Rights and the Rule of Law", and one was a report of his retirement from the Bench in Hong Kong. These three occasions carried with them principles which were fundamental to Sanguinetti's worldview. Li told the graduates: "I don't know why he chose yesterday to give this to me but it was serendipitous." Later in her speech, she chose to quote from his Gibraltar speech. She concluded from it:

> We can see that you and I stand in a long and unbroken tradition based on the lawyer's role in maintaining the rule of law, no matter in what time or where in what circumstances and however unpopular the cause.

This role was probably Sanguinetti's greatest contribution to the Bar.

At the end of her address, Li said: "I would like to come back to what Albert Sanguinetti said about fear. 'Fear is not a good companion.'" Behind Sanguinetti's sense of humour and rapier wit lay courage.

He was very proud of his Bar life membership. He kept the minutes of the Bar Association's Annual Meeting of 2008 in conjunction with a Bar mess dinner in which he is listed as being the sole life member present. By 2004, there were only two of them left. In a talk at the Helena May that year,[11] Patrick Yu told them he was one of the two survivors. The other was Sanguinetti, "whom you probably know or of whom may at least have heard. There used to be five of us. Unfortunately only the good die young. Alberto and I are the only ones left to boast of our age."

Sanguinetti was looked up to by people of all ranks, many of whom were grateful to him for his help and guidance. Wong Yan Lung, after his appointment as Secretary for Justice, responded to Sanguinetti's congratulations in a letter dated 24 October 2008.[12] At the bottom of this, next to his signature, Wong had written: "I will firmly bear in mind your advice regarding impartiality, transparency and fairness." David Leonard on being made a High Court judge wrote in October 1991 to express his hope that Sanguinetti's wise counsel would be something available to him in the future as it was in the past. In the same vein, Grenville Cross took silk and wrote to thank Sanguinetti for his support on 17 March 1990[13]—he had written a warm letter of formal support for Cross to Chief Justice Yang but also a back door one telling Yang that he had been checking around to confirm his good view of Cross.[14] Arjaan Sakhrani, later a High Court judge, wrote to Sanguinetti on 28 July 1986, stating: "I have been privileged to have had a friend like you at the Bar. It has made life a lot easier." Adrian Huggins applied for silk in December 1990, and in a letter on the 28th, he apologised to Sanguinetti for not having given "you and other elders and betters due and proper notice"—it is a courtesy for members of the junior Bar applying for silk to inform "elders and betters".

Some of this correspondence was pro forma "one-liners", and Sanguinetti received a succession of them, many of them keenly delivered, including from Anthony Neoh, Robert Ribiero, Alan Hoo ("in my folly" in the tradition of self-deprecation), and likewise Robert Kotewall ("after immature reflection").[15]

One barrister, who had been rejected for silk twice for reasons he found implausible, told Sanguinetti of a rumour that anyone supported by or known to be friendly with him would not get it. Sanguinetti may have enjoyed a small flash of the old anti-establishment notoriety, but the barrister's rumour lacked one point of substance—Sanguinetti had refused to be his referee because he did not know him well enough. From the most junior end of the profession came a letter of gratitude in June 2005 from the parents of Antonio M. Da Roza, followed up by one from Antonio himself, for the recommendation Sanguinetti made to the Court of Appeal that he should serve there as a marshal.

His affection for the Hong Kong Bar did not lead him to be in any way cosseting or restrictive. In September 1984, he supported a proposal that the English silk Alan Tyrell should be admitted to defend a criminal case. Sanguinetti believed that if the client wanted Tyrell, then he should have him—it is a free market. However, this was hotly contested by the Bar Council, and the chairman, Henry Litton, was opposed. The acting Chief Justice Huggins ruled against Tyrell.

One of the arguments Sanguinetti used in favour of admitting Tyrell was that having English silks coming to Hong Kong was good for the junior Bar. If he was protective, it was of the junior Bar and its health. At a Bar dinner night in November 2007, he urged the welfare of struggling members of the junior Bar on Rimsky Yuen, later Secretary for Justice, whom he supported for the Bar chairmanship.[16] He also involved Andrew Li, the Chief Justice, who replied on 2 August 2008. Both replies were reassuring though short on specifics. Li concluded: "Ultimately, competitive market forces would be at work." In his letter to the Chief Justice, Sanguinetti had mentioned his own failing energy. Pencilled on the Chief Justice's reply was the note: "He sent more than this letter. A basket of fruit."

Only a few years earlier, in May 2003 when his energy may not have been so drained, he wrote a letter to Andrew Li which began, portentously: "You may well think that in writing this letter I am highly impertinent." It is written in capital letters. The second stroke in his letter D is particularly sweeping. When writing on matters of importance, he always used capitals. He probably knew how testing his long hand script was for the reader.

He began the letter by heaping praise, especially upon his choice of commercial law silks, but he went on to state that no private practitioners at the junior Bar had been made silks for two years. This he thought was odd, given how so much of court work is criminal law. Two of the rejected were honest, straight-forward, and of high calibre. If selected, they would have been able to compete

> with some (not many) of the unscrupulous, irresponsible and money grabbing so-called "Leaders" of the criminal Bar. Regrettably, there is a feeling amongst a large number of

practitioners, especially those practicing at the criminal Bar, that you appear to be biased against them.

He had no doubt that this was not the case. Then he quoted Second Corinthians 11:17–22: "Shall I commend you in this? No I shall not." Throughout his life, at telling moments, he quoted scripture. Like many educated and culturally inculcated non-believers, he could not resist the ethical and literary appeal of the Bible.

He ended this affectionate but undoubted admonishment by saying: "As one of the three Hon. Life Members of the HK Bar Assoc., I take a lively interest in all matters that concern the Bar." As the Gray's Inn writer had observed, free of the need to earn money or preferment, he could speak truth as he saw it to power. This "lively interest" seems to have been his main calling in his final years.

Chief Justice Li rejected the criticism of his appointments, considering it a "fair regime, operated fairly" and was saddened to hear that he appeared biased, which he was not. However, he fully accepted Sanguinetti's motive in writing to be of service to him. "It is a service which is very much valued and appreciated as it comes from an old friend of great experience, much wisdom and complete integrity." For Sanguinetti, this appreciation was a justifying and gratifying change from those more unsteady times of Chief Justice Hogan.

His last involvement with the Hong Kong Bar Association was an invitation on 1 December 2008 to attend the Bar mess dinner to be held at the Hong Kong Club in the coming February.[17] A Bar dinner at the club, what could have been more delightful? "Accepted" he wrote on the letter, but he was not to make it to the event.

He remained steadfast in his belief that, with the British gone, Hong Kong would become a happier place under Chinese sovereignty. His mantra continued to be "the sooner, the better". Since the early days of his friendship with Percy Chen, he had been a member of the Marco Polo Club, a Xinhua News Agency sponsored dining club for explaining

Mainland culture and ethics as well as aspects of New China to compatriots and foreign friends. It met on the last Thursday of each month for a black tie European meal in a private room at the Mandarin Hotel. For a while, it was the only place in the world where Westerners could meet informally and have discussions with representatives of the People's Republic of China. There were usually about 30 Party cadres present.[18] On 28 November 1996, he attended the 40th anniversary meeting under the chairmanship of Philip Wong, the Legislative Councillor for the business sector.

On the penultimate day of British rule in 1997, he looked out from his Elizabeth House apartment in Causeway Bay at the sunset beyond the Exhibition Centre, which was to be the location of the handover ceremony. He wrote a memo to mark the moment, pointing out that the Exhibition Centre workers had demonstrated that day over not being paid as agreed, which must have gone down as one of the very last shortcomings of British rule. He wrote: "Over 99.5% of the Chinese are extremely proud that HK is being embraced by the Motherland. The cloud of shame has gone after 156 years of alien rule."

One of his last collaborations with Elsie Tu was in defence of the consistently pro-Beijing Secretary for Justice, Elsie Leung Oi Se. She was roughly treated by students on a visit to the Chinese University of Hong Kong for what they saw as her acts of commission and omission in the legal process in favour of the Mainland, including refusal to prosecute the owner of the *Hong Kong Standard*, Sally Aw Sian, for being involved with false circulation figures. Sanguinetti co-signed a letter to the newspaper on 28 October 1999 with Patrick Yu and Brian McElney condemning the students and supporting Leong. This was followed by a letter from Elsie Tu, endorsing their letter and saying that the students had been "grossly misled by a small group of heartless politicians bent on creating trouble for anyone connected with the [Special Administrative Region] government", an interesting observation from an expert in such an exercise.[19] Leong wrote gratefully to Sanguinetti the day following: "Living amongst friends is comforting."[20]

The defence of Elsie Leung Oi Se knew no bounds for Sanguinetti. He was quoted in the *South China Morning Post* earlier, on 8 February,[21] for this issue kept its heat for a long time, saying that one may consider her mistaken for not prosecuting Sally Aw Sian in the public interest but that Leong need not resign. He went on to say:

> I am not scared of the rule of law provided that an institution exists for private prosecution … if anyone cannot agree with this matter, there is nothing to stop them from bringing a private prosecution in the magistrates' court.[22]

This was almost politically disingenuous, but Sanguinetti was no politician. His only attempt at political office ended honourably but not in victory. He stood to be a member of the Election Committee for the Legal Subsector of the Legislative Council in May 2000. He came 23rd out of 36 candidates. Considering that he did no canvassing and out of all the candidates, he was the only one without a fax number, it is remarkable he came ahead of 13 of them. In a letter to Sanguinetti, replying to some gesture of goodwill, solicitor Maurice Lee, who came sixth, said: "You are too good to be part of the game. You have nothing to lose when you do not take part in this game."

Sanguinetti does not seem to have been particularly disappointed at the loss. He appears to have been just out for a stroll. What might have been more hurtful was the refusal of an offer to be part of the Basic Law Drafting Committee. Elsie Tu proposed him to Elsie Leong. Any personal regard Leong may have had for Sanguinetti must have been overpowered by the risks of this outspoken and free-thinking personality being as out of step with the Party drill as he had been back on parade in Gibraltar. In May 1997, she wrote to Tu:

> Space and organisation structure do not permit us from [*sic*] making Albert part of the drafting team. However I shall call on

him for advice from time to time before the bills are presented so as to avoid mistakes in the drafting.[23]

The logic in excluding a man from a drafting team who could avoid mistakes in drafting indicates an excuse over which not much time was spent. There is no record of him being called upon, at any time.

His optimism about the liberation romance continued, nonetheless. He expressed this to the *Gibraltar Chronicle* on 21 September 2001, saying that everyone was better off in Hong Kong since the departure of the British and there was considerably more democracy for the Hong Kongese. To the People's Republic, he continued to be helpful, even mysteriously so. In a brief handwritten note in his files, he says:

> I met two of the fact finding officials from the [People's Republic] of China at their request on Saturday July 12th 2003. The meeting took place in the Thai restaurant behind Elizabeth House from 2.30 pm–3.30 pm. I expressed my views on matters raised by them.[24]

These matters are explained no further. The date is significant though. It is only 11 days after the mass demonstration against the proposed introduction of Article 23 security laws, of which Sanguinetti says nothing. The central government is known to have been taken by surprise by the demonstrations. Talking to Sanguinetti may have been part of a programme of consultations with friends of China to find out what was going on. One wonders what insights romantics of his generation could give into a new generation of Hong Kong identity which had been coming of age in their advanced years. It is most likely that whatever he advised, it would have been to tread softly.

With age came health problems. He needed a valve inserted into his heart. He underwent the procedure at Grantham Hospital, a specialist cardiothoracic hospital. Sanguinetti was shaken by this, becoming extremely conscious of what he ate, rarely eating meat, and exercising frequently. He never understood why he was always overweight though, perhaps due to the many times he was invited out and his insistence on going to buffets that allowed him to eat as much as he could and, in most cases, to take some home. By the middle of 1995, the valve had worn out, and it needed replacing with a metal one. The operation was again done at the Grantham Hospital. According to Brian McElney, his room was like a flower shop, with all the bouquets from his friends. He recovered from the surgery well enough, but the metal replacement had drawbacks. He had to take the anti-rejection drug Warfarin, also used as a rat poison, for the rest of his life. This drug complicated his life more. He had to be monitored frequently, and some of the foods on those buffets were now forbidden to him.

The diagnosis of a heart ailment put a stop to the pipe smoking Sanguinetti had continued since his university days. To those who saw him in later life, meticulously prepared every morning with skin creams and fragrances and dressed in vivid colours and silks with the ubiquitous monocle, this would have been like the Prince Regent filling and lighting a Calabash. His pipe smoking had started in London where it went well with his more conservative period of pin stripes, waistcoat, and bowler hat, and by the time he reached Hong Kong, it had become habitual. Many of his friends remember the mess he left behind from it, filling his pipe repeatedly and dropping tobacco all over the floor. Like many pipe smokers, his habit was more about this process and the optics than actually smoking the pipe. So frequent were his pipes that his bottom front teeth became worn by the pipe stem. He was given gifts of stunning gold Cartier and Dunhill lighters and pipes—one he loved in particular was a Savinelli Giubileo D'oro pipe, given out of appreciation for winning a case.

Convalescing from the heart valve surgery, Sanguinetti took a cruise with Brian McElney on the rivers and canals between St Petersburg and Moscow. St Petersburg is a tsarist showcase, and he was in his element telling tales of Catherine the Great and the later tsars, and of Prince Yousoupoff and Rasputin whom he had read about extensively.

In the rejection of doctrine, some sentiments of faith lay restlessly in Sanguinetti. After leaving St Petersburg, the vessel sailed on to the Moscow Orthodox Christian centre of Yaroslav, located just before Moscow. Outside the main door of the cathedral, an Orthodox priest barred the way demanding US$1 per head for entry. Sanguinetti accused him of turning the house of God into a den of thieves. The priest ignored him. The group from the vessel had spotted an open side door and when they emerged ten minutes later, Sanguinetti was still haranguing the priest who suddenly stood to an impressive height and declared, in impressive English: "I quite agree with you, Sir." Sanguinetti never saw the inside of the cathedral. Fuming still, he left the precinct, found a board and a nail, wrote that they had made the house of God into a den of thieves, and hung the board on the gate in imitation of Martin Luther.[25]

Sanguinetti could obviously be a testy traveller. On another cruise to Iceland, the Faroe Islands, and Norway, he did not enjoy the company on board—circumstances easily found on cruises and probably inevitable for one who had intellectual expectations of the company he kept. He deliberately did not dress for dinner and spent much of the time complaining as he ate it. Traveling with Sanguinetti in his later years, his Hong Kong companion recalls how, on their first trip together to Bangkok, Sanguinetti insisted on touring markets while he wanted to see temples. "No more after that", he reports with realism rather than any hard feelings. "On holidays, we went our separate ways."

Sanguinetti did not travel after 2004. In the last few years of his life at home, he enjoyed going to exhibitions of auction houses and greeting the shop owners in strolls along Hollywood Road, which he had patrolled, along with Cat Street, for bargains for 50 years. His favourite type of shopping was to pick out small gifts for friends and then meticulously wrap them himself. Occasionally, he would go to see movies that interested him, and his tastes in popular music were Francophile, with affection for the singing of Yves Montand and Charles Trenet. He might stay indoors for a day or two, but then he would foray out. A favourite destination became the High Court Library in Admiralty where he could read the British newspapers. As with elderly gentlemen in reading rooms the world over, he would nod off to sleep and have to be given a gentle shake at closing time. A regular calling spot for reading the press became the reception area at Johnson, Stokes & Master and great was his lament when they decided to no longer offer the British daily papers. He did not just go to the solicitor's to read. He was forever assessing and reassessing his complex list of assets and changing his will, adding codicils depending on his involvements at the time. It was estimated that he did that at least 20 times, though he always left the core benefactions to friends and family unchanged.

He kept in close touch with the survivors from his generation in Gibraltar, in particular with Willie Piccone who would telephone him in the evenings quite frequently. With his nearby Hong Kong friends, he would try out new restaurants. The Century Hotel in Wan Chai, near his home, now provided his favourite buffet target at weekends. His preference by then seems to have settled on Western food.

The Hong Kong Club's range from haute cuisine to British comfort food was just one of the reasons he enjoyed going there. He never actually joined the club because he regarded the entrance fee as too high, but he had limited access to it from his London Oriental Club's reciprocal arrangement and the generosity of his friends who were members, particularly Peter and Audrey Ho, solicitors and former colleagues of Brian McElney. Here, he could be among many of his old legal colleagues. Members of the Bar and of that former colonial establishment which he had upbraided so often would stop by his table to talk. Audrey Ho recalls an occasion when Lawrence Lok, once a junior Sanguinetti had helped win a case and now a senior counsel, introduced his retinue of juniors and pupils, one by one. This scene—with Sanguinetti raising his hand, decorated with a dark and prominent ring showing his family crest, and the younger men inclining down, almost seeming to kiss it—made Ho think of a presentation to the pope. Given his claimed papal forebear, this seems appropriate.

Ho recalls Sanguinetti's sharp, even harsh, wit as well as his gentle sympathy. Once, while he was smoking his pipe (when he still could) after dinner next to a table with noisy children, the father asked him if he would please mind not smoking. Sanguinetti asked in return if he would please mind not having so many children. He obviously found the riposte irresistible, but he was not averse to children. Memories of his own warm family made him sympathetic to others. "He was always very encouraging to me during the trials and tribulations and pressures of being a mom to young children", says Ho.

Sanguinetti's invitations to people to view public holiday fireworks from his vantage point apartment went down particularly well with the Ho children. Their son Matthew's childhood impression for a long time was that Uncle Albert was responsible for arranging the viewing of fireworks in Hong Kong from his home and that his family watched them for free because we were luckily his friends.

"I recall Albert lending his wig to Matthew for a day to take to his kindergarten for 'show and tell' about professions", says Ho. "A barrister's wig is very precious and normally never leaves a barrister." Putting on the battered wig in front of his classmates would have been pure Sanguinetti play acting and something may have entered the child's soul. Matthew went on to read law at university.

During one of their lunches, Sanguinetti told Audrey Ho that he had bladder cancer.

> He was very stoic about it and went about his treatment positively. Whenever our long-time driver was free, he would drive Albert to the hospital which he greatly appreciated. I visited him at the hospital regularly and he was always cheerful, even

towards the very end. He still had a very good memory of people and places and his intellect, wit and humour never faded.

He checked into a private room at Queen Mary Hospital in July 2009. His turbulent years on the Hong Kong Bench and full health coverage in the retirement privileges he had fought for were giving him a final pay off. It was a comfortable place for him, and he had no need to travel back and forth for treatment. For some years, he had been looked after in Elizabeth House by a devoted Filipino manservant, Anover Ireneo. He now came to the hospital every day, assisting Sanguinetti with his morning toilette, and stayed on hand until he went to sleep. Despite the convenience of it, some of his friends became concerned over this voluntary confinement and the dangers of immobility. Sanguinetti's interest in movement had waned though. He was stoic in front of friends, but the cancer had collapsed his world. He was finding this difficult to accept, and his will to live was slipping. This private hospital privilege consoled him. He no longer wanted to be in Causeway Bay. An inexhaustible precession of friends came to visit and re-visit him at the hospital. Then, eventually, they came to say goodbye.

On 27 October 2009, Sanguinetti died from sepsis in his sleep. He was unconscious from the morphine given to dull the pain, and he passed away at dawn with his nephew James, his manservant Ireone, and his partner at his bedside.

Sanguinetti had made it quite clear that there was to be no religious ceremony of any sort, but there was a restrained and elegant cremation at the Cape Collinson crematorium to which nephews, nieces, great-nephews, and great-nieces came from across the world, as well as old friends. The reception at the Hong Kong Club afterwards featured a comprehensive and touching photographic account of his life. Guests were addressed by his nephew James Gordon and Gladys Li, SC. They were a congregation of Hong Kong's eminent citizens including no less than 21 judges and very many of his colleagues at the Bar. The esteem in which he was held was on august display.

Sanguinetti died a wealthy man, and he disposed of that wealth generously across a wide spread of people and organisations. His will had certain preferences and strictures. The money he left to his "difficult sister" should be halved by the executors if they considered that she was interfering with the execution of it. Any charitable donations were only for the poor and victims of misfortune and were not to be made to charities to do with education or the arts. Recipients included Amnesty International, Project Orbis, the China Coast Home, and charities combatting slavery, for the handicapped, and for earthquake relief. The Hong Kong Bar was left a sum to assist young Chinese barristers, whom Sanguinetti knew were the ones who struggled most. It could not be accepted worded in those terms but the executors were able to re-craft the legacy as a more general donation.

To his partner, he demonstrated generous care, and he was also kind to his dedicated manservant Ireneo, with a money bequest and by letting him live on in Elizabeth House for six months until he found a new position. To his long-time friend Hiromu in Japan he left money and what was described as a Japanese Shugu (Erotic) hand scroll. All his nephews, nieces, and cousins were provided for, and so too were the Gordons and McBeaths,[26] including the niece who had cared for his late sister despite her having defaulted on the electricity bill, as well as Michael Cumming, the step-son of his beloved cousin Lourdes Cumming. Children of his close friends and colleagues were also remembered. For example, Judge Kemal Bokhary's daughters were each left a sum by "Uncle Albert".

After he had dispensed with the money and property, the will went on to distribute his antiques collection, very precisely and to many people, which makes the later clauses read like an auction catalogue. One of his executors, Gladys Li, SC, was much favoured artistically. She received Cantonese fans, a Thai prince's ring, an intaglio ring with a bloodstone, and several crucifixes with long lineages. Mr Justice Kemal Bokhary was given rare Chinese embroidery and a gold pendant with an inscription from the Koran which had been a present from Princess Pari Arfa of Iran. In Gibraltar, Willie Piccone got a statue of the Goddess of Mercy, while a cousin received an Asprey silver cigarette case "originally bought by or for Wallis Simpson".[27] In England, Brian McElney received a donation and a scroll for his Museum of East Asian Art in Bath, as well as the George III silver tea caddy, as promised 50 years before. In America, inlaid Chinese scroll boxes went to the Los Angeles County Museum of Art.

In the will, he said that he did not want to be of trouble to anyone in the disposal of his ashes but expressed a general preference for them to be scattered at sea either in Hong Kong or Gibraltar, or both. Both the South China Sea and the Mediterranean received him.

Eight years after his death, in a message of welcome to Abraham Chan who was taking silk in June 2017, Chief Justice Geoffrey Ma quoted from a chapter of the Bar Associations 50th Anniversary, which states: "Life at the Bar was exciting because the Bar comprised of colourful characters like Albert Sanguinetti."[28] The Chief Justice read his name out alongside those of Charles Ching, Henry Litton, and Patrick Yu, "a joy for the budding barrister to watch and learn from".

None of his colleagues at the Bar or friends across the world or his admiring local public saw Sanguinetti's garrulous charm and florid manner—that "joy to watch"—as anything but authentic. It was sincerely him—what he was all about. The monocle, the considered scruffiness in court, the sartorial showmanship outside, the grandiloquent passion for justice and liberty, the raised voice for the poor and unfortunate, the implacable opposition to those considered unworthy, even the self-denigrating miserliness, were accepted as essential to the man. Glorious, hilarious, theatrical, and disconcerting sometimes—it was all from the heart.

A brave and moving view was taken of Sanguinetti by Mr Justice Kemal Bokhary in the Bar Association Newsletter of

January 2010.[29] This would certainly have agitated Sanguinetti into an argument, but because it came from someone close to being a brother, it would have been taken well and so it can be ventured here. Bokhary wrote:

> It is undeniably true that he was not a religious man. Indeed he would become very angry if anyone suggested that he was at all religious. But he had a philosophy so good, so kind and so inclusive as to be difficult to distinguish from religiosity of the most admirable type. So maybe.[30]

Notes

Chapter One: Childhood on the Rock

1. W.G.F. Jackson, *The Rock of the Gibraltarians*, Gibraltar: Gibraltar Books, 1987, p. 282.

2. *Ibid.*, p. 282.

3. Sanguinetti papers.

4. Sanguinetti papers.

5. Pere Ferrer Guasp, *Joan March, la cara oculta del poder* [*Juan March: The Hidden Face of Power*], Edicions CORT, 2004.

6. John Julius Norwich, *The Popes: A History*, London: Chatto & Windus, 2011.

7. Brian McElney, Sanguinetti papers.

8. The conditions in Gibraltar prevent any widespread farming, leaving inhabitants reliant on neighbouring Spain and nearby Morocco for their food supply. The sovereignty of Gibraltar has historically been a point of contention between Britain and Spain, with disputes resulting in the periodic blockade of supplies between Spain and Gibraltar. For more on these disputes and blockades, see Jackson, 1987; Ernle Bradford, *Gibraltar: The History of a Fortress*, New York: Open Road Integrated Media, 1971; Chris Grocott and Gareth Stockey, *Gibraltar: A Modern History*, Cardiff: University of Wales Press, 2012.

9. Sir Joshua Abraham Hassan (1915–1997), nicknamed "Salvador" (Saviour), was a Gibraltarian politician and the first Mayor and Chief Minister of Gibraltar, serving four terms as Chief Minister

for a total of 20 years in office. He was a key figure in the civil rights movement in Gibraltar and played an important role in self-government. He was a successful lawyer and his chambers, Hassans International Law Firm, are the largest in Gibraltar.

10. A "day boy" refers to the students attending a boarding school who did not board but instead went home after lessons.

11. "On being a boy in 1950s Gibraltar", *Broadsides—A collection of bits and pieces*, Blog, available at: https://broadsidesdotme.wordpress.com/2012/01/13/on-being-a-boy-in-1950s-gibraltar/, accessed on 1 June 2022.

12. Sanguinetti papers.

13. Sir Alfred Vasquez was Speaker of the Parliament from 1970 to 1992, holding the office longer than anyone else to date. He worked as a senior partner at a law firm with J.E. Triay. He died on 3 July 2012. See *The Global Legal Post*, "Leading Gibraltar lawyer and politician dies", 12 July 2012, available at: www.globallegalpost.com/news/leading-gibraltar-lawyer-and-politician-dies, accessed on 1 June 2022.

14. William "Willie" Piccone is a Gibraltarian businessman and hotelier who is the proprietor of the Bristol Hotel in Gibraltar. He remained a close childhood friend of Sanguinetti.

15. Sanguinetti papers.

Chapter Two: Scattered by War

1. Peter Bond, *300 Years of British Gibraltar: 1704–2004*, Gibraltar: Peter-Tan Ltd for the Government of Gibraltar, 2003.

2. Jackson, 1987.

3. Brian McElney, Sanguinetti papers.

4. Jackson, 1987.

5. *Ibid*.

6. Gladys Veronica Li, born in 1948, was formerly a barrister in England and became a senior counsel at the Hong Kong Bar with a constitutional law and human rights practice. She was chairman of the Hong Kong Bar Association in 1995 and 1996, and she is a founding member of the Hong Kong Civic Party.

7. The book was inscribed at the front with "University College, London" and dated sometime in 1947.

Chapter Three: London Calling

1. Interview with Willie Piccone, Sanguinetti papers, Correspondence Box 4.

2. Sanguinetti papers, Box 1.

3. Lasting from the 5th to the 9th of December in 1952, the smog was thick enough to bring transportation to a stop and had lethal effects on the population. About 4,000 are thought to have died in the immediate aftermath, followed by another 8,000 over the subsequent year. The Great Smog had a significant effect on air pollution regulations worldwide, including the passing of the Clean Air Act of 1956. For a recent discussion, see Laura Robson-Mainwaring, "The Great Smog of 1952", *The National Archives*, Blog, 19 July 2022, available at: https://blog.nationalarchives.gov.uk/the-great-smog-of-1952/, accessed on 30 July 2022.

4. Interview with Mesod Massias, Sanguinetti papers.

5. Interview with Willie Piccone, Sanguinetti papers.

6. Interview with Mesod Massias, Sanguinetti papers.

7. Interview with Willie Piccone, Sanguinetti papers.

8. Interview with Raphael Massias, Sanguinetti papers.

9. Interview with Raphael Massias, Sanguinetti papers.

10. Andrew Mitchell, "Cripps, (Richard) Stafford", in John Ramsden (ed), *The Oxford Companion to Twentieth-century British Politics*, New York: Oxford University Press, 2002.

11. Born in Gibraltar in 1931 and educated in England, J.E. Triay was called to the Middle Temple and the Bar in Gibraltar in 1952 and became a Queen's counsel in 1982. J.E. and his brother, J.J., inherited their father's law firm, later to become Triay & Triay. He was controversial for his prominent part in advocating a settlement with Spain in 1968 when Spanish leader Francisco Franco was campaigning to recover Gibraltar. Their brother Louis also became a prominent lawyer.

12. Interview with J.E. Triay, Sanguinetti papers, Box 4.

13. Simon Fook Sean Li was a graduate of the University of Hong Kong and University College, London. He was called to the Bar at Lincoln's Inn in 1951. He became a Crown counsel in Hong Kong in 1953, judge of the District Court in 1963, and the first Chinese judge to be appointed to the High Court in 1971. He was made a Justice of Appeal and was the first Chinese to be appointed as the vice-president of the Court of

Appeal in 1984. He married Marie Veronica Lillian Yang, and both were close with Sanguinetti.

14. Numerous texts have been published about colonial Hong Kong and the handover from Britain to China in 1997. For instance, *History.com* states: "In 1898, Britain was granted an additional 99 years of rule over Hong Kong under the Second Convention of Peking. In September 1984, after years of negotiations, the British and the Chinese signed a formal agreement approving the 1997 turnover of the island in exchange for a Chinese pledge to preserve Hong Kong's capitalist system. On July 1, 1997, Hong Kong was peaceably handed over to China in a ceremony attended by numerous Chinese, British, and international dignitaries." See *History.com*, "Hong Kong returned to China", 24 November 2009 (last updated 29 June 2021), available at: www.history.com/this-day-in-history/hong-kong-returned-to-china, accessed on 1 June 2022.

15. Interview with Gladys Li, Sanguinetti papers.

16. Interview with Leolin Price, Sanguinetti papers.

17. Quoted in Sanguinetti's obituary by Anthony J.P. Lombard, *Gibraltar Chronicle*, Issue 12 December 09, Sanguinetti papers, Box 3.

18. Sir Isaac Hai "Jack" Jacob (1908–2000), born in Shanghai, was a lawyer and civil procedure academic. He built a promising legal practice in London before moving to become Queen's Bench master. As a master and senior master of the High Court and Queen's remembrancer (1957–1980), he reformed civil court procedure and enriched the academic understanding of it. He was knighted and given honorary silk.

19. The death of Sir Jack prompted a touching exchange with Robin in which Robin expressed those simple deep sadnesses you can confide to an understanding ear. Of his father, he wrote: "I miss telling him things." Sanguinetti was unfailing and thoughtful in sending letters of condolence on the death of all his friends. See Jacobs R. letter, Sanguinetti papers, Box 3.

20. Sanguinetti papers, Box 3.

Chapter Four: A Different Kind of Colony

1. Sir Sidney Solomon "Solly" Abrahams served as chief justice of several British colonies and ultimately as Chief Justice of Ceylon (Sri Lanka) from 1936–1939. He was later senior legal assistant to the

Commonwealth Relations Office. He was an Olympic athlete and older brother of famed Olympian Harold Abrahams.

2. *Chariots of Fire*, directed by Hugh Hudson, original screenplay by Colin Welland, produced by David Puttnam, distributed by 20th Century Fox, London: Enigma Productions, 1981.

3. Sanguinetti papers, Box 3.

4. Levi I. Izuakor, "Kenya: Demographic constraints on the growth of European settlement, 1900–1956", *Africa: Rivista trimestrale di studi e documentazione dell'Istituto italiano per l'Africa e l'Oriente*, Anno 42, No. 3, 1987, pp. 400–416.

5. For more on the formation of the KLFA and local politics at the time, see Frank Furedi, *The Mau Mau War in Perspective*, Athens, OH: Ohio University Press, 1989; Tabitha Kanogo, *Squatters and the Roots of Mau Mau (1905–1963)*, Athens, OH: Ohio University Press, 1987; Anaïs Angelo, *Power and the Presidency in Kenya: The Jomo Kenyatta Years*, Cambridge: Cambridge University Press, 2020.

6. Jennifer Rosenberg, "1952: Princess Elizabeth becomes Queen at 25", *ThoughtCo*, 28 August 2020, available at: www.thoughtco.com/princess-elizabeth-becomes-queen-1779354, accessed on 1 June 2022.

7. For additional information about the Mau Mau Rebellion, see David Anderson, *Histories of the Hanged: The Dirty War in Kenya and the End of Empire*, New York: W.W. Norton & Company, 2005.

8. These cases are listed in various issues of the *Kenya Gazette*, which can be accessed at https://gazettes.africa/gazettes/ke/ and in an electronic format at https://books.google.co.ke/books/about/Kenya_Gazette. html?id=SiZddRcP0BcC. In the list of cases, "s/o" means "son of". The case dates provided here appear in Sanguinetti's files and notes from his time and work in Kenya. In some cases, the date differs from the issue date of the Gazette in which the case appears.

9. Chris McGreal, "G2: Shameful legacy: In the early 1950s, Mau Mau rebels murdered 32 people in an uprising against colonial rule in Kenya. Britain's response was brutal: 150,000 Kenyans were detained in camps where, survivors claim, prisoners were beaten, tortured, sexually abused and even murdered. Fifty years on, a handful of them are suing the British government", *The Guardian*, 13 October 2006. The article cites these figures from letters from Members of Parliament objecting to the executions for offences other than murders written to a senior Kenyan cabinet minister of the government.

10. Interview with Lydia Armstrong, Sanguinetti papers.

11. Interview with Kemal Bokhary, Sanguinetti papers.

12. John Lonsdale, "Mau Maus of the Mind: Making Mau Mau and Remaking Kenya", *The Journal of African History*, 1990, Vol. 31, No. 3, pp. 393–421; A.B. Assensoh, *African Political Leadership: Jomo Kenyatta, Kwame Nkrumah, and Julius K. Nyerere*. Malabar, FL: Krieger Publishing Company, 1998.

13. Anderson, 2005.

14. Sanguinetti papers, Box 1, File 1949–1995.

15. Jeremy Murray-Brown, *Kenyatta*, New York: Fontana, 1974.

16. *Ibid.*

Chapter Five: Home to Higher Office

1. Interview with Cecil Isola, Sanguinetti papers.

2. Bruce Trigger, *Revolutions in Archaeology*, New York: Columbia University Press, 1980, p. 154.

3. John Garcia, *The Modern Political and Constitutional Development of Gibraltar, 1940–1988*, PhD Thesis, University of Hull, 1991.

4. Sanguinetti papers, Box 1, File 1949–1996.

5. Interview with Louis Andlaw, Sanguinetti papers.

6. Sanguinetti papers.

7. *R v Associated Periodicals Ltd and Others, ex p. the Attorney General*, Supreme Court, 1812–1977 GibLR 157, 27 November 1956.

8. *Pizarello v Attorney General*, Supreme Court, 1812–1977 GibLR 160, 29 January 1957.

9. Anthony J.P. Lombard, *Gibraltar Chronicle*, Issue 12 December 2009, Sanguinetti papers, Box 3.

10. Sir Charles had a distinguished military career, serving in the Second World War and in later operations, including acting as the commander-in-chief of "Operation Musketeer", the moniker used for the Anglo-French invasion of the Suez in 1956. For additional information about the attack and Keightley's role, see Wilfred P. Deac, "Suez Crisis: Operation Musketeer", *HistoryNet*, 12 June 2006, available

at: www.historynet.com/suez-crisis-operation-musketeer/, accessed on 1 June 2022.

11. Sanguinetti papers, Box 1, File 1949–1995.

12. While it is not possible to be completely certain, this is most likely referring to William Isola, Dr Cecil Isola's brother who had joined their father Albert's legal practice in 1947. William was a member of Gibraltar's City Council from 1958 to 1969 and a member of the Gibraltar House of Assembly from 1969 to 1976, serving as a Government Minister from 1969 to 1972. See the Isolas LLP website, "About Us: Our History", available at: https://gibraltarlawyers.com/isolas/our-history/, accessed on 1 June 2022; and Cecil Isola, *An Autobiography of a Colonial Doctor*, Bloomington, IN: Author House, 2011.

13. Sanguinetti papers, Box 1, File 1949–1995.

14. Interview with Cecil Isola, Sanguinetti papers.

Chapter Six: Hong Kong: On the Bench

1. Sanguinetti papers.

2. The figures summarised in this paragraph are from John M. Carroll, *A Concise History of Hong Kong*, New York: Rowman and Littlefield, 2007.

3. Patrick Yu, *Tales from No. 9 Ice House Street*, Hong Kong: Hong Kong University Press, 2002. Born in 1922 and educated in Hong Kong, Yu became the first Chinese person to be appointed Crown counsel in 1951. He resigned and commenced a private practice, becoming a top criminal lawyer. He helped establish the Faculty of Law at the University of Hong Kong and received an Honorary Doctor of Laws (LLD) degree. He declined several offers of judgeships and refused to apply to be a QC. He retired in 1993 and subsequently published his popular memoir.

4. Brian McElney, Sanguinetti papers.

5. "Police sergeant and ex-constable freed: Found not guilty of conspiracy and demanding money", *South China Morning Post*, 27 November 1958, p. 7.

6. Brian McElney, Sanguinetti papers.

7. "New Magistrate", *South China Morning Post*, 8 November 1958, p. 6.

8. "Govt posts: Appointments and Transfers Gazette Notice", *South China Morning Post*, 18 April 1959, p. 6.

9. Sanguinetti papers, Box 1, File 1949–1995.

10. Sanguinetti papers, Box 4.

11. Sanguinetti papers, Box 3.

12. "Twenty-two-year-old man convicted thirty times", *South China Morning Post*, 20 April 1961, p. 7.

13. *Ibid.*

14. A.J.J. Sanguinetti, "A plea for abolition", *South China Morning Post*, 2 May 1978, p. 8.

15. *Au Yeung Ming v The Queen*, Court of Appeal, Criminal Appeal No. 846 of 1969; Sanguinetti papers, Box 2, File 1.

16. Deane, Daniela, "Use of 'the cane' lives on: In parts of Asia, flogging still exists", *LA Times*, 18 June 1989.

17. "Warning to unlicensed food stall owners", *South China Morning Post*, 22 February 1962, p. 8.

18. Sir Ti Liang Yang moved briefly to Hong Kong, then to England, after reading law in China from 1946–1949. He graduated with a Bachelor of Laws (LLB) from University College, London, and was called to the Bar at Gray's Inn. He returned to Hong Kong as a magistrate in 1956. Yang was appointed a Justice of Appeal in 1981, and in March 1988, he was appointed Chief Justice of Hong Kong, the first time an ethnic Chinese had held that office.

19. The details of the case are also recorded in the officer's appeal. See *Shum Hung v Tam Fun*, Supreme Court, Criminal Appeal No. 338 of 1961.

20. "Woman's complaint denied by policeman", *South China Morning Post*, 4 July 1961, p. 13.

21. "Summons for assault dismissed", *South China Morning Post*, 1 August 1961, p. 8.

22. "'Sympathies ran away with magistrate': Allegation", *South China Morning Post*, 18 October 1961, p. 9.

23. *Shum Hung v Tam Fun*, Supreme Court, Criminal Appeal No. 338 of 1961.

24. Sanguinetti papers, Box 2, File 1960–1974.

25. *R v Wong Hing Shan*, District Court, Criminal Case No. 39 of 1960. See also "Constable innocent of wounding charge", *South China Morning Post*, 2 June 1960, p. 7.

26. "Magistrate indicts constable: False testimony in traffic case", *South China Morning Post*, 9 March 1960, p. 6; "Policeman fined $15 for false testimony", *South China Morning Post*, 5 April 1960, p. 9.

27. "Magistrate criticises police", *South China Morning Post*, 5 April 1961, p. 6.

28. "Promotion does not depend on arrests, police warned", *South China Morning Post*, 26 February 1963, p. 1.

29. A. Sanguinetti, "Increase needed in police force", *South China Morning Post*, 14 April 1972, p. 10.

30. See *The Attorney General v Man Chi Kin and Another*, Appellate Jurisdiction, Criminal Appeal No. 205 of 1964. The "magistrate" is not named in the case, but this is made clear by the press coverage of the case.

31. "Power to grant pardon comes from legislative authority, Crown says", *South China Morning Post*, 10 April 1964, p. 8.

32. "Queer things happened when Muslim took oath without first having bath", *South China Morning Post*, 27 July 1960, p. 7.

33. *Ibid.*

34. Sanguinetti papers, Box 2, File 1960–1976. "Evidence of demand for money: Ex-cashier of Indian company accused of using threats", *South China Morning Post*, 31 October 1959, p. 12;

35. Humphrey Richardson, *The Sexual Life of Robinson Crusoe*, Paris: The Olympia Press, 1955. Other information about the film was not found.

36. Quoted anecdotally in Matthew Brooks, "HK's 'Rumpole' was tireless in the search for justice", *South China Morning Post*, 8 November 2009, p. 4.

37. "Wigs for judges termed ridiculous", *South China Morning Post*, 5 October 1967, p. 9.

38. Sanguinetti papers, Box 1, File 1958–1985, 5 February 1964, translation. Later in the trial, the story was similarly covered in the English press. See, for example, "Magistrate expresses concern over constable's action", *South China Morning Post*, 11 March 1964, p. 8.

39. Sanguinetti papers, Box 1, File 1958–1985.

40. Sanguinetti papers, Box 1, File 1949–1995.

41. Sanguinetti papers, Box 1, File 1958–1985.

42. *George C.S. Liang Trading as Wood & Co v Lee Kau Yan*, District Court, Action No. 2132 of 1959.

43. *Tsang Shiu Tim & Tsang Hung Tim v Wong Kee Trading as Kee Hup Metal-ware Dealers and Cheung Kwan*, District Court, Appeal No. 3 of 1960.

44. *Yeung Yu Long and Others v The Sun Sun Wineshop*, District Court, Action No. 1136 of 1960.

45. *Au Tak Chen v Li Hon Ming*, District Court, Action No. 1271 of 1960.

46. Sanguinetti papers, Box 1, File 1958–1985. For more on the case, see "Magistrate takes trial of Asst Revenue Officer into Kowloon Hospital", *South China Morning Post*, 26 July 1960, p. 7.

47. Sanguinetti papers, Box 1, File 1958–1985. For more on the case, see "The Courts: Two death certificates on boy, Inquest jury told", *South China Morning Post*, 21 March 1963, p. 12.

48. "The Courts: Blasting procedures vary, Inquest told", *South China Morning Post*, 9 March 1963, p. 13; "Worker's death: Covers 'inadequate' at blasting site", *South China Morning Post*, 12 March 1963, p. 8.

49. Coroners Inquiry, Sanguinetti papers, Box 2, File 1960–1975. See also "Coroner critical of hospital's procedure: Urges authorities to devise system ensuring treatment", *South China Morning Post*, 1 July 1960, p. 1.

50. *Hong Kong Standard*, 19 March 1961.

51. *Hong Kong Standard*, 20 March 1961. Sanguinetti papers, Box 1, File 1949–1995.

52. Sir Michael Joseph Patrick Hogan (1908–1986) was an Irish-qualified barrister who served in multiple British imperial jurisdictions. He was Chief Magistrate and later Solicitor General in Palestine, Attorney General in Aden, and Solicitor General then Attorney General of Malaya, where he acted as Administrator of Malaya after the High Commissioner was assassinated. He was appointed Chief Justice of Hong Kong in 1955. From 1964, he concurrently held the post of Chief Justice of Brunei. Hogan and Sanguinetti clashed over various issues.

53. "Ambush: Official Story", *The Straits Times*, 8 October 1951, p. 1. Other details about Sir Henry's assassination are compiled in Tan Teng Phee, "The Case of Tras New Village and the Assassination of Henry Gurney during the Malayan Emergency", *Biblioasia* (National Library, Singapore), January 2011, available at: https://biblioasia.nlb.gov.sg/files/pdf/vol-6/issue-4/v6-issue4_HenryGurney.pdf, accessed on 1 June 2022. For a recent discussion about the Malayan Emergency in general, see Karl Hack, *The Malayan Emergency: Revolution and Counterinsurgency at the End of Empire*, Cambridge: Cambridge University Press, 2021.

54. Meaning truth and force, "satyagraha" was a form of civil non-violent resistance brought by Mahatma Ghandi against British rule in India

between 1920 up to independence in 1947. For more, see Ramachandra Guha, *Gandhi: The Years that Changed the World, 1914–1948*, New York: Alfred A. Knopf, 2018; Barbara D. Metcalf and Thomas R. Metcalf, *A Concise History of Modern India* (third edition), New York: Cambridge University Press, 2012.

55. Sanguinetti papers, Box 1, File 1949–1995.

56. *Ibid.*

57. *Ibid.*

58. *Ibid.* A Legal Opinion is formally expressed advice based on expert knowledge of a professional lawyer or judge. Providing such advice is a well-established practice in common law jurisdictions.

59. Sanguinetti papers, Box 1, File 1949–1995.

60. *Ibid.*

61. "Magistrate critical of circular: 'It is contrary to judicial functions and duties'", *South China Morning Post*, 10 March 1964, p. 1.

62. Sanguinetti papers, Box 1, File 1949–1995. See also "The Courts: Judge's reply to remarks by magistrate", *South China Morning Post*, 14 March 1964, p. 8.

63. "Storm in a teacup", *South China Morning Post*, 14 March 1964, p. 10.

64. Sanguinetti papers, Box 1, File 1949–1995.

65. *Ibid.*

66. *Ibid.*

67. Born in 1932, Brian S. McElney was a senior partner in the Hong Kong solicitors' firm of Johnston, Stokes & Master. He was president of the Hong Kong Law Society and founded the Museum of East Asian Art in Bath, England, in 1990.

Chapter Seven: To the Bar

1. For more on General Hassan Arfa, see his entry in Encyclopaedia Iranica, available at: www.iranicaonline.org/articles/arfa-hasan-iranian-general-born-in-tiflis-in-1895, accessed 1 June 2022. The history of the Pahlavi family and the final days of the Shah's reign in Iran are covered in Andrew Scott Cooper, *The Fall of Heaven: The Pahlavis and the Final Days of Imperial Iran*, New York: Henry Holt and Company, 2016.

2. Sanguinetti papers.

3. Interview with James Gordon, Sanguinetti papers.

4. "Former magistrate admitted to bar", *South China Morning Post*, 4 April 1965, p. 4.

5. After graduating from Cambridge University in 1959, David Leonard trained as a solicitor. He later became a District Court judge then High Court judge in Hong Kong until 1967. He was an adjudicator on the United Kingdom Immigration and Asylum Tribunal. He also served on the High Court of Brunei and has been a judge of the Supreme Court there since 2010.

6. D. Leonard, 1977 Memorandum, Sanguinetti papers, Box 4.

7. *In the Matter of the Canton Trust and Commercial Bank Ltd*, Supreme Court, Companies (Winding-up) Petition No. 10 of 1965. See also "Financial Secretary has right to petition—Judge", *South China Morning Post*, 22 May 1965, p. 6.

8. Sir Alan Armstrong Huggins (1921–2009) was a British colonial judge who served in Uganda, Hong Kong, and Brunei. He served for 40 years in Hong Kong, ultimately as the vice-president of the Court of Appeal from 1980 to 1987. From 1997 to 2000, he was a non-permanent Hong Kong judge of the Court of Final Appeal. His son Adrian would later become a QC and was also close with Sanguinetti.

9. *The Attorney General v Chow Sau-sing*, Full Court, Criminal Appeal No. 522 of 1965; Sanguinetti papers, Box 2, File 1.

10. *Cheng Chung Yat v The Queen*, Court of Appeal, Criminal Appeal No. 676 of 1969; Sanguinetti papers, Box 2, File 1.

11. "Businessman is found guilty of rape bid", *South China Morning Post*, 13 March 1970, p. 7; "Executive gets 20 months for rape bid", *South China Morning Post*, 9 April 1970, p 6.

12. Sanguinetti papers, Box 2.

13. *Cheng Kam Man v The Queen*, Court of Final Appeal, Criminal Appeal No. 426 of 1969; Sanguinetti papers, Box 2, File 1.

14. *Li Ming-kwan and Another v The Queen*, Full Court, Criminal Appeal No. 367 of 1972.

15. Quoted from the trial transcript for the *Li Ming-kwan* case, Sanguinetti papers, Box 2, File 1960–1976.

16. *Chung Kam-to v The Queen*, Supreme Court, Criminal Appeal No. 393 of 1969; Sanguinetti papers, Box 2, File 1.

17. "$7,000 compensation award for assault", *South China Morning Post*, 3 February 1970, p. 6.

18. *Au Yeung Ming v The Queen*, Court of Appeal, Criminal Appeal No. 846 of 1969; Sanguinetti papers, Box 2, File 1.

19. The case had been in trial for several months already. See "Three on trial for falsification of documents", *South China Morning Post*, 24 April 1965, p. 8.

20. In Justice Li's 1974 judgement for *Wide World Exports Ltd v Henry Victor Ardy*, High Court, Action No. 2835A of 1971, he states: "A variety of textbooks, legal authorities were cited in support of his contention. Mr. Jackson-Lipkin, learned counsel for the Plaintiff, had replied equally with comments on the textbooks and foot-notes cited by Mr. Sanguinetti." This list of references is one that possibly included the English appeal in which Jackson-Lipkin was criticised.

21. Lindy Course, "Jackson-Lipkin entry in 'Who's Who' raises some questions about who's who", *South China Morning Post*, 2 March 1987, p. 1; Ravina Shamdasani, "Jurist with a penchant for generating controversy", *South China Morning Post*, 25 May 2005, available at: www.scmp.com/article/501874/jurist-penchant-generating-controversy, accessed on 1 June 2022.

22. *HKSAR v Jackson-Lipkin Lucille Fung and Another*, Court of First Instance, Magistracy Appeal No. 173 of 2007. The case also received a lot of media coverage. See, for example, Teddy Ng, "Hong Kong judge, wife jailed", *China Daily*, 27 January 2005, p. 3, available at: www.chinadaily.com.cn/china/2007-01/27/content_794274.htm, accessed on 1 June 2022. They were both freed after serving only four months of their sentences. See Nick Gentle, "Disgraced judge and wife freed in act of mercy", *South China Morning Post*, 26 May 2007, available at: www.scmp.com/article/594353/disgraced-judge-and-wife-freed-act-mercy?module=perpetual_scroll_0&pgtype=article&campaign=594353, accessed on 1 June 2022.

23. Sanguinetti papers, Box 2.

24. Sanguinetti papers, Box 1, File 1958–1985.

25. "Legal Aid Bill: 'Bar Association in favour of measure", *South China Morning Post*, 10 November 1966, p. 10. Notably, Sanguinetti was against this particular proposed Legal Aid Bill as it did not extend to criminal courts.

26. "Criticism of HK Court System", *South China Morning Post*, 28 February 1970, p. 7.

27. Sanguinetti papers, Box 1, File 1949–1995.

28. Sanguinetti papers, Box 1, File 1958–1985.

29. Elsie Elliott (1913–2015), later Elsie Tu, was a British teacher and social activist in Hong Kong. She was an elected member of the Urban Council from 1963 to 1995 and a member of the Legislative Council from 1988 to 1995. She was appointed to the Beijing-controlled Provisional Legislative Council from December 1996 to June 1998. She was a reappearing figure in Sanguinetti's life in Hong Kong.

30. D. Leonard, 1977 Memorandum, Sanguinetti papers, Box 4.

31. Brian McElney, Memoir, Sanguinetti papers.

32. "Sir Alan Huggins", *The Telegraph*, 8 February 2010, available at: www.telegraph.co.uk/news/obituaries/law-obituaries/7190749/Sir-Alan-Huggins.html, accessed on 1 June 2022.

33. Quoted anecdotally in Matthew Brooks, "HK's 'Rumpole' was tireless in the search for justice", *South China Morning Post*, 8 November 2009, p. 4.

34. "Wig maker acquitted", *South China Morning Post*, 16 August 1967, p. 7.

35. *Ibid.*

Chapter Eight: Riot and Reform

1. It had been discovered that Godber had accrued HK$4.3 million, largely through corrupt and illegal means. After hearing of the allegations and that he was under investigation, Godber and his wife fled Hong Kong before further questioning, leading to a man-hunt. Godber was later found in Britain, arrested, and eventually extradited back to Hong Kong for trial. The story was extensively covered in the local press. See, for example, "Interpol alerted: Police search for missing officer", *South China Morning Post*, 12 June 1973, p. 1; "Godber tracked down", *South China Morning Post*, 19 June 1973, p. 1; "Godber left with $4.3m", *South China Morning Post*, 29 December 1973, p. 9; "Evidence may lead to Godber's return", *South China Morning Post*, 14 January 1974, p. 7; "HK rejoices over arrest", *South China Morning Post*, 1 May 1974, p. 1; "Two charges of corruption laid", *South China Morning Post*, 8 January 1975, p. 9; "Godber goes to jail for 4 years", *South China Morning Post*, 26 February 1975, p. 1. The trial was presided over by Briggs, McMullin, and Pickering (*Peter Fitzroy Godber v The Queen*, Appellate Jurisdiction, Criminal Appeal No. 181 of 1975). The scandal identified issues with the colony's and London's extradition laws and

was a significant driver of the establishment of the Independent Commission Against Corruption (ICAC) in Hong Kong. See "Govt sets up office to fight corruption in the Colony", *South China Morning Post*, 29 December 1973, p. 9. For more on the Hong Kong police force, corruption, and the ICAC, see Kevin Sinclair, *Asia's Finest: An Illustrated Account of the Royal Hong Kong Police*, Hong Kong: Unicorn, 1983; H.J. Lethbridge, *Hard Graft in Hong Kong: Scandal, Corruption, the ICAC*, Oxford: Oxford University Press, 1985.

2. Carroll, 2007, Ch. 6, p. 150.

3. Sanguinetti papers, Box 4, Star Ferry Riots File.

4. "Lo Kei tells Inquiry he was never paid by Mrs Elliott", *South China Morning Post*, 24 May 1966.

5. Sanguinetti papers, Box 4, Star Ferry Riots File.

6. 1 Corinthians, Chapter 11, verses 28–31, King James Bible.

7. Sanguinetti papers, Box 1, File 1949–1985.

8. Sanguinetti papers, Box 1, File 1986–2008.

9. Sanguinetti papers, Box 3.

10. Sanguinetti papers, Box 1, File 1949–1985.

11. Sanguinetti papers, Box 1, File 1949–1995.

12. Sanguinetti papers, Box 3.

13. Sanguinetti papers, Box 4, Amnesty and Justice File.

14. In 1976, Elsie Elliott actually recommended Sanguinetti for the job of ombudsman. See "Ombudsman: All-rounder call", *South China Morning Post*, 11 June 1976, p. 7.

15. "Legal Aid Bill: 'Bar Association in favour of measure", *South China Morning Post*, 10 November 1966, p. 10. Notably, Sanguinetti was against this particular proposed Legal Aid Bill as it did not extend to criminal courts.

16. Sanguinetti papers, Box 4, Amnesty and Justice File.

17. *Ibid.*

18. *Ibid.*

19. *Ibid.*

20. *Ibid.*

21. *Ibid.*

22. *Ibid.*

23. *Ibid.*

24. *Ibid.*

25. *Ibid.*

26. *Ibid.*

27. *Ibid.*

28. *Ibid.*

29. See, for example, "Korean Spy Put His Foot To It", *South China Morning Post*, 30 November 1972, p. 1. Notably, the paper misspells Soh Sung's name as "Saw Sung".

30. Sanguinetti papers, Box 4, Amnesty and Justice File.

31. King Hassan II (1929–1999) took power in 1961 after the death of his father. His attempts to democratise the Moroccan political system were criticised for their autocratic nature. He is reported to have survived two assassination attempts. See "Moroccan King's escape from assassination attempt is second in 13 months", *The New York Times*, 17 August 1972, p. 10, available at: www.nytimes.com/1972/08/17/archives/moroccan-kings-escape-from-assassination-attempt-is-second-in-13.html, accessed on 1 June 2022.

32. See "Morocco executes 11 for role in plot to assassinate Hassan", *The New York Times*, 14 January 1973, p. 24, available at: www.nytimes.com/1973/01/14/archives/morocco-executes-11-for-role-in-plot-to-assassinate-hassan-appeal.html, accessed on 1 June 2022.

33. Peter Birkett, *Gibraltar Sunday Telegraph*, 20 August 1972.

34. Sanguinetti papers, Box 4, Amnesty and Justice File.

35. See, for example, "Court told of fire which left two dead", *South China Morning Post*, 27 April 1973, p. 8; "Weeping mother tells of killer fire", *South China Morning Post*, 28 April 1973, p. 7.

36. "Murder trial ends: Three to die", *South China Morning Post*, 14 July 1973, p. 6.

37. *Chan Hing-Cheung and Others v The Queen*, Full Court, Appellate Jurisdiction, Criminal Appeal No. 579 of 1973.

38. *Ibid.*

39. Sanguinetti papers, Box 2, File 1960–1974.

40. *Chan Lee Kuen v Chan Siu Fai*, Supreme Court (Divorce Jurisdiction), Action No. 23 of 1966.

41. *Ibid.*

42. *Ibid.*

43. *The Attorney General v Pat Chiuk-Wah and Others*, Full Court, Appellate Jurisdiction, Criminal Appeal No. 639 of 1968.

44. *The Queen v Chan Yam Yick*, Court of Appeal, Criminal Appeal No. 103 of 1985.

45. "Penalised for 'stupidity'", *South China Morning Post*, 12 November 1976, p. 14.

Chapter Nine: Hard Work and High Points

1. Sanguinetti papers, Box 1, File 1949–1995.

2. "Human cargo intercepted after chase", *South China Morning Post*, 5 June 1974, p. 28.

3. For a brief history of the Vietnam War and the Paris Peace Accords, see www.history.com/topics/vietnam-war/vietnam-war-history, accessed on 1 June 2022.

4. "S. Vietnam wants 119 illegal immigrants back", *South China Morning Post*, 7 June 1974, p. 1.

5. Kevin Sinclair, "Refugee route—Saigon to Jordon Road", *South China Morning Post*, 22 June 1974, p. 1.

6. "Govt seeking talks over refugees' fate", *South China Morning Post*, 15 July 1974, p. 1.

7. "Refugees will be sent back to S. Vietnam", *South China Morning Post*, 15 June 1974, p. 1.

8. Harold Chan and Tommy Lewis, "Vietnamese refugees flown home", *South China Morning Post*, 17 June 1974, p. 1.

9. "Deportees not being harshly treated", *South China Morning Post*, 28 June 1974, p. 22.

10. "Refugees' death denied", *South China Morning Post*, 29 July 1974, p. 6; "Saigon denies Amnesty charges", *South China Morning Post*, 10 August 1974, p. 1.

11. "Vietnam refugees in hell-hole prison?" *South China Morning Post*, 26 June 1974, p. 1.

12. Sanguinetti papers, Box 4, Amnesty and Justice File.

13. *Ibid.*

14. *Ibid.*

15. For more about Vietnamese refugees in Hong Kong and other areas of Southeast Asia, see Les Bird, *Along the Southern Boundary: A Marine Police Officer's Frontline Account of the Vietnamese Boatpeople and Their Arrival in Hong Kong*, Hong Kong: Blacksmith Books, 2022; Jana K. Lipman, *In Camps: Vietnamese Refugees, Asylum Seekers, and Repatriates*, Oakland, CA: University of California Press, 2020; Yuk Wah Chan, *The Chinese/Vietnamese Diaspora: Revisiting the Boat People*, New York: Routledge, 2011.

16. Sanguinetti papers, Box 4, Amnesty and Justice File.

17. Sanguinetti papers, Box 1, File 1958–1985.

18. The group was led by Mao's wife, Jiang Qing. For more about the Gang of Four and the Cultural Revolution generally, see Frank Dikötter, *The Cultural Revolution: A People's History, 1962–1976*, New York: Bloomsbury Publishing, 2016; Alexander C. Cook, *The Cultural Revolution on Trial: Mao and the Gang of Four*, Cambridge: Cambridge University Press, 2016.

19. Sanguinetti papers, Box 1, File 1958–1985.

20. Sanguinetti papers.

21. Sanguinetti papers, Box 1, File 1958–1998.

22. Sanguinetti papers, Box 1, File 1949–1995.

23. Numerous media sources have covered stories involving Brenda and Kai-bong Chau, including interviews and descriptions of their presence at social events. For a personal description of the couple, see, for example, Fionnuala McHugh, "Kai-bong and Brenda Chau", *South China Morning Post*, 21 September 1997, available at: www.scmp.com/article/212252/kai-bong-and-brenda-chau, accessed on 1 June 2022.

24. Sanguinetti papers, Box 3.

25. Thomas Kwok Ping-kwong is a Hong Kong billionaire and the former co-chairman of Sun Hung Kai Properties. He was later arrested with his brother on corruption and bribery charges. See www.forbes.com/profile/kwok/?sh=7a4f23fe5b20, accessed on 1 June 2022. Cecil Chao, also a Hong Kong billionaire, is the owner of Cheuk Nang Holdings Ltd. His elaborate lifestyle, rumours about having sex with 10,000 women, and

his offer of a HK$1 billion dowry for his lesbian daughter Gigi have kept him in the social spotlight. See, for example, Eric Wilson, "Property Tycoon Cecil Chao and His Daughter Gigi on Building a Lasting Legacy", *Tatler Asia*, 2 September 2020, available at: www.tatlerasia.com/power-purpose/business/cecil-chao-gigi-chao-family-legacy-interview, accessed on 1 June 2022.

26. Interview with James Gordon, Sanguinetti papers.

27. Interview with Mesod Massias, Sanguinetti papers.

28. Brian McElney, Sanguinetti papers.

29. Sanguinetti revealed this gem of economy and architecture to John Mao, Wendy Mao's son, who had remained a good friend after Sanguinetti represented him in a trial involving a check scam at Dollar Credit (*The Queen v John Mao Kai Yuan*, Court of Appeal, Criminal Appeal No. 440 of 1985). John also visited him in Japan.

30. Brian McElney, Sanguinetti papers. Possibly referring to Malcolm Stacey's *Super Scrooge: 3000 Sneaky Ways to Save Money*, London: Quiller Press, 1991.

31. David Leonard, Memorandum 2010, Sanguinetti papers, Box 4.

32. Elsie Elliott, *The Avarice, Bureaucracy and Corruption of Hong Kong*, Hong Kong: Friends Commercial Printing Factory, 1971.

33. "Mongkok shooting: Coroner appeals for witnesses", *South China Morning Post*, 12 February 1976, p. 7.

34. "Ah Sir" or 阿Sir, is a colloquial Cantonese phrase to show respect. Its widest use seems to be for police officers and, sometimes, Western men, particularly by older generations because they were so often inspectors. For more about this, see "Why Do Some People Get Called 'Ah Sir' in Hong Kong", *HK Magazine—South China Morning Post*, 17 March 2016, available at: www.scmp.com/magazines/hk-magazine/article/2037746/why-do-some-people-get-called-ah-sir-hong-kong?module=perpetual_scroll_0&pgtype=article&campaign=2037746, accessed on 1 June 2022.

35. "Shooting victim—hit twice in back—bled to death", *South China Morning Post*, 13 February 1976, p. 10.

36. "Mongkok shooting: Coroner appeals for witnesses", *South China Morning Post*, 12 February 1976, p. 7.

37. *Hong Kong Standard*, 12 February 1976.

38. "Shooting witness says 'never again'", *South China Morning Post*, 21 February 1976, p. 6.

39. *The Star*, 10 March 1976.

40. "Counsel told to calm down at inquest", *South China Morning Post*, 11 March 1976, p. 7.

41. *The Star*, 11 March 1976.

42. "Witness objects to statement", *South China Morning Post*, 12 March 1976, p. 8.

43. *Hong Kong Standard*, 12 March 1976.

44. "Lawyer threatens to withdraw from inquest", *South China Morning Post*, 13 March 1976, p. 7.

45. *Ibid.*

46. "Woman breaks down at inquest", *South China Morning Post*, 10 April 1976, p. 8.

47. "Lai verdict: Review possible", *South China Morning Post*, 21 May 1976, p. 1.

48. *Au Pui-Kuen v The Attorney General*, Privy Council, Appeal No. 39 of 1977; Sanguinetti papers, Box 4, Au Pui-Kuen File.

49. The term *"sub judice* circumstances" refers to circumstances that cannot be publicly discussed outside of the court. Sanguinetti papers, Box 4, Au Pui-Kuen File.

50. Sanguinetti papers, Box 4, Au Pui-Kuen File.

51. Sanguinetti papers, Box 3, Cheng Huan File.

52. Sanguinetti papers.

53. *Chan Kwong v The Queen* , Court of Appeal, Criminal Appeal No. 191 of 1982.

54. Duffy's statement was made during the trial of John MacLennan, in which Sanguinetti was also involved. The case, and Sanguinetti's role in it, is discussed in more detail in a later chapter. Other information can be found in Nigel Collett, *A Death in Hong Kong: The MacLennan Case of 1980 and the Suppression of a Scandal* (second edition), Hong Kong: City University of Hong Kong Press, 2020.

55. *R v Watson* [1980] 2 All ER 293 (Criminal Appeal).

56. Sanguinetti papers, Box 2, File 1960–1976.

57. Sanguinetti met one of the defendants again 30 years later as well as the police officer in 2005 at the Jockey Club. The police officer was now a PhD and a management consultant.

58. *Yeung Chiu v The Queen*, Supreme Court, Criminal Appeal No. 1043 of 1975; Sanguinetti papers, Box 2, File 1960–1976.

59. Albert Sanguinetti, "Two Pints into a Quart Pot?" *Hong Kong Law Review*, 1975, Vol. 5, p. 78.

60. *Chan Ka-shing v The Queen*, Full Court, Appellate Jurisdiction, Criminal Appeal No. 1122 of 1974; Sanguinetti papers, Box 2, File 1960–1976.

61. Sanguinetti papers, Box 2, File 1960–1976.

62. "Prisoner's death: Man freed", *South China Morning Post*, 18 April 1975, p. 6.

63. Sanguinetti papers, Box 2, File 2.

64. *Chan Kwong ming v The Queen*, Supreme Court, Criminal Appeal No. 1172 of 1977.

65. "Penalties on hawkers too tough: Judge", *South China Morning Post*, 10 December 1977, p. 1.

66. *Lam Chau kwai v The Queen*, Supreme Court, Criminal Appeal No. 1237 of 1977. The case is also mentioned in the "Penalties on hawkers too tough: Judge" article, but the values are incorrect.

67. *Ibid.*

68. "Magistrate rapped in hawker appeal", *South China Morning Post*, 30 March 1978, p. 10. For the legal proceeding for three of these hawkers, see *Chu Hon v The Queen*, High Court, Criminal Appeal No. 199 of 1978.

69. *Au Po lo v The Queen*, Supreme Court, Criminal Appeal No. 226 of 1978; Sanguinetti papers, Box 2, File 2.

70. Sadly, there is nothing further about the student's life after this.

71. *Wu Man kwok v The Queen*, Supreme Court, Criminal Appeal No. 317 of 1978.

72. "Blackmail appeal won", *South China Morning Post*, 26 May 1978, p. 12.

73. Sanguinetti papers.

Chapter Ten: Two Reports

1. "Elsie: Prisons can beat homes", *South China Morning Post*, 3 April 1978, p. 1.

2. Elliott-Sanguinetti Report, Sanguinetti papers, Box 4.

3. Quoted from the Police Force Ordinance, Cap. 232, section 51, available at: www.elegislation.gov.hk/hk/cap232?xpid=ID_1438402865374_001, accessed on 1 June 2022.

4. Also known as Ma Po Ping Prison, situated at Tong Fuk on Lantau Island. It was also previously referred to as the Ma Po Ping Addiction Treatment Centre. See "Prisons Order", *Historical Laws of Hong Kong Online*, available at: https://oelawhk.lib.hku.hk/items/show/2936, accessed on 1 June 2022.

5. Elliott-Sanguinetti Report, Sanguinetti papers, Box 4.

6. *Ibid.*

7. "The Elliott-Sanguinetti Report", *South China Morning Post*, 10 May 1978, p. 2.

8. Letter, Elliott to MacLehose, May 1978, Sanguinetti papers, Box 4.

9. Elliott-Sanguinetti Report, Sanguinetti papers, Box 4.

10. *The Mikado* is a comic opera by Gilbert and Sullivan that satirises British politics through a Japanese setting.

11. "Lawyer's home looted", *South China Morning Post*, 21 November 1977, p. 1

12. Brian McElney, Sanguinetti papers.

13. *Miami Vice* was an innovative mid-1980s American crime drama TV series. Many of the fashion styles and trends in the show are now considered symbolic of the stereotypical image of 1980s pop culture.

14. MacLennan inquiry papers, Sanguinetti papers, Box 4.

15. Collett, 2020, p. 302. Hercules Poirot and Jane Marple are fictional detectives created by Agatha Christie.

16. *Ibid.*, p. 330.

17. *Ibid.*, p. 265.

18. Not to be confused with John Richard Duffy who's claim from prison had, in part, initiated this sequence of events.

19. Commission of Inquiry into Inspector MacLennan's Case, "Papers of the Inspector MacLennan Inquiry, 1980–81" [Commission Transcript], donated by D.M.E. Evans, previously owned by Mr A.J.J. Sanguinetti, University of Hong Kong Library, MSS 345.2052 H7 M1, Part VII, pp. 12,027–12,030. See also Collett, 2020, p. 327.

20. Collett, 2020.

21. *Ibid.*, p. 327.

22. High Court 5357 of 1980; Sanguinetti papers.

23. Syed Kemal Shah Bokhary, born in Hong Kong in 1947, received his early education there and his legal education in London. He was called to the English Bar in 1970 and was appointed Queen's counsel in 1983. In 1989, he was appointed a judge of the High Court and then to the Court of Appeal in 1993. Bokhary served as a Permanent Judge of the Court of Final Appeal of the Hong Kong Special Administrative Region from 1997 to 2012. He married former High Court judge Verina Saeeda Bokhary. They have three daughters.

24. Quoted from email correspondence between Bokhary and the author.

25. "Libel suit settled for $60,000", *South China Morning Post*, 19 May 1981, p. 12.

26. Sanguinetti papers.

27. David Leonard, Memorandum 2010, Sanguinetti papers, Box 4.

28. Brian McElney, Sanguinetti papers.

Chapter Eleven: The Golden Years

1. Sanguinetti papers, Box 1, File 1949–1995.

2. *Ibid.*

3. Brian McElney, Sanguinetti papers.

4. *Ibid.*

5. Magistracy Court, Criminal Appeal No. 383 of 1986; Sanguinetti papers, Box 1, File 2.

6. *The Queen, Respondent v Li Kin Wai, 1st Appellant, Chan Wing Sam, 2nd Appellant*, Supreme Court, Magistracy Criminal Appeal No. 102 of 1985; Sanguinetti papers, Box 1, File 2.

7. *In an Application by Tse Cho for Orders of Certiorari and Prohibition*, High Court, Miscellaneous Proceedings No. 91 of 1979.

8. "Vice verdict quashed", *South China Morning Post*, 17 February 1978, p. 7.

9. *The Queen v Tam Kwok-yeung and Others*, Court of First Instance, Magistracy Appeal No. 926 of 1988.

10. *Chan Man and Others v The Queen*, High Court, Criminal Appeal No. 26 of 1976.

11. "Sex Literature 'is Important for Society'", *South China Morning Post*, 21 June 1985, p. 17.

12. Sanguinetti papers.

13. *Szeto Yuk-man v The Queen*, Court of Appeal, Criminal Appeal No. 60 of 1982.

14. Sanguinetti papers, Box 3.

15. *Ibid.*

16. *Ibid.*

17. For more about King Zog and Queen Geraldine, see Neil Rees, *A Royal Exile: King Zog and Queen Geraldine of Albania*, Chesham: Studge Publications, 2010. Queen Geraldine died in 2002. See Douglas Martin, "Geraldine of Albania, 87, Queen with US ties, is dead", *The New York Times*, 27 October 2002, p. 45, available at: www.nytimes.com/2002/10/27/world/geraldine-of-albania-87-queen-with-us-ties-is-dead.html, accessed on 1 June 2022.

18. Sanguinetti papers, Box 1, File 1958–1985.

19. John Mao, drafted by Brian McElney, Sanguinetti papers.

20. Brian McElney, Sanguinetti papers.

21. Sanguinetti papers, Box 3.

22. *Ibid.*

23. Sanguinetti papers, Box 1, File 1958–1985.

24. *Ibid.*

25. A.J. Sanguinetti, "Raising retirement age of CJ", *South China Morning Post*, 8 May 1976, p. 7; Sanguinetti papers, Box 1, File 1949–1995.

26. Lindy Course, "Judiciary admits to 'technical error'", *South China Morning Post*, 15 April 1988, p. 1.

27. "Lawyers 'ignored' on age extension", *South China Morning Post*, 8 May 1976, p. 5.

28. Lindy Course, "Judges back Findlay", *South China Morning Post*, 22 March 1990, p. 1.

29. Letter dated 26 March 1990, Sanguinetti papers, Box 1, File 1949–1995.

30. Jim Biddulph, "From the Gallery: A lot of sound produces little impact on debates", *South China Morning Post*, 3 May 1990, p. 7; Sanguinetti papers, Box 1, File 1949–1995.

31. *The Queen v John Mao Kai Yuan*, Court of Appeal, Criminal Appeal No. 440 of 1985.

32. For more on the ICAC, see H.J. Lethbridge, *Hard Graft in Hong Kong: Scandal, Corruption, the ICAC*, Oxford: Oxford University Press, 1985.

33. *The Queen v Cheung Hay Din and Others*, Court of Appeal, Criminal Appeal No. 623 of 1988.

34. "Inspector denies dealing unfairly with solicitor", *South China Morning Post*, 12 October 1988, p. 6.

35. *Ibid.*

36. Sanguinetti papers, Box 1, File 1949–1995.

37. *Ibid.*

38. A brief history and image of the board members can be found at York Lo, "Conic (康力)—IIK Electronics Giant of the Late 1970s, Early 1980s", *The Industrial History of Hong Kong Group*, 17 November 2017, available at: https://industrialhistoryhk.org/conic-hk-electronics-giant-of-the-late-1970s-early-1980s/, accessed on 1 June 2022.

39. *The Queen v Tam Chung-Shing and Others*, Court of Appeal, Criminal Appeal No. 405 of 1988; *The Queen v Tam Chung-Shing and Another*, Court of Appeal, Miscellaneous Proceedings No. 2448 of 1987.

40. *The Queen v Wu Tung Lam*, Court of Appeal, Criminal Appeal No. 1367 of 1983.

41. *Lo Kwong-hing v The Queen*, Court of Appeal, Criminal Appeal No. 593 of 1979.

42. *Chan Kwok-hing v R*, Court of Appeal, Criminal Appeal No. 103 of 1994.

43. "Damage conviction quashed", *South China Morning Post*, 10 October 1987, p. 4.

44. *The Queen v Hsu Jen Young*, Court of First Instance, Magistracy Appeal No. 951 of 1988.

45. *Au Hang and Another v Chow Chi Hung*, Court of Appeal, Criminal Appeal No. 399 of 1987.

46. *The Queen v Chan Yan To and Another*, Court of Appeal, Criminal Appeal No. 32 of 1988.

47. *R v Lo Shu-keung and Others*, Court of Appeal, Criminal Appeal No. 155 of 1991.

48. *The Queen v Leung Kam Wah*, Court of First Instance, Magistracy Appeal No. 78 of 1992.

49. *The Queen v Siu Yuk Shing*, Court of First Instance, Magistracy Appeal No. 172 of 1993.

50. *The Queen v Mak Yuet-hang*, Court of Appeal, Criminal Appeal No. 399 of 1987.

51. *The Queen v Cheung Hong-yeung*, Court of Appeal, Criminal Appeal No. 132 of 1992.

52. Sanguinetti papers.

53. Sanguinetti papers, Box 2, File 3.

Chapter Twelve: Retirement

1. Sanguinetti papers, Box 3.

2. Sanguinetti papers, Box 1, File 1990–2004.

3. Referring to a crowd collapse causing 20 deaths by crushing in a popular bar area in Hong Kong on New Year's Eve. Over 100 others were injured in the stampede which involving 20,000 people congregating in the area to celebrate the holiday. See Tommy Lewis, "20 Dead in Crush of New Year Revellers: 100 Injured as Crowd Counts to Midnight", *South China Morning Post*, 1 January 1993, p. 1.

4. Interview with Kemal Bokhary, Sanguinetti papers.

5. High Court 5357 of 1980; Sanguinetti papers.

6. Sanguinetti papers, Box 1, File 1986–2005.

7. *Ibid.*

8. Sanguinetti papers, Box 1, File 1990–2004.

9. Sanguinetti papers.

10. A transcript of the speech is held in the Sanguinetti papers, Box 1, File 1986–2008.

11. Sanguinetti papers, Box 1, File 1990–2004. The Helena May is a social club and historical building located on Garden Road in Central, Hong Kong. For more information, see The Helena May Website at: www.helenamay.com/?doing_wp_cron=1654154962.746876955032348 6328125, accessed on 1 June 2022.

12. Sanguinetti papers, Box 1, File 1986–2005.

13. Sanguinetti papers, Box 1, File 1949–1995.

14. *Ibid.*

15. Sanguinetti papers, various files.

16. Sanguinetti papers, Box 1, File 1986–2005.

17. Sanguinetti papers, Box 1, File 1986–2008.

18. Christine Loh, *Underground Front: The Chinese Communist Party in Hong Kong*, Second Edition, Hong Kong: Hong Kong University Press, 2019, p. 88.

19. Sanguinetti papers, Box 1, File 1990–2004.

20. *Ibid.*

21. Angela Li, "Sally Aw Private Action Mooted", *South China Morning Post*, 8 February 1999, p. 6.

22. *Ibid.*

23. Sanguinetti papers, Box 1, File 1990–2004.

24. *Ibid.*

25. Luther was a German-born monk most widely known for his "95 Theses" attacking the Catholic Church, which he is believed to have nailed to the door of the Wittenberg Castle church in 1517, sparking the Protestant Reformation. For more, see *History.com*, "Martin Luther and the 95 Theses", 29 October 2009 (last updated 1 November 2021), available at: www.history.com/topics/reformation/martin-luther-and-the-95-theses, accessed on 1 June 2022.

26. Sanguinetti's sister Maria Lourdes's family.

27. Wallis Simpson, Duchess of Windsor (1896–1986), was an American socialite and wife of the Duke of Windsor, the former King-Emperor Edward VIII. The Duke was her third husband, and her status as a divorcée created significant scandal for the Crown, leading to Edward's abdication from the thrown and the Queen's ban of the title "Duke of Windsor". For more, see Andrew Morton, *Wallis in Love: The Untold Life of the Duchess of Windsor, the Woman Who Changed the Monarchy*, New York: Grand Central Publishing, 2018; Andrew Lownie, *Traitor King: The Scandalous Exile of the Duke and Duchess of Windsor*, New York: Pegasus Books, 2022.

28. This quote appears in a chapter titled "The Golden Age" by Corinne Remedios and Mohan Bharwaney. A transcript of Ma's speech can be

found at: www.hkcfa.hk/filemanager/speech/en/upload/1187/cj_speech_20170610_en.pdf, accessed on 1 June 2022.

29. "A Tribute to Albert Sanguinetti by the Hon Mr Justice Bokhary PJ", *The Bar Newsletter: Publication of the Bar Council, Hong Kong Bar Association*, Issue 1, 1 January 2010, p. 20. Available online at: www.hkba.org/sites/default/files/2010.1_Issue%201.pdf, accessed 1 June 2022.

30. *Ibid.*

References

Archive: Sanguinetti papers
The majority of the quotations cited in the text can be found
in the Sanguinetti papers held in Gibraltar. These include four
boxes of Sanguinetti's correspondence, research, court case
files and transcripts, personal notes, and photographs.

    Box 1
        File 1949–1985
        File 1949–1995
        File 1949–1996
        File 1958–1985
        File 1958–1998
        File 1986–2005
        File 1986–2008
        File 1990–2004
        File 2
    Box 2
        File 1960–1974
        File 1960–1975
        File 1960–1976
        File 1
        File 2
        File 3
    Box 3
        Cheng Huan File
        Jacobs R. letter

Box 4
>Amnesty and Justice File
>Au Pui-Kuen File
>David Leonard, Memorandum 2010
>D. Leonard, 1977 Memorandum
>Star Ferry Riots File

Drafts and Interviews

The files also include early manuscript drafts and notes by Brian McElney and Virginia Blackburn, as well as records from various interviews with:
>Louis Andlaw
>Lydia Armstrong
>Kemal Bokhary
>James Gordon
>Cecil Isola
>Gladys Li
>Mesod Massias
>Raphael Massias
>Brian McElney
>Willie Piccone
>Leolin Price
>J.E. Triay

Legal Cases

Various legal cases are cited in the notes. In some instances, the official case numbers are not provided as the text is based on the informal notes and transcripts found in Sanguinetti's personal files.

Books, Articles, and Websites

Anderson, David, *Histories of the Hanged: The Dirty War in Kenya and the End of Empire*, New York: W.W. Norton, 2005.

Angelo, Anaïs, *Power and the Presidency in Kenya: The Jomo Kenyatta Years*, Cambridge: Cambridge University Press, 2020.

Assensoh, A.B., *African Political Leadership: Jomo Kenyatta, Kwame Nkrumah, and Julius K. Nyerere*, Malabar, FL: Krieger Publishing Company, 1998.

Bird, Les, *Along the Southern Boundary: A Marine Police Officer's Frontline Account of the Vietnamese Boatpeople and Their Arrival in Hong Kong*, Hong Kong: Blacksmith Books, 2022.

Bradford, Ernle, *Gibraltar: The History of a Fortress*, New York: Open Road Integrated Media, 1971.

Bond, Peter, *300 Years of British Gibraltar: 1704–2004*, Gibraltar: Peter-Tan Ltd for the Government of Gibraltar, 2003.

Carroll, John M., *A Concise History of Hong Kong*, New York: Rowman and Littlefield, 2007.

Collett, Nigel, *A Death in Hong Kong: The MacLennan Case of 1980 and the Suppression of a Scandal*, Hong Kong: City University of Hong Kong Press, 2018.

Commission of Inquiry into Inspector MacLennan's Case, "Papers of the Inspector MacLennan Inquiry, 1980–81" [Commission Transcript], donated by D.M.E. Evans, previously owned by Mr A.J.J. Sanguinetti, University of Hong Kong Library, MSS 345.2052 H7 M1.

Cook, Alexander C., *The Cultural Revolution on Trial: Mao and the Gang of Four*, Cambridge: Cambridge University Press, 2016.

Cooper, Andrew Scott, *The Fall of Heaven: The Pahlavis and the Final Days of Imperial Iran*, New York: Henry Holt and Company, 2016

Deac, Wilfred P., "Suez Crisis: Operation Musketeer", *HistoryNet*, 12 June 2006, available at: www.historynet.com/suez-crisis-operation-musketeer/.

Dikötter, Frank, *The Cultural Revolution: A People's History, 1962–1976*, New York: Bloomsbury Publishing, 2016;

Elliott, Elsie, *The Avarice, Bureaucracy and Corruption of Hong Kong*, Hong Kong: Friends Commercial Printing Factory, 1971.

Furedi, Frank, *The Mau Mau War in Perspective*, Athens, OH: Ohio University Press, 1989.

Garcia, John, *The Modern Political and Constitutional Development of Gibraltar, 1940–1988*, PhD Thesis, University of Hull, 1991.

The Global Legal Post, "Leading Gibraltar Lawyer and Politician Dies", 12 July 2012, available at: www.globallegalpost.com/news/leading-gibraltar-lawyer-and-politician-dies.

Grocott, Chris, and Gareth Stockey, *Gibraltar: A Modern History*, Cardiff: University of Wales Press, 2012.

Guasp, Pere Ferrer, *Joan March, la cara oculta del poder* [*Juan March: The Hidden Face of Power*], Edicions CORT, 2004.

Guha, Ramachandra, *Gandhi: The Years that Changed the World, 1914–1948*, New York: Alfred A. Knopf, 2018.

Hack, Karl, *The Malayan Emergency: Revolution and Counterinsurgency at the End of Empire*, Cambridge: Cambridge University Press, 2021.

The Helena May Website, available at: www.helenamay.com/?doing_wp_cron=1654154962.7468769550323486328125.

History.com, "Martin Luther and the 95 Theses", 29 October 2009 (last updated 1 November 2021), available at: www.history.com/topics/reformation/martin-luther-and-the-95-theses.

History.com, "Hong Kong Returned to China", 24 November 2009 (last updated 29 June 2021), available at: www.history.com/this-day-in-history/hong-kong-returned-to-china.

Hong Kong Special Administrative Region Government, *Police Force Ordinance*, Cap. 232, section 51, available at: www.elegislation.gov.hk/hk/cap232?xpid=ID_1438402865374_001.

Isola, Cecil, *An Autobiography of a Colonial Doctor*, Bloomington, IN: Author House, 2011.

Isolas LLP website, "About Us: Our History", available at: https://gibraltarlawyers.com/isolas/our-history/.

Izuakor, Levi I., "Kenya: Demographic constraints on the growth of European settlement, 1900–1956", *Africa: Rivista trimestrale di studi e documentazione dell'Istituto italiano per l'Africa e l'Oriente*, Anno 42, No. 3, 1987.

Jackson, W.G.F., *The Rock of the Gibraltarians*, Gibraltar: Gibraltar Books, 1987.

Kanogo, Tabitha, S*quatters and the Roots of Mau Mau (1905–1963)*, Athens, OH: Ohio University Press, 1987.

Lethbridge, H.J., *Hard Graft in Hong Kong: Scandal, Corruption, the ICAC*, Oxford: Oxford University Press, 1985.

Lipman, Jana K., *In Camps: Vietnamese Refugees, Asylum Seekers, and Repatriates*, Oakland, CA: University of California Press, 2020.

Lo, York, "Conic (康力)—HK Electronics Giant of the Late 1970s, Early 1980s", *The Industrial History of Hong Kong Group*, 17 November 2017, available at: https://industrial historyhk.org/conic-hk-electronics-giant-of-the-late-1970s-early-1980s/.

Loh, Christine, *Underground Front: The Chinese Communist Party in Hong Kong*, Second Edition, Hong Kong: Hong Kong University Press, 2019.

Lonsdale, John, "Mau Maus of the Mind: Making Mau Mau and Remaking Kenya", *The Journal of African History*, 1990, Vol. 31, No. 3, pp. 393–421.

Lownie, Andrew, *Traitor King: The Scandalous Exile of the Duke and Duchess of Windsor*, New York: Pegasus Books, 2022.

Ma, Geoffrey, "CJ's Address at Ceremony for the Admission of the New Senior Counsel", 10 June 2017, available at: www.hkcfa.hk/filemanager/speech/en/upload/1187/cj_speech_20170610_en.pdf.

Metcalf, Barbara D., and Thomas R. Metcalf, *A Concise History of Modern India* (third edition), New York: Cambridge University Press, 2012.

Mitchell, Andrew, "Cripps, (Richard) Stafford", in John Ramsden (ed), *The Oxford Companion to Twentieth-century British Politics*, New York: Oxford University Press, 2002.

Morton, Andrew, *Wallis in Love: The Untold Life of the Duchess of Windsor, the Woman Who Changed the Monarchy*, New York: Grand Central Publishing, 2018.

Murray-Brown, Jeremy, *Kenyatta*, New York: Fontana, 1974.

Norwich, John Julius, *The Popes: A History*, London: Chatto & Windus, 2011.

"On being a boy in 1950s Gibraltar", *Broadsides—A collection of bits and pieces*, Blog, available at: https://broadsidesdotme.wordpress.com/2012/01/13/on-being-a-boy-in-1950s-gibraltar/.

"Prisons Order", *Historical Laws of Hong Kong Online*, available at: https://oelawhk.lib.hku.hk/items/show/2936.

Rees, Neil, *A Royal Exile: King Zog and Queen Geraldine of Albania*, Chesham: Studge Publications, 2010.

Richardson, Humphrey, *The Sexual Life of Robinson Crusoe*, Paris: The Olympia Press, 1955.

Robson-Mainwaring, Laura, "The Great Smog of 1952", Blog, *The National Archives*, 19 July 2022, available at: https://blog.nationalarchives.gov.uk/the-great-smog-of-1952/.

Rosenberg, Jennifer, "1952: Princess Elizabeth Becomes Queen at 25", *ThoughtCo*, 28 August 2020, available at: www.thoughtco.com/princess-elizabeth-becomes-queen-1779354.

Sanguinetti, Albert, "Two Pints into a Quart Pot?" *Hong Kong Law Review*, 1975, Vol. 5, p. 78.

Sinclair, Kevin, *Asia's Finest: An Illustrated Account of the Royal Hong Kong Police*, Hong Kong: Unicorn, 1983.

Tan Teng Phee, "The Case of Tras New Village and the Assassination of Henry Gurney during the Malayan Emergency", *Biblioasia* (National Library, Singapore), January 2011, available at: https://biblioasia.nlb.gov.sg/files/pdf/vol-6/issue-4/v6-issue4_HenryGurney.pdf.

Trigger, Bruce, *Revolutions in Archaeology*, New York: Columbia University Press, 1980.

Yu, Patrick, *Tales from No. 9 Ice House Street*, Hong Kong: Hong Kong University Press, 2002.

Yuk Wah Chan, *The Chinese/Vietnamese Diaspora: Revisiting the Boat People*, New York: Routledge, 2011.

Newspapers and Periodicals

Far East Economic Review
Gibraltar Chronicle
The Gibraltar Sunday Telegraph
The Guardian
Hong Kong Law Review
Hong Kong Standard
Kenya Gazette
LA Times
The New York Times
South China Morning Post
The Star
The Telegraph
Vox